PEOPLES OF THE WORLD
Eastern Europe and the Post-Soviet Republics

PEOPLES OF THE WORLD

Eastern Europe and the Post-Soviet Republics

Joyce Moss • George Wilson

The Culture, Geographical Setting, and Historical Background of 34 Eastern European Peoples

FIRST EDITION

Gale Research Inc. • *DETROIT* • *WASHINGTON DC* • *LONDON*

Joyce Moss
George Wilson

Gale Research Inc. staff

Coordinating Editors: Linda Metzger, Kenneth Estell

Production Manager: Mary Beth Trimper
Production Associate: Mary Winterhalter

Art Director: Cindy Baldwin
Keyliner: C.J. Jonik

The paper used in this publication meets the minimum requirements of American National Standard for Information Sciences—Permanence Paper for Printer Library Materials, ANSI Z39.48-1984. ∞ ™

Printed in the United States of America
Published in the United States by Gale Research Inc.
Published simultaneously in the United Kingdom
by Gale Research International Limited
(An affiliated company of Gale Research Inc.)
10 9 8 7 6 5 4

Contents

Country Briefs

Preface

Through the centuries, hundreds of societies have formed and faded in Eastern and Central Europe. Some created new languages, the remnants of which are major clues to the existence of societies lost in the battleground of Europe and in the ancient struggle between East and West.

At various times, Greeks, Romans, Hungarians, Austrians, Poles, Turks, and Russians have dominated major parts of the region and changed the societies, attempting to impose their own language and culture on the other residents. The process was illustrated in an 1802 book written by a Vlach priest in Greece, who exhorted Albanians, Bulgars, and Vlachs—those who spoke an "alien tongue"—to change their barbaric language to speak and write in Greek. The implication was that, by turning to Greek, these strangers would take a first step toward foregoing their old customs as well as their language.

Thus the people of Eastern Europe were subjected to forces that would Hellenize, Romanize, Turkicize, Mongolize, Germanize, and Russianize them. They were torn between Eastern and Western versions of Christianity, while being introduced to the newer religion of Islam. As they struggled over religion and met with wave after wave of newcomers from the east and north, cultural boundaries shifted, resulting in shared common influences and common words in today's societies.

But societies grew independently of these external influences. Poles, Czechs (Moravians), Hungarians, Serbs, and Bulgarians all developed powerful independent states. Although each fell into periods of darkness, each reemerged in the nineteenth and twentieth centuries, albeit with vastly different national boundaries than in the past as new countries were created. Even when the people were able to exert their own forces for independence, they often found themselves subservient to German local leaders or landowners who had gained control of many of the communities in the region.

Throughout every effort to homogenize or reorganize the region, strong societies have held to traditional beliefs and customs—beliefs and customs that reemerge whenever there is a changing of the guard. The changing canopy of Central and Eastern Europe alters the bounds of cultural identities so that societies override national boundaries. A Hungarian living in Romania, for example, considers himself no less Hungarian than the resident of Budapest; a Pole in Ukraine, no less a Pole than a resident of Kraków.

A changing of the guard is taking place today as the former Soviet republics struggle to realign while holding their influence in Europe. Already, the old Soviet republics are declaring their identity by re-establishing old languages, changing names of states and cities, and constructing their own governments.

Throughout all the domination by outsiders and the shifting national boundaries within Central Europe, local and national groups have clung to their old tenets. Education, long highly respected in Eastern and Central Europe, has produced great achievements in science, art, literature, and music. Indeed, great cultures have grown through thousands of years among the people of this region. Their legacies have been carried throughout the world by migrants from the troubled areas; the impact of the Slavic, Magyar, and Turkic peoples and their neighbors on world thought has been felt in art, architecture, science, literature, medicine, and philosophy.

It is the strength of these peoples and their contributions to the lives of all of us that the authors hope to emphasize in this book.

Acknowledgements

The authors are deeply indebted to Dr. Ivan Berend, Professor of East-Central European History, University of California at Los Angeles, for his careful review of the entire manuscript and for his aid in locating sources of information. For his specific review of foreign words in the manuscript, gratitude is extended to Dr. Henning Andersen, Professor of Slavic Languages, University of California at Los Angeles.

The authors also appreciate the assistance of Shiva Rea Bailey, Denise Berger, Monica Gyulai, and Colin Wells. Their contributions in compiling research and preliminary writing of some of the entries made the entire project possible.

A special thank-you is extended to Eugene Brycki, who brought his experiences as a worker for Solidarity to the entry on the Polish people, and to Fred Moss and Martin Weiss, whose recollections of Eastern European Jewish life and concentration camp procedure added vivid details that helped recreate the cultural experience. Thank you also to Rabbi Stanley F. Chyet for his refinements on the Eastern European Jews.

Introduction

They came in waves—Magyars, Goths, Huns, Romans, Avars, Franks, Vlachs, Bulgars, Slavs, Mongols. In their early history, some settled to farm the land or herd sheep and cattle; others came as raiders and warriors. Each took a turn at establishing a great kingdom in Central and Eastern Europe. Roman militia spread across the areas of present-day Romania, Hungary, and Czechoslovakia beyond the Elbe River to the Oder, and both north and south of the Danube. As elsewhere in Europe, Romans left a mark on the land that remains to this day.

Slavs spread across the north from Poland to Russia and south to the Danube. For a time, Slavs dreamt of a great Slavic Empire, a dream that has turned to an interest in separatism today. But Avars from the east cut off the Slav move southward and took their turn as rulers of the region. In turn, they were defeated by the Franks under Charlemagne, whose influence spread north and east through present-day Poland.

Poland grew to great strength and merged in the age-proven manner: intermarriage of ruling families. After one merger with Lithuania, the great Polish and Lithuanian states were transformed into the Grand Duchy of Lithuania, which spread its influence from the Baltic to the Black seas. But eventually, the powerful Poles succumbed to the pressures of a growing Slav state in Russia and to Austrian and Prussian pressures on the north and south. In the end, the great Polish Empire was divided as spoils among its neighbors.

Magyars ruled in a Hungary that was a major force in the land as a single kingdom. It became a dominant force through a union with Austria to form the powerful Austro-Hungarian Empire.

Paganism was followed by Roman Catholicism encouraged by the Teutonic Knights, champions of the great Italian-German Holy Roman Empire, by Eastern Orthodox Catholicism, and then by Islam, brought to the area through Turkish dominance in the days of the Ottoman Empire. Finally, through such zealots as Jan Hus (a Czech protestant), a foment of protestantism found a place in Central Europe and the Baltic States.

A Region of Unrest and Achievement

Throughout all of this, a variety of nobles cut out their own territories and ruled over landless serfs by the grace of their own strength and the goodwill of their neighbors and the church. But here, at least as strongly as in any other region, the serfs exhibited their own power to control, keeping their own religious orders when their overlords were changing theirs for expediency or for territorial gain.

Societies rose, fell, and merged with others to form new societies with new cultural identities and new languages. Often, the origins of peoples were obscure; the earliest recorders, the Romans, took note of only those people in their paths of conquest. Mountain dwellers such as the early Vlachs were ignored, as were the southeastern Kyrgyz in the great Mongol sweep across the continent. But most societies were caught in the great milling of peoples and the eventual sweep westward. Even though some claimed Roman languages and called themselves Romans, they mostly disappeared into the mixing bowl of assimilation.

The various peoples constructed great public buildings, mosques, and churches. They developed rich literary traditions in the multitude of Slavic and Turkic dialects. Trade routes were well established between East and West. Rivers provided highways, and mountain ranges, shelters.

Despite the almost constant unrest, this region has produced great musical developments and outstanding scientific research. Education is highly regarded, with some of the world's oldest and greatest universities, such as the University at Prague. It was in Poland where Copernicus defined the movements of the planets, and where Casimir Funk produced outstanding research, including identifying and naming the vitamins. From this region, the first astronaut circled the earth, and some of the world's finest mathematicians and philosophers produced works that affect all of us today.

Changing Map

Great wars have changed the map of the region—wars between Avars and French, Russians and Turks, Catholics and Protestants, Christians and Muslims. More recently, World Wars I and II spread throughout the region, forced nations to take sides, and resulted in reshaping national boundaries. Only from the late 1940s to 1990 have the national boundaries held as the maps of 1990 showed them. But this is a region of great accomplishments and great changes, and the fomentation continues. In 1991 the Soviet Union withdrew from its commitment to communism, and the Union began to disintegrate.

Similar struggles in East-Central Europe have occurred since the Soviet Union imposed its will on its western neighbors, forcing the adoption of communism and pledges of mutual support through the Warsaw Pact of 1955. Yugoslavia, Bulgaria, Albania, and Poland all freed themselves in the years leading to the general collapse of communist management from 1989 to 1991. Croats and Serbs are at once demanding separate states and fighting to keep the old union alive. Bohemians and Slovaks in Czechoslovakia are expressing their interest in separation.

The unrest and capriciousness of the governments of the portion of the world from the Baltic to the Black and Caspian seas and from the Elbe River to the Ural Mountains makes this region a challenging one about which to write. But the accomplishments of the peoples in literature, music, science, philosophy, and religion make the challenge worth risking.

The Contents of This Book

The authors have used a broad brush in attempting to describe the peoples of Eastern Europe and the post-Soviet republics. The historical stirring and mixing of peoples in this region have blended the earlier cultures so that today most cultures are distinguishable only on a national level, except in the vast expanse of Russia, that land once called the Russian Federation of Soviet Socialist Republics. Here more than 100 languages still reflect the assimilation of peoples first undertaken by the Russian tsars. For many years these people were Russianized—dominated by Russian leaders and indoctrinated with Russian cultural patterns and language. Only in the 1990s have they begun a reawakening of their own unique cultures. In describing the peoples of the post-Soviet republics, we have, for the most part, concentrated on national cultures and on those cultures strong enough to have sustained a separate republic within the former union.

Format and Arrangement of Entries

Peoples of the World: Eastern Europe and the Post-Soviet Republics is divided into three sections: Old Cultures, Cultures of Today, and Country Briefs. The section on the old cultures provides a brief overview of the region's ancient peoples, which includes peoples who appeared in greatest strength as recently as the fifteenth and sixteenth centuries A.D.

Organized alphabetically by culture names, Cultures of Today includes the dominant cultures of the region today. The entry for each of the groups is arranged as follows:

A dictionary-style definition introduces the entry, providing a key to pronunciation of the people's name, describing the group in brief, and furnishing the key facts of population, location, and language. (Populations are estimates based on the best and most recent available data.)

Following this introduction are detailed descriptions under three main headings: Geographical Setting, Historical Background, and Culture Today.

For quick access to information, subheadings appear under main headings. The Culture Today section, for example, may include these categories: Food, clothing, and shelter; Religion; Education; Family life; The Arts; Recreation; and Language. (Subheadings vary according to the unique experience of each group.)

Each entry in Cultures Today concludes with a section headed For More Information, which is a selective guide for readers wanting to conduct further research on the society. This section lists reading materials and appropriate organizations to contact.

The entries in the third section, Country Briefs, contain information about population, languages, and cities, describe the nation's topography, and relate current events and issues within each country.

Other Helpful Features

To assist readers in understanding details, each entry includes a map that highlights the current geographical distribution of the featured society. Photographs illustrate the entries. All quoted material is identified parenthetically within the text of the entry; for complete bibliographic identification, the reader should consult the Bibliography included in the book's back matter.

Although every effort has been made to explain foreign or difficult terms within the text, a Glossary has been compiled as a further aid to the reader. A comprehensive Subject Index provides another point of access to the information contained in the entries.

Comments and Suggestions

Your comments on this work, as well as your suggestions for future Peoples of the World volumes, are welcome. Please write: Editors, Peoples of the World, Gale Research Inc., 835 Penobscot Bldg., Detroit, Michigan 48226-4904.

Table of Cultures and Countries

The table below illustrates the relationship of Eastern European countries to the societies described in this book.

Country	Cultures
Albania	Albanians, Greeks
Armenia	Armenians, Azeri, Russians
Azerbaijan	Armenians, Azeri, Georgians, Russians
Bulgaria	Bulgarians, Turks
Byelarus	Byelarussians, Poles, Russians, Ukrainians
Czechoslovakia	Czechs, Germans, Magyars, Slovaks, Ukrainians
Estonia	Estonians, Russians, Ukrainians
Georgia	Armenians, Azeri, Georgians, Russians
Hungary	Croats, Germans, Magyars
Kazakhstan	Kazakhs, Russians, Ukrainians
Kyrgyzstan	Kyrgyz, Russians, Ukrainians, Uzbeks
Latvia	Latvians, Russians, Estonians
Lithuania	Lithuanians, Poles, Russians
Moldova	Moldovans, Romanians, Russians, Ukrainians
Poland	Germans, Poles, Ukrainians
Romania	Magyars, Romanians, Russians, Ukrainians
Russia	Russians (100 ethnic groups including Tungus, Yakut, and Amursk)
Tajikistan	Russians, Tajiks, Ukrainians
Turkmenistan	Turkmen, Russians, Uzbeks
Ukraine	Ukrainians, Byelarussians, Russians, Moldovans
Uzbekistan	Kazakhs, Russians, Tajiks, Uzbeks, Ukrainians
Yugoslavia	Albanians, Croats, Montenegrins, Romanians, Serbs, Vlachs

SOME ANCIENT CULTURES

AVARS
(a' vars)

People of Mongol or Turkish origin who migrated to the
area of the Caspian Sea, the Don and Volga Rivers, and thence
throughout Europe.

Population: Unknown.
Location: Eastern Europe, from the Volga River to the Elbe River
and the Baltic Sea.
Language: Avar, an oriental language.

Geographical Setting

Before A.D. 800, the Avars occupied various lands on either side of
the Caucasus Mountains in what is now Ukraine and Austria. Some
historians place the earliest identifiable Avars in this region in the
year 568. The land of this area is varied from mountains, to steppes,
to broad plains. At the time of the Avars it was occupied by a number
of small kingdoms, or serfdoms, that had been conquered by the
Romans and divided into provinces in their Empire. Upon the decline of the Roman Empire and its eastern counterpart, Byzantium,
the region that had been the Roman provinces of Dacia, Dalmatia,
and Thracia reverted to a number of small kingdoms.

Historical Background

Early history. Historians describe two groups of Avars, one in Asia
and one in Europe. Both groups seem to have originated in central
Asia. Before A.D. 461, one group of people were driven out of their
homeland and moved westward toward Europe. By that year they
had overcome a Turkish tribe, the Ulgurs, and assimilated them. The

new society began the European Avars. Until 555 this society dominated the steppes around the Volga River in what is now Ukraine. In that year, the Avars were defeated by the Turks and retreated north of the Caucasus Mountains. In their movements, the Asian Avars captured or lived peacefully side-by-side with European early inhabitants of the Carpathian Basin and elsewhere. As a result, the name Avar really refers to a lifestyle adopted by a mix of peoples.

Pleading in Rome with the pope for assistance against the Turks, the Avars were instead hired by the Roman emperor Justinian to fight the Slavs and Bulgars, who were threatening the empire. They were supported in this battle by continual tributes paid by Justinian. Successful in their campaign against the Slavs, the Avars expanded their influence from the Volga River to the Elbe River (now in Czechoslovakia and Germany), and as far north as the Baltic Sea.

Romans and Byzantines. Ten years later (565), the Roman emperor Justinian discontinued his tribute to the Avars, forcing them to ally themselves with the southern Lombards. This alliance defeated the surrounding peoples, and it then fell apart. The Lombards moved south and west to Italy, while the Avars occupied the Danube Basin. Here, their king (*khagan*), Bayan, became the strongest ruler in Europe, demanding and receiving tribute from the Byzantine rulers in return for discontinuing attacks on the eastern Roman Empire. The tribute was enormous: 120,000 pieces of gold, an elephant, and a bed of gold, among other items. Bayan continued to demand and receive this tribute until his death in the year 600. After his death, however, the Avar dynasty declined.

Disintegration of the Avar kingdom. Bayan's death was followed by years of war, attrition, and compromise. Over the next 30 years, the Avars suffered losses to the Greeks and Slavs. The kingdom of Moravia (now part of Czechoslovakia) became independent of Avar rule. In 626 the Avars joined Slavs and Bulgars in a costly battle with the forces of Constantinople. By 635 Bulgaria and Croatia (until recently part of Yugoslavia) had broken away and become independent. Still the Avars continued raids into what is now Germany and Italy.

Franks. By 797 Charlemagne, ruler of the Franks, had begun to build a new empire in western Europe and came into conflict with the Avars. The defeated Avars were forced to move to an area that is now eastern Austria and to become vassals of the Franks. The unhappy Avars revolted against Frank domination in 799 and again in 803, but both efforts failed. The Avars then ceased to exist as a people, but had left their marks on most of the cultures of Eastern Europe.

Culture

The Avars seem to have had no written language. At least no records of their lives or raids have been found. What is left of this culture are some fence rings in Austria and nearby countries where Avar groups developed settlements. Much of present-day information has been learned through excavations of Avar cemeteries near these established villages.

These graves reveal a wide range of body and skull shapes, indicating that the Avars, who were originally horse-riding nomads, had mixed with the peoples they raided. The importance of the horse in this culture is demonstrated by the existence of graves for horses near the human cemeteries.

Avar communities. While some of the Avars were probably fishermen and farmers as a result of their assimilation by people they conquered, the Avars were nomads whose chief occupation was raiding other people. Divided into small units, Avars raided the people of present-day Germany and others to the south, carrying off food and wealth, and demanding tributes in trade for peace. They returned to their villages of huts, which were protected from retaliations by a wooden fence. These fence rings indicate how large the villages were. One ring has a circumference of 38 miles.

Disorganization. The large villages notwithstanding, Avars were slow to develop a distinct culture of their own other than the reputation as horsemen. When they were defeated by Charlemagne, the Avars were described as so culturally disorganized that they did not even know what to do with the loot gathered from their raids. The armies of Charlemagne found large stocks of wealth and household tools that had been stored for long periods of time.

Clothing. Avar clothing consisted of a single gown, usually belted, with beaded or ornamented necklaces and headbands. As the Avars became more stationary, some women's dresses were ornamented with detailed embroidery and pleated skirts. The Avar wore earrings and paste-bead necklaces.

Other indications from the graves. Avars were sometimes buried with their belongings or with food for the hereafter. Iron swords have been found in the graves along with the remains of eggs and the bones of fowl. That the Avar had an interest in music is seen from the crude horns that have been found in the cemeteries.

The Avars were long-experienced in absorbing customs from their captives. When the Avars disintegrated as a people after their losses in 803, they were absorbed into the societies of their victims, who now reappeared as distinct peoples. Thus the Avar people contributed to the characteristics of many Eastern European societies.

For More Information

Lipták, Pál. *Avars and Ancient Hungarians.* Budapest: Akadémiai Kaidó, 1983.

Pirenne, Henri. *A History of Europe.* New Hyde Park, New York: University Books, 1955.

COSSACKS
(koss' acks)

Russian tribesmen in the days of the tsars who served as soldiers for the empire in lieu of paying taxes.

Population: 2,500,000 in 1880 (estimate).
Location: Southern Ukraine, southern Russia, central Asia, and Siberia.
Languages: Ukrainian, Russian.

Geographical Setting

The Russian steppes, or wooded grassy plains, extend in a broad belt across Russia, reaching from north of the Black and Caspian seas nearly to Lake Baikal in southern Siberia. To the north and northwest lay the forests of Russia and Poland; to the west rise the rugged Carpathian Mountains; to the east, rolling plains and desert stretch to Mongolia and China. Several rivers flow south through the steppes from the northern forests. Of the four most important rivers, the Dnieper and the Don flow into the Black Sea, and the Volga and Yaik into the Caspian Sea. While summers are temperate, strong winds, frigid cold and heavy snowfall make winters harsh on the steppes.

Historical Background

In feudal times, the many rulers of small territories of Europe frequently protected themselves and their land by hiring mercenaries. These mercenaries were given the status of a lower nobility in order to exempt them from some oppressive taxations and from the tedious work of the serfs who supplied the regimes with needed food, clothing, and weapons. Often these mercenaries were settled in a separate, protected community. The Cossacks are described here as representative of these several groups of paid soldiers.

Tatar renegades. The first Cossacks were not Russians at all, but descendants of Asian conquerors called Mongols. These warlike horsemen swept into Russia in the 1200s from the eastern steppes, plundering villages and appointing Russian princes to collect tribute for them. Not at home in the forests, the Mongols held sway over the Russians by the constant threat of invasion. By the 1400s, the princes had become powerful enough to resist, and Tatar (a Mongol people) unity had been weakened by constant feuding between chiefs. The Russians were thus able to hire renegade Tatar bands to protect them from raiders. A member of such a band was called a kazak, a Mongol word meaning "guard" and later "adventurer" or "frontiersman." The word remained the same in Russian; "Cossack" is the English form.

The "Wild Country." As the Russian rulers (tsars) expanded their power southward, they recruited Russians and other Slavs to man watchposts along the frontier. The recruits were called town Cossacks; other Russians adopted the nomadic, freewheeling lifestyle of the Tatar horsemen and were called free Cossacks. These roving bands, preying on both Russian and Tatar travelers, as well as others, gradually came to occupy the western steppes from the Dnieper to the Yaik rivers, a region called the "Wild Country" (dikoye polye).

Cossack communities. In the 1500s increasing numbers of Russians came to the "Wild Country." Most often, those who sought refuge there included religious dissenters, peasants fleeing from oppression by their masters, and outlaws avoiding the authorities. By the late 1500s they had established several communities. One such settlement was the Zaporozhian Sech, or the "clearing beyond the rapids." Strategically situated in the forested area below the lower Dnieper's violent rapids, the Zaporozhian Cossacks became one of the largest and most famous Cossack groups. Another renowned community, the Don Cossacks, arose on the lower Don River. In 1581, one group of Dons crossed the Ural Mountains and began the subjugation of the people of Siberia. Over the next three centuries, other communities were established, tending to push farther south and east: on the Terek and Kuban rivers in the Caucasus Mountains, on the southern reaches of the Volga and Yaik rivers, and finally in southern Siberia as far as the Sea of Japan.

Struggles for independence. The Cossack communities had an ambivalent relationship with the tsars. On the one hand, they provided needed military support in the tsars' constant clashes with neighbors such as Lithuania, Poland, and Turkey, as well as protection from Tatar raids. In exchange for this support, the tsars paid the Cossacks and supplied them with food, gunpowder, and cloth. On the other hand, the Cossacks valued their independence, often raiding Tatar or Turkish areas without the tsars' approval, and resisting attempts to control them. In 1630, for example, the Don Cossacks killed an emissary who had been sent by Tsar Michael to demand their obedience.

In the 1600s and 1700s, Cossack heroes led a number of revolts against the growing power of the tsars. The revolts often took on the character of popular uprisings, as peasants joined the Cossack forces. The greatest two revolts were led by Sténka Rázin (died 1671), a Don Cossack who became a Russian folk hero, and Yemelyán Pugachév (died 1775), also of the Don, who was called "the peasants' tsar."

Servants of the tsar. All the revolts ultimately failed, and by the 1800s the Cossacks were firmly under the control of the tsar's War Ministry. From this time until the Russian Revolution of 1917, they were a combination military and police force, a tool for the tsars' aggressive policies abroad and for the repression of Jews and peasants at home. Organized into 11 corps (*voisks*), Cossacks were dedicated to military service. In the early 1900s men were required to serve 12 years in active service in the military and five years in reserve. The corps were sometimes large military units. A Kuban viosk was made up of six battalions of infantry and 15 batteries of artillery. Although organized to support the tsar, Cossack troops sparked the Russian Revolution in 1917 by refusing to fire on a demonstrating crowd in Petrograd. Cossacks fought on both sides in the revolution, but when the Communists came to power, many Cossacks were treated harshly. Many fled to Turkey, Europe, or America. Others became settled Soviet citizens, working as peasant farmers and then as workers on collectives, finding no special place among the new citizenry. In a final bid for independence, exiled Cossack general Krasnov allied himself with Germany during World War II. After the failure of the German invasion of Russia and the ultimate defeat of the Nazis,

Krasnov and his leaders were turned over to the Soviets, who tried and executed them. The last revolt had failed, but the old ways of the Cossacks had long since disappeared.

Culture

The Cossacks were never a distinct ethnic or national group. Though most were ethnic Russians, many married Tatar women, and Cossack life was more influenced by the open steppes of the Tatars than the forests of Russia. Aside from the dominant Russians, Cossacks included Tatars, Ukrainians, Poles, Persians, and Lithuanians. While some were pirates on the rivers and inland seas of southern Russia, and others eventually became settled farmers, the image of the "pure" Cossack is that of a warrior on horseback, with fur hat and colorful costume, brandishing a saber, whip, or pistol and galloping across the bleak and empty steppe. This almost mythical figure occupies a central place in Russian culture, celebrated in the novels of Tolstoy (*The Cossacks*) and Sholokhov (*And Quiet Flows the Don*), in the poems of Pushkin and Yevtushenko, in the paintings of Repin, and in the music of Musorgsky and Shostakovich.

Food, clothing, and shelter. The nomadic early Cossacks often lived by plunder, raiding trade caravans or small groups of travelers. Those who came to the "wild country" fished or hunted the plentiful game to be found there: geese, pheasants, partridges, wild boar, deer, antelope, and many varieties of fish. Rivers like the Don, Kuban, Terek, Volga, and Yaik (now called the Ural) supplied carp, barbel, salmon, and giant herring. Sturgeon 30 feet long were reportedly taken from the Yaik. Fish—dried, smoked, and salted as well as fresh—was a staple for the early Cossacks. They traded fish, caviar (the eggs of sturgeon), fur, hides, honey, and beeswax for grain to make bread, for cloth, nails, and weapons. At first, the unsettled life and the danger of raids kept the Cossacks from raising livestock. In the 1700s, however, Yaik and Zaporozhian Cossacks herded large flocks of sheep.

Cossack costumes reflected their diverse origins, blending Russian styles with those of various tribal groups of the south and east. While early Cossacks wore skins and rough, patched cloth, later costumes became rich and highly decorative. The loose, baggy pants of the Tatars were convenient for long hours on horseback, as was the *burka*, a waterproof, ankle-length cloak of goat- or camel-hair which doubled as a blanket. Each group evolved its own style. Terek Cossacks wore

A Cossack in the classical dress of this warrior group. *Courtesy of the National Anthropological Archive of the Smithsonian Institution.*

the *cherkeska*, an open jacket with wooden cartridge pockets sewn diagonally on each side of the chest. Whereas the Zaporozhians shaved their heads in the nomad style and wore top-knots and huge mustaches, Terek and Yaik Cossacks grew bushy beards. Most wore fur hats in different styles and leather boots. In the 1800s, the costumes became military uniforms. Cossack women wore brightly colored blouses and skirts, with braided hair under scarves.

Cossack shelters varied with the territory. Often, Cossack groups would build fortified villages of barrack-like structures or grouped houses. The wooden dwellings might have roofs of hide like the tents of the nomads. In the 1700s, as divisions between rich and poor

Cossacks became wider, the comfortable European-style homes of the wealthy contrasted with the communal barracks of the poor in which the men slept crosswise on the dining tables.

Government. The early Cossack communities were essentially military establishments. They were called *voiska* ("armies" or "hosts"). A democratic system evolved, in which every man was equal, and decisions were made in a popular assembly known as the *krug* (among the Don, Terek, and Yaik) or *rada* (among the Zaporozhians). The boisterous and often violent assemblies divided spoils, sent out embassies, and elected the leaders. The leader, called *ataman* or *hetman,* kept order and administered justice, relying on his personal reputation. He might easily be deposed, or worse. A Yaik ataman, for instance, was beaten to death in the 1600s for accepting unpopular orders from Moscow. As the communities grew, this loose organization became more rigid, with power resting more in the hands of a few. The voiska became too large for an assembly to be efficient, and eventually the ataman answered more to the tsar than to his followers.

Family life. At first, the voiska were mostly male communities. Women were captured in raids upon neighboring tribes. Today, many Russians show the high cheekbones, flat features, or slanted eyes of Tatar women thus taken. As the settlements became more secure, new arrivals brought their wives and children with them, balancing out the sexes. Cossack women were relatively free and self-reliant, often fighting and drinking along with the men. When the men were away on campaign, the women managed the affairs of the community and saw to its protection.

Religion. While some groups were Muslim or pagan, most were followers of the Russian Orthodox Church. Among them were a large number of long-standing believers in the church who had fled persecution (see RUSSIANS). The rough-and-ready men were simple in their religious practices, and the Russian-dominated groups, such as the Don and Zaporozhians, welcomed Muslims and others.

Today, the Cossacks survive only in Russian art and literature. Some of their practices have continued, such as trick-riding, displayed now in Russian circuses. The Cossack dance, called the *hopak*, is performed by folk ensembles, and "Cossack" choirs sing the old ballads. But the performers are trained professionals, rather than the unruly and vanished horsemen of the steppes.

For More Information

Longworth, Philip. *The Cossacks.* New York: Holt, Rinehart, and Winston, 1970.

McNeal, Robert H. *Tsar and Cossack, 1855-1914.* New York: St. Martin's Press, 1987.

Seaton, Albert. *Horsemen of the Steppes: The Story of the Cossacks.* New York: Hippocrene Books, 1985.

HUNS
(huns)

Mongols who invaded China about 200 B.C. and entered Europe about 325 A.D., where they sometimes sided with the Goths in their westward movement.

Population: Unknown.
Location: Eastern and Central Europe.
Languages: Probably various tribal languages related to Finnish.

Geographical Setting

The people called Huns originally entered Europe through the steppes north of the Caspian Sea and spread west of the region of the Visigoths in north-central Europe and south into Bulgaria. From these bases, they made military excursions, attacking the Roman Empire as far away as present-day France, and extending their raids southeast into Persia.

Historical Background

Origin. Some historians place the origin of the Huns in China as part of a group called the Hsuing-nu who established themselves in northern China as early as 200 B.C. This group caused such difficulty for the emperor of China that he was forced to make a treaty with them. Over the next century, the Chinese empire strengthened and the Huns were forced to move north and then west. Others ascribe the term Hun to a collection of tribes emerging from the steppe region of present-day Russia to wage war on the people of eastern Europe. They may not have been a unified group until the expert warrior, Attila took command. After much success and then defeat, scattered Huns may have been the forerunners of today's Bulgarians and Hungarians.

In Europe. By A.D. 372, the Huns had established themselves on the steppes north of the Caspian Sea. They expanded their influence by raiding, defeating, and then absorbing other peoples they encountered. By 374 they had invaded the northern kingdom of the Ostrogoths, had subjected this group, and moved westward to encounter the Visigoths. Dislodged by the Hun hordes, the Visigoths were forced to seek sanctuary within the Roman Empire, where they eventually contributed to the downfall of the Empire.

Huns and the Roman Empire. From 400 onward, the Huns were at once allies of Rome and enemies of the empire. In 409 the Huns joined the Romans who crossed the Danube into present-day Bulgaria. So powerful did the Huns become and such a threat to the Roman Empire that, by 432, the Hun King Rugila was able to sell Hun services to the Romans for a tribute of 350 pounds of gold annually. By that year, Rome and the Huns were quarreling over control of other small groups in the region.

Attila. About 432, King Rugila died and his two sons, Attila and Bleda, assumed command of the Huns. By 445, Bleda had died, killed by Attila, and Attila began to lead the Huns to their greatest strength. Immediately, Attila moved his armies to fight the Romans at Thermopylae, Gallipoli, and Constantinople. So successful were his raids that he was able to exact a triple tribute from the Eastern Roman Empire—2,100 pounds of gold annually.

Defeat. Absorbing the defeated peoples into his army, Attila was able to gather more than half a million warriors to fight the Romans and Goths on the plains of France. In 451, the forces of Attila were turned back with great losses in this battle, but regrouped and directed an attack on Italy that began in 452. However, Attila died in 453 before this struggle was resolved, and the rule of the Huns fell to his several sons. These sons were not able to agree on sharing power and the Hun dynasty quickly disintegrated. The captured groups began to withdraw from the union and the Roman Empire helped with the breakup, placing some Huns under the government at Scythia, and some under Dacia (the Roman province that is now mostly Romania). Some Huns retreated to Russia.

Many Central and Eastern Europeans descend from the Huns, as well as the Avars, the wave of Asian horsemen who followed the Huns. At their height, the Huns were instrumental in bringing down the Roman Empire both in Rome and in Constantinople. They cleared the way for later Slavic states to rise and grow.

Culture

Records. Through his long controversies with the Romans, Attila, the leader of the Huns at the peak of their power, had many exchanges and bargaining sessions with Roman emissaries. While the Huns left no records, the accounts of these ambassadors from Rome and Constantinople provide views of life among the Huns.

Villages and families. Visitors to Attila described an enclosed village in which at least some of the houses were of smoothed planks and logs. Some walls contained carved planks for decoration. Women counted as merchandise among the Huns as they did in much of Europe at that time. A wife was to serve the husband at his call but was to live in a separate house. Still, there was some loyalty between husband and wife. The wife of Attila, named Kreka, lived in a home in which the earthen floor was covered with mats of wool. Her servants were described as skilled in embroidery, which they used to ornament clothes worn over the more rustic traveling costume.

Assimilation. At first, the Huns were hunters, then raiders—preferring to raid their neighbors than to till the soil or tend herds. But as the Huns' influence grew, and they began to capture and assimilate other peoples, there were accounts of sheepherding among them. The Huns, like the later Avars, without a strong culture of their own, often adopted the ways of the people they conquered. In turn, many of these people were put to work providing for the vast army of the Huns. And this army itself swelled as the defeated soldiers joined the victor.

Food and recreation. Hun encampments were often filled with songs of valiant deeds performed in battle. Wine was a popular drink among the Huns, most often consumed from wooden cups. Wooden serving bowls held the food, which was eaten off wooden plates. In times of great show, as between nobles or with emissaries from other rulers, gold and silver table settings were used. Wine-drinking was often a symbol of the order of the society, with the highest-ranking officer drinking first, and followed by others in order of their rank. This military life dominated the Huns.

Hun society as seen at Attila's funeral. Some of the customs of the Huns were revealed at Attila's death. Men who discovered the death cut themselves so that Attila's passing would be mourned with the spilling of warrior blood rather than with tears. The body was laid out under a silk tent for those who would pay homage. The best horsemen rode around the body chanting a funeral song that lauded his victories over Scythians and German realms, and his extracting of tribute from the Roman Empire. The body was buried in three coffins, iron, silver, and gold, and buried at night to protect it from enemies. Some arms and wealth gained in combat were included. Those who completed the burial were slaughtered to keep secret the exact location of the wealth and the body.

After Attila's death, as was the custom, the power of government passed to his sons. But these sons (three by the wife Kreka) fell to quarreling among themselves. By 454, when the Gepid tribes and the Ostrogoths had withdrawn their allegiance and engaged the Huns in the Battle of Nedao, the Huns were badly beaten and broken into many small and non-offensive tribes.

For More Information

Dahmus, Joseph. *The Middle Ages: A Popular History.* New York: Doubleday, 1968.

Gordon, C. D. *The Age of Attila.* Ann Arbor: University of Michigan Press, 1960.

SLAVS
(slavs)

The general name of various peoples speaking related languages who early inhabited eastern and central Europe and are still the dominant people in that area.

Population: Unknown.
Location: Europe from Germany east through Russia, and from the Balkans to Finland.
Language: Slavic.

Geographical Setting

The early Slavs were an agricultural people living in the lowland plains of eastern Europe. These plains extend north to the Baltic Sea and east beyond the Caspian Sea to the Ural Mountains. Much of this land is arable, with moderate rainfall, and cool temperatures that rise to 80 degrees Fahrenheit in summer and drop much below freezing in long winters. The land rises gently from the Baltic Sea to the foothills of the Carpathian Mountains.

Later the Slavs spread to the more mountainous regions south of the Carpathian Mountains into the present-day Balkan states of Bulgaria and Yugoslavia.

Historical Background

Who are the Slavs? The Slavic people are represented today by Russians, Ukrainians, Byelarussians, Serbs, Croats, Bohemians, Bulgarians, Sorbs, Slovaks, Slovenes, Moravians, and Poles. The name for the early peoples did not appear until the ninth century A.D., and their disdain of strong government left little firm record of their activities. Even the name indicates some generality. Slav may have come from *slovo*, which means "word," as opposed to the Slavic name for foreigners *nemcy* or "dumb" (that is, not understanding the language). Still, the path of the Slavs has been traced in all directions from a region north of the Carpathian Mountains between the Vistula and Dnieper rivers. These people were surrounded by neighbors who were somewhat more unified than they: Lithuanians, Prussians, Letts, Finns, Persians, Thracians, and the German Gothic tribes.

Spread over Europe. By the fourth century Slavic people had crossed the Danube south into the Balkan region. By the fifth century they had spread southwest to the Elbe River, and by the sixth century had spread to the Roman areas of Thracia and Macedonia. By this time, some of the Slavs had been organized into two nations—the Sclaveni and the Antes—north and left of the Danube River. Gradually, the Slavs divided into the various groups and languages known today.

Division. This differentiation was stimulated by the land barriers to communication, by other peoples such as the Avars, who divided the Slavs north and south for a time, and by Christianity, which divided the Slavs between the church at Rome and that at Byzantium. The Slavs became organized into kingdoms through their associations with others. Some were dominated by the Avars, who the Slavs later joined in attacks on Constantinople. These attacks resulted in a trade treaty with the eastern Roman capital in 860. Before this time, waves of Slavs had moved north and east into present-day Russia.

Christianity. By 811 the leader of the Bulgars who had conquered Slavs in the southern area, adopted Christianity and elected the eastern form of the religion. In this century, the Christian missionaries Cyril and Methodius visited the Slavs, created an alphabet for the Slavic people, and began the first Slavic writing. In 989 the Slavic king Vladimir was baptized and chose to follow the Roman Catholic Church. Thus the separation of various units of the Slavs continued.

Numbers. By the early 1800s, there were estimated to be 55,000,000 Slavic people in Central and Eastern Europe. In 1830 there was an effort to unite the people through a pan-slavic movement. The desire for an encompassing Slavic nation is still spoken of in the 1990s.

Culture

Organization. The early Slavs were seminomadic farmers. Communal tribal units formed self-governing villages, farmed the area, and then moved to other little-used land to begin again. The families and villages were patriarchal and the Slavs disdained war. This love of peace and refusal to organize into larger units made them easy prey for Mongols, Avars, and Magyars, with whom they became assimilated, from whom they borrowed language and customs, and to whom they passed on their traditions. Later, Christianity was introduced by the Roman emperor Justinian, by the Franks, who demanded tribute from the Slavs, and by missionaries from Constantinople. Thus, without a strong government or universally held customs of their own, the Slavs spread their influence widely, and often through the organizing abilities of outside peoples who ruled them.

Family and village life. Slavic families were based on monogamy, and the village families were bound by commonly held land. In the first Slavic communities, religion and political leadership were combined, with priests also serving as rulers of the community known in Russia as *mir* and in Serbian areas as *zadruga* (terms meaning a society of people working together on a basis of equal political, economic, and social rights).

Religion. Before Christianity, the Slavic religion was a complex belief in many gods and in immortality, but with little idea of a state after death except for its being a journey for which the dead needed supplies. Slavic gods were both universally accepted and chosen by local groups. Some appear to be borrowed from the Romans. *Perin*, god of thunder, was one of the generally accepted deities, as were *Svarog* (god of the heavens), *Dazbog* (god of the sun), and *Stribog* (god of wind and weather). There were also goddesses such as *Vesna* (of spring) and *Morana* (of death). Some of these gods became *Svintovint, Radipest,* and *Svintrivint* in the Baltic States, and *Bielobog* and *Chornobog* (gods of light and dark) in Silesia. The Slavic religion also worshiped gods of justice (*Prava*), love (*Lado* and *Lada*), and language (*Diovana*).

The images of their gods were sometimes influenced by the neighbors of the Slavs. There were a three-headed god, which may have been influenced by early introductions to Christianity, and four-headed or four-faced gods reminiscent of the idols of India.

Economy. Slavs were herders of cattle and farmers. They were also gatherers of honey, some of which they turned into a drink called mead. As the Slavic people spread, they became tradesmen as well, exchanging goods along the rivers and traveling as far as the great trading center at Kiev.

Celebrations. Slavic feasts followed the seasons, as did most important agricultural events. Great banquets celebrated the coming of the new year (the holiday of Kaliody), summer (Kupaly), and mourning for the dead (Trizna). These feasts and other celebrations were the occasion for music. The early folk music of the Slavs was like the folk music and dance of Russians today.

A people whose vague history is one of disunity and influence by others, the Slavs gave birth to many of the political and cultural groups of today's Eastern Europe.

For More Information

Dahmus, Joseph. *The Middle Ages: A Popular History.* New York: Doubleday, 1968.

Pirenne, Henri. *A History of Europe.* New Hyde Park, New York: University Books, 1955.

VLACHS
(walachs)

A Latin or latinized people who early spread from the Adriatic Sea to the Bug River in Russia, but were mostly concentrated in the Transylvania area of modern-day Hungary and Romania.

Population: 11,000,000 (estimate at the beginning of World War I).
Location: Romania, Hungary, Moldavia, Greece, Turkey.
Languages: Romanian, and other languages of the countries in which Vlachs settled.

Geographical Setting

The Vlach people inhabited what is now Romania and part of Hungary during the reign of the Roman Empire and were dominant in southern Romania, parts of Hungary, and Moldavia. Originally located in the Transylvania Mountains and the plains south of them, Vlachs spread into the Danube valley and across the mountains to valleys drained by northern tributaries to the Danube. The low coastal land of the Black Sea rises gradually in the west, forming a fertile plain that is cut in the north by the Carpathian Mountains and then drops in altitude again toward Hungary. The Carpathian Mountains sweep north to south to join the east-to-west Transylvanian Alps in the center of the area. It was in these mountains that the Vlachs located at the time the Romans withdrew from their Dacian province in A.D. 262.

Historical Background

Dacia. Before the Romans took command of the region of Central Europe between the Carpathian Mountains and the Danube River, there had formed the loosely knit nation of Dacia. In A.D. 107, Roman forces claimed this nation, then inhabited by peaceful farmers and a few nomadic tribes who had spread from Greece, Turkey and as far west as present-day Hungary. Dacia became a province of the Roman Empire and the residents there merged with a rush of Roman immigrants, blending their language with the language of the newcomers.

Origin. The actual origin of the Vlachs is obscure. Some scholars, particularly Hungarians, claim that the Vlachs emerged south of the Danube after the year 1000 and are therefore relative newcomers to the land. Others, particularly Romanians, claim the Vlachs to be a blend of very early settlers and their Roman rulers. (This theory of "Daco-Roman continuity" was first proposed in the 1700s.) The Hungarian position is that the mixing of populations was nearly impossible in the 160 years the Romans remained in the region. When the Romans quit Dacia in 262, Vlach people seem to have gathered in the mountain regions of present-day Romania. The term Vlachs was given to them by their Slavic neighbors. The people themselves prefer to be called Romani, a reminder of their assimilation of the customs and language of their Roman overlords.

Roman influence. Bands of distinctly Romanized (the Vlach language is of Roman derivation) people were known to live in the mountains as early as the 900s, and were scattered south of the Danube from Greece to Hungary by the 1100s. By 1184, the Vlachs had joined Bulgarians in a short-lived empire of Vlachs and Bulgarians and by the thirteenth and fourteenth centuries had established the states of Walachia (now part of Romania) and Moldavia (now partly Romanian and partly a republic of the former Soviet Union), and had spread to the mountain areas of Bulgaria and Greece. The Vlachs reached their greatest power at the end of the fourteenth century and the beginning of the fifteenth century under King Mircea the Great. This king succeeded in uniting the feudal nobles enough to command the land from the Black Sea to the great bend of the Danube River, and from that river to the Carpathian Mountains.

Governments. However, Vlachs were nearly always united or divided at the whims of neighboring rulers. Governed by local nobles called boyars, Vlachs were easy targets for invaders as these local rulers formed agreements with stronger area leaders in order to survive. Even the strong king Mircea signed a treaty of submission to the

Turks in 1417 and the Vlachs were soon caught up in disputes between Greeks, Hungarians, Turks, Russians, and Germans, and in Christian crusades against the Muslim Turks.

Vlad the Impaler. The most well-known of the Vlach leaders, although certainly not the most influential, has become a symbol of villainy. Vlad II, Prince of Walachia, who ruled that region as a vassal of Sigismund the German emperor in the middle of the 1400s, has been immortalized in the stories of Count Dracula based on his life. (Vlad was a member of the Order of the Dragon [*draco*], from which the name Dracula arose.) Vlad II, or Vlad the Impaler, reflects the mix of influences on the Vlachs. Vlad I, his father, had been "educated" at the court of Emperor Sigismund and had allied himself with the Polish king Ladislaw II before becoming ruler of the Vlachs. Raised a prince of this Vlach king, the ten-year-old Vlad II was sent to a Turkish capital as assurance that his father would keep his bond with the Turks. Vlad was educated by the Turks for eight years before being released. He then joined Germans and Hungarians to battle the same Turks. A contemporary of Vlad II, John Hunyadi, who was also of Vlach heritage, joined Hungarian forces and was so successful as a battle leader that he became governor of Hungary and was later able to name his son king of the Hungarians.

Effects of Vlachs. Thus the effects of the Vlachs were felt from Austria to Greece and Turkey and on both sides of the Danube River. Today Vlachs are a small percentage of the population in Hungary, yet are the largest populations of Romanian Walachia and the former Soviet republic of Moldavia. Small groups of Vlach descendants live in Turkey and Greece.

Culture

Nomads. In their earliest history, Vlachs were nomadic people who depended on herding animals for their livelihood. Once settled they lived for centuries as peasants in near poverty, ruled by wealthy boyars in the manner of European feudal states. Most of the people were uneducated and their boyars were often preoccupied with war and defense. As a result, few records remain of the lives of most Vlachs. Most of the records are in the remains of great forts built to stem the advances of Turks and Germanic peoples. Some evidence of their life-patterns is to be seen in a few scattered villages in the

mountains of Greece and Bulgaria. Here the Vlachs are today seminomadic shepherds, living among other peoples in the villages and
moving with their herds to lower lands in winter.

Nobles. The medieval noblemen lived in great stone palaces with
tiled roofs inside fortresses, some of which were small villages within
massive turreted walls. One of these fortresses has been estimated to
have been 3,000 feet on each side. Built on difficult-to-ascend mountain slopes or on hilltops, these palaces overlooked fields where peasants used primitive tools to till fields owned by the nobles. These
peasant farmers lived in huts of stone, wood, or thatch, and paid for
the land they used with provisions for the fortresses that protected
them from neighboring lords.

Noblemen dressed in finery reflecting both Roman and Turkish
influences. The Eastern influence was seen also in the habits of nobles
who frequently took more than one wife or concubine. Daughters
were chattel, often given in marriage to other nobles to maintain
peace or to strengthen alignments.

Warriors and tillers. While boyars and their warriors fought with
Turks, Hungarians, Germans, and among themselves, peasants tilled
the land to raise crops, most of which were paid to the noble who
claimed to be protector and owner of the land. For the most part,
these peasants lived in squalor and dressed in the most simple homespun clothing. Still, nobles and peasants joined frequently in enjoying
great fairs, open-air theatrical performances, and the antics of street
performers.

Rich and poor. The division between wealthy and poor remained
into the twentieth century, at which time most Romanians were still
below the poverty line in annual income and 4 percent of Hungarians
owned 50 percent of the land. The heritage of the Vlachs and their
Central European neighbors prepared the people for revolt and adoption of a Communist plan to divide the land among the peasants.

Vlachs today. Today, most Vlach people have merged with their
neighbors and are no longer readily identified except in the few villages scattered through the Balkan states in which sizeable groups of
Vlach-speaking people reside. These people may number as few as
50,000 and live in mountain villages such as Samarina and Perivoli
in the Pindus Mountains of Greece.

For More Information

Florescu, Radu and Raymond T. McNally. *Dracula, Prince of Many Faces: His Life and His Times*. Boston: Little Brown, 1989.

Pirenne, Henri. *A History of Europe*, New Hyde Park, New York: University Books, 1955.

CULTURES OF TODAY

ALBANIANS

(al bay' knee uns)

People—related to the Greeks—now living throughout the world, but mostly in Albania, a country north of Greece.

Population: 4,000,000 (1990 estimate), of which 3,208,000 live in Albania.
Location: Albania, Yugoslavia, Italy, and Greece.
Language: In Albania, Albanian, an Indo-European language with two distinct dialects: Ghez and Tosk.

Albanians

Geographical Setting

The largest population of Albanians live in the country of Albania bounded on the north and east by former Yugoslavian states and on the southeast by Greece. Across the Adriatic Sea from the "heel" of Italy, and just north of the rocky limestone country of Greece, a range of the Alps Mountains breaks into a fan of 6,000- to 8,000-foot ranges. The Albanian Alps separate Albania and Yugoslavia in the north. This range has several branches that extend into southwestern Albania, forming a high plateau. Centrally, there are three mountain ranges that slope first to hill country, then to a low, silty marshland near the sea. The result is that two-thirds of the homeland of the Albanians is mountainous. For Albania's size (just 215 miles north to south and 50 to 90 miles across), the climate, along with the terrain, is quite varied. Heavy rains fall in the north. The mountains endure extremes of heat and cold, and the land along the Adriatic Sea enjoys a more moderate climate. The rugged terrain has served as a barrier for the residents of the mountain plateaus against the Greeks from whose land these "Albanians" originally migrated.

Historical Background

Origins. People from Greece had migrated to the mountain valleys in what is now Albania by 300 B.C. and had established tribal groups there, isolated from other Greeks and from each other by the mountain ranges. Before that date, Greek trading towns had been established along the Adriatic Sea. By 300 B.C., some of these central groups had been united into the first Albanian kingdom, Illyria. The separation from the Greeks resulted in a separate identity for the Albanians, while the plateaus sheltered by the ranges of mountain peaks made it difficult for potential invaders. However, these barriers also made it difficult for various Albanian groups to unite in their own defense. Romans commanded part of the country by 167 B.C., Serbs conquered the Albanians in A.D. 640, and Bulgarians ruled the land from 976 to 1014. The Albanians fell under Byzantine rule from 1014 to 1204, at which time the land became part of an empire called Epirus that was ruled by Michael Comnenus. While the government initiated by Comnenus ruled part of the land until 1358, a series of Sicilian kings ruled the central highlands of Albania between 1271 and 1368, except for a brief period when most of the land was ruled by the Serbian leader Stephen Dushan. In every rule, the isolated groups of Albanians were difficult to reach and control, and were actually ruled by their own feudal lords. When in the 1300s Venetians seized Albanian coastal towns, one of the lords appealed to the Turks for aid. After 1385, Turks began to claim rule over many parts of Albania.

Albanians under the Turks. By 1431 Turks had captured Albania and united it under George Castriota (known as Skanderbeg) as part of the Ottoman Empire. However, the Albanians in their mountain strongholds continued to resist foreign dominations. Revolts against the Turks were frequent. Skanderbeg led resistance forces for 20 years during the fifteenth century and temporarily led the country to independence. He is now a symbol of Albanian spirit and unity. Finally, led by Mekmed Buslati, the Albanians again temporarily drove out the Turks in 1760. The mountain separations this time worked against Albanian unity. Claimed, but again not dominated, by the Turks, it was not until the Russian defeat of the Turks in 1877 that Albanians were freed from Turkish rule, although they were now divided into two parts. And not until 1879 was Albania united, forming the Albanian League. Language was then a divisive influence. Albanians in the north spoke Gheg while those in the south spoke a related, but different dialect, Tosk. There was no common written language. A series of language conferences in 1895 and 1897 attempted to remedy this problem. A common Latin alphabet was accepted at another conference in 1908, and eventually Tosk became the official written language.

Independence. In 1908, threats from other parts of Europe caused the Albanians to align themselves once again with the Turks. But the promised help and freedom did not develop and the Albanians withdrew from the alliance with the Ottoman Empire in 1912, after more than 400 years of Turkish dominance, retaining only half their homeland. In 1925, the Albanian people established a republic in their remaining land and Ahmed Bey Zogu became prime minister. Although Albania remained a republic in name, it was actually a dictatorship directed by Zogu (who became King Zog I in 1928) until it was overrun by Italy at the beginning of World War II (1939). The association with Italy resulted in the second-largest group of Albanians forming communities on Italian soil, particularly in Sicily. After the war Albania reorganized as a communist state. Enver Hoxha, who had led 70,000 Albanians in battle against Italy and Germany, became leader of the country and aligned it with Russia. Hoxha led the country in his role as Communist party chairman until his death in 1985. After his death, Ramiz Alia became party chairman and leader of the country.

Breaks with Russia and China. In the 1950s Albania distanced itself from the Soviet Union, feeling that the Union had over-liberalized the programs of Stalin. Albania held to the old communist line, moving toward greater cooperation with China than with the USSR. For a time, Albanians were dominated by Yugoslavia, and there were suggestions of creating a Yugoslav province from Albania, but that proposal was abandoned. The Chinese alliance also proved unsatisfactory; Albania severed its Chinese affiliation and became an independent communist community in 1986. A break in Albanian isolation came when the country began to renew associations with Greece and Britain, while still refusing to admit people of other nations such as the United States into their country. This, however, did not shelter Albanians from the central European shakeup with the fall of the Soviet Union. Long the poorest of the central European states, Albanians suffered greatly in the shaken economy of 1991. By early 1992, Albanians were suffering severe shortages of food and other necessary materials and were airing their frustrations through strikes and demonstrations against the government. By March 1992 more than 100,000 Albanians had left the country to seek jobs and security in other countries, particularly Italy.

Culture Today

Outside influences. The lifestyles of the Albanians bear signs of the many people who have controlled the land. There are mosques (the result of Turkish influence), forts of the Romans, old castles, and Roman theaters. Remains of a prosperous Greek city, Apollonia, remain on the Adriatic coast. The Turkish influence is seen in the capital city of Tiranë, named by a Turkish general after the Middle-Eastern city of Teheran, the site of one of the general's most recent conquests. The Middle-Eastern influence has left the traditional bazaar in Tiranë, along with the Islamic policies of welcoming visitors and secluding women.

    Religion. However, the lives of Albanians are influenced by the Turkish overlords mostly in the area of religion. In the 1940s and 1950s, following its Soviet model, the government of Albania attempted to discourage religious practices. Church properties were confiscated and some church leaders were purged. Under this heavy pressure, the religious affiliations of Albanians persisted, but religion is still not recognized by the Albanian government. Sixty-five percent of the Albanians who remain in Albania are Muslim. Twenty-three percent are Christians of the Orthodox Church, reflecting the division between east and west in Byzantine days, while a smaller minority is Roman Catholic. In addition, older ideas still influence religious practice. In many areas popular tradition revolves around the *dreqci* (demon). The demon enters the bodies of people who are evil and causes them to terrorize others. Vampires are believe to be condemned souls. *Shtrigat* (witches) are warded off with special rituals in the month of March. Still, Muslim holy days and Christian holidays are celebrated throughout Albania. Other signs of Greek, Roman, and Turkish influences can be seen in the foods and traditions of the country. However, as in other countries influenced by the communism of the USSR, religion has been discouraged in Albania, yet remains a strong influence among the people. Meanwhile, Russian influences in dress, law, and literature have a strong hold on the country.

Food, clothing, and shelter. The largest city in Albania is Tiranë, a community of 250,000, and there are few cities of more than 100,000 population. Until the advent of communism, most Albanians were farmers, although only 11 percent of the land can be farmed. President Hoxha began a program of land reform and of agricultural modernization. The land belonging to large landowners was confiscated and redistributed to the workers, who were then organized into collectives. The government held title to all the land. With increased farm productivity and expansion of petroleum and other mineral industries, there was a move to the cities. Today fewer than one-fourth of the people work in agriculture.

The remaining farmworkers live in the fertile mountain valleys and grow a variety of crops depending on the altitude of the land. Crops vary from maize in the valleys to fruit such as olives, oranges, and lemons. Corn, wheat, and oats are principal products, while barley, rye, and vegetables are also produced in large quantity. The diets of Albanians reflect these products of the fertile farmlands. Salads are a major diet item. A typical dinner might be salad, meat (chicken or mutton), rice, and a second meat dish. Coffee is served at nearly

Holidays in Albania are occasions to dress in traditional finery; red bandeleros embroidered in gold, white and black shirts, and a fringed jacket are topped by a red fez. *From the Library of Congress.*

all meals, and is a favorite restaurant drink over which to hold conversations.

Clothing in the city is Westernized, but in the country some people still dress in traditional robes or loose-fitting shirts and pants. Even longer-standing traditional costumes are seen on festive days. The ancient costume for men was the kilt, sometimes worn with a *zhurdu* (typically a red and yellow waistcoat). Over time, the kilt was replaced by an all-white pant-and-shirt suit with colored trimming. Albanian women still enjoy full skirts and long white shirts with wide sleeves. The shirts are embroidered heavily and sometimes reflect the area in which the person lives. Most women wear a *kesa*, a head-cloth, which is white for married women.

City Albanians live in stone, brick, or concrete houses with tiled or shingled roofs. Some live in large concrete apartments. Country homes are small, brick, stone, or wood-frame buildings, sometimes with thatched roofs.

Language and literature. In the periods of Turkish rule attempts were made to banish the Albanian language. The Albanians resisted, but books and papers in the Albanian language were banned. It was not until 1908 that the Albanians agreed on a universally accepted written language. The Turkish actions and their own slow progress in establishing a common language resulted in widespread illiteracy. Although today there is a university in Tiranë, many Albanians cannot read or write. Since it was illegal for Albanians to read or write in their own language while under Turkish rule and the adoption of Soviet communism drove many elite out of the country, much popular Albanian literature has come from Albanians in exile. Poet Jeronim de Rada and folkwriter Zef Schiro wrote in Italy, Anton Zako-Cajupi in Egypt, and Fan Noli in America. As Albanians became more fully independent, authors such as dramatists Mihal Grameno and Kristo Floqil began to write in Albania using the Latin alphabet and the Tosk dialect first made popular in *Istoria e Skënderbeut* (The Story of Skanderbeg), written by Naim Fraşeri in 1898.

Arts. The same restrictive forces limited Albanian production of theatrical works. An exception was the northern region where the largest city is Scutari. There Roman Catholicism was dominant and the priests held special privileges. Pask Vasa Pash was the first playwright to work in Albania. He wrote *The Jew's Son* in 1879. In 1901 the first drama influenced by growing nationalism was *Besa*, written by Sami Bey Fásgëri in 1901, a play about a pledge of honor. Recent works are limited to social statements that adhere to the Stalinist line of communism.

Early Albanian art was heavily influenced by the Greeks and Romans. Remains of the early architecture are seen in ruins of Apollonia and in the Roman center of Buthrotum. Typical Islamic mosques replace many of the old church buildings during five centuries of Turkish rule. In the nineteenth and twentieth centuries, these mosques came to be highly decorated with Byzantine-style paintings and carvings. More recent structures and works of art reflect the influence of Italian and Russian domination.

Education. Before President Enver Hoxha came into power and the country of Albania became a communist state, Albanians had no national educational system, although about 45,000 elementary students did attend some form of organized school. The communist government set about immediately to create a sound educational program. Now elementary school is compulsory for Albanians, and more than 200,000 elementary school students attend state-run schools. The state also set out to create a national system of higher education. This began with the establishment of training schools in areas where technical skills were needed. The training institutions were later integrated into the national University of Tiranë.

Holidays. National holidays in Albania include New Year's Day, January 1; the celebration of the beginning of the republic, January 11; May Day (Labor Day), May 1; the celebration of the victory of the socialist revolution, November 7; the proclamation of independence (Independence Day), November 28; and the day of liberation in 1944, November 29.

Traditions. Albanians today are solidly communistic and this has had an impact on the lives of the people. Traditionally, Albanians lived together in extended family units of such size (50 people or more) that the groups resembled small tribes, and frequently established their own law. Local law was more important than national law. In the Albanian ethic, theft and murder came to be less serious crimes than breaking a promise. This concern for a person's word resulted in an oral code of conduct that endured even in the long periods of blood feuds. As recently as the 1950s, disagreements among Albanian families was settled by armed executions. In this arena of guns, conduct was governed by a bond, the *bessa*. Under the bessa, women were protected from any harm; so were men while they were accompanying women as well as all children too young to bear arms.

Industry. Today, a steel industry and an oil industry are growing in Albania and people are moving to the few cities. Coal, too, is a major mineral resource of the Albanian mountains. Mineral resources and fertile farmland are so bountiful in Albania that an old folktale still recounted tells of the time God revisited the earth to check on the

This Albanian boy is carrying a typical rural bed—a three-ply straw mat that will be rolled out on the bedroom floor. *From the Library of Congress.*

progress of the creation. He found depressing scenes everywhere until visiting Albania, where the land remained as it had been planned in the creation.

Change. Albanians are a changing group, but outside knowledge of the change is limited by the very closed state in which they live. Only very well-monitored groups of visitors are allowed into the land and then only on tours carefully arranged with government approval. Still, in 1990, there were reports emanating from Yugoslavia of unrest in some Albanian cities. The president of Albania announced some slight modifications in the government, including elections with more than one candidate—albeit all candidates endorsed by the communist government.

For More Information

Logoreci, Anton. *The Albanians: Europe's Forgotten Survivors*. London: Gollancz, 1977.

Robyns, Gwen. *Geraldine of the Albanians*. London: Muller, Blond, and White, 1987.

ARMENIANS

(ar me' knee uns)

A much-persecuted people of the Near East, particularly located in Turkey and Armenia.

Population: 4,634,900 in Armenia and adjacent countries; 3,580,000 in Armenia (1990 estimate).
Location: Armenia, Azerbaijan, and Georgia. One-third of all Armenians are dispersed throughout the world.
Languages: Armenian, Russian.

Geographical Setting

Bordered by Azerbaijan, Iran, Turkey, and Georgia, the small country of Armenia (now the Republic of Armenia) was once part of Turkey

and the Soviet Union. It is a high plateau, with the land lying between 6,000 and 8,000 feet above sea level. Rugged volcanic mountains are cut by many short, fast-flowing streams. Mountain valleys are fertile, producing grains and cotton, while the mountains yield copper ore. The rivers provide energy for industries. In the Georgia-Armenia-Azerbaijan region, three mountain ranges converge to form a changing and unstable mass: the Greater Caucasus Mountains, the Lesser Caucasus Mountains, and the Surami Mountains. The area has extreme hot and cold temperatures and moderate rains.

Historical Background

Origins. Having endured centuries of persecutions, struggling for a homeland, and being forced to flee in great numbers from Turkey, Armenians are now spread throughout the world. There are 1,400,000 Armenians living in the former Soviet Union states outside the Republic of Armenian. There are also large Armenian populations in other countries near their Eastern European bases: 45,000 Armenians live in Greece, for example, 6,000 in Bulgaria, 4,000 in Egypt, 90,000 in Syria and Lebanon, 14,500 in Iraq, and 2,500 in Palestine. In addition, nearly 500,000 Armenians live in the United States. About 50,000 Armenians still live in Turkey. This article refers mostly to those Armenians who live in the Republic of Armenia.

Armenians and Greeks. Armenians are thought to have come to the land they now inhabit during the sixth century B.C. By 325 B.C. the various groups of Armenians had fallen under the conquest of Alexander the Great. They remained Greek subjects for 200 years until gaining independence under the Artaxias dynasty (190 B.C. to 55 B.C.). In this period, the Armenian Empire reached the height of its power, covering a vast area from the Caucasus Mountains to Lebanon and Syria.

Armenians and Romans. After 55 B.C. the power of the empire and its rulers was curbed by the Romans who brought the territory under their control while maintaining the Armenian government. However, the Artaxias dynasty ended in 1 B.C. By A.D. 70 the populace had been divided into Armenia Minor and Armenia Major. Armenia Minor remained a Roman province and was thereafter governed by Romans, Byzantines, Arabs, and Persians, finally becoming part of

Turkey in 1541. Meanwhile, Armenia Major was taken by Persia and later fell under the control of various other groups.

The Armenians adopted Christianity as their official religion in A.D. 301. Shortly thereafter, they abandoned the use of the Greek language in the church. The two actions served to isolate the Armenians from their non-Christian neighbors and, at the same time, to build an Armenian identity.

Armenians, Persians, Turks, and Russians. Armenians played a key role in the Byzantine (eastern Roman) Empire of the Middle Ages, providing many of its leaders. From the twelfth to the eighteenth centuries, the Armenians were dominated by Persian and Turkish rule and surrounded by the religion of Islam. Persia and Turkey struggled for control of Armenian lands, and in 1514 they divided the territory, with the Turks acquiring a major portion. In 1828, Russia conquered the portion of Armenia controlled by the Persians. Under all these different rulers, Armenians tenaciously established their own communities and preserved their own culture.

Turkish-Armenian differences. In the late 1800s the Turks embarked on a policy of domination that culminated in the massacre of approximately 200,000 Armenians. Then, in 1915, the Armenians sided with Russia in a dispute with Turkey, and Turkish leaders decided to remove all Armenians in Turkey to Syria. Many of those driven or led out of Turkey found equally harsh treatment from the Kurds, over whose land they were forced to pass. The campaign succeeded in sending one-third of the Turkish Armenians to Syria, and in the massacre a million Armenians died. Many others fled to countries throughout the world. The land occupied by the Armenians was subsequently occupied by Turks, and there began an exodus from that country into the Soviet Union and other areas of the world. Today the Armenian population in Turkey has been reduced to 50,000.

The Armenian Soviet Socialist Republic. After World War I, Turkey promised reform in its treatment of Armenians and an international committee was appointed to help in the solution. With pressure for land from both Russia and Turkey, the committee declared a small portion of Turkish land to be Armenian. After that, promises to the Armenian people were largely forgotten in repairing the damage of the war, and Armenians turned for support to their long-time associate, Russia. The Armenian Soviet Socialist Republic was organized in 1917 and joined the Union of Soviet Socialist Republics on December 20, 1922. Since then, and until the demise of the Soviet Union, there was sporadic Armenian guerrilla resistance to Soviet rule, but the Soviets managed to industrialize and collectivize Armenian life.

One writer, Manoog Abeghian, described the Armenian point of view (Baliozian 1980, p. 43):

It has been the destiny of the Armenian people to wage a struggle against foreign nations for the protection of their physical and spiritual life.

With little history to change its view, the Armenians remained separate from other ethnic groups in the Soviet Union and retained many of their distinct traditional practices. However, with government support, the Armenians developed their industrial potentials to become one of the most prosperous regions in Eastern Europe. This prosperity was dampened in 1988 when the region was struck by a series of earthquakes. These earthquakes were felt in Georgia and Azerbaijan as well, but the strongest, measuring 10 on the Soviet earthquake scale, destroyed large parts of Armenia. Overall, 24,807 Armenians were killed and 514,000, nearly one-third the population, were left homeless. Also, 130,000 Armenians took refuge in the less-damaged Azerbaijan. Already burdened with 500,000 Armenians who had moved from their homeland, the additional earthquake refugees in Azerbaijan strained relationships between the two peoples. In 1989 through 1991 the two areas were at war over a part of Azerbaijan now predominantly occupied by Armenians.

With the 1991 downfall of the Soviet Union, Armenia became an independent nation, but was one of the first to join in the Union's replacement, the Commonwealth of Independent States.

Culture Today

Personal Traits. The Armenians are sometimes described as aristocratic, honest, self-confident, and stubborn adherents to their own principles. Some Armenian proverbs express the taciturn yet expressive nature, caring, humor, and respect for quick-mindedness that are part of the Armenian culture. Examples of Armenian proverbs include:

- Teaching consists of opening the mind; the mouth opens by itself.

- A wise man needs few words, a fool needs many.
- He is so cunning that he even knows where the devil sleeps.
- Crime for the rich, punishment for the poor.
- A wealthy man is only a thief who has not yet been caught.
- To the poor, everyone is generous with advice.

Economy. Armenians raised a number of food ingredients on collective farms, mostly for their own consumption, but also some for trade, including grain, sugar beets, potatoes, and grapes. Livestock (cattle, pigs, poultry, and sheep) are raised for food and wool. Wool and other fibers are processed in textile factories near the larger cities.

Other light industries in Armenia include chemical, cement, and machine manufacturing. Over one-third of Armenia's labor force is employed in metal work and in the production of metal-cutting lathes and other machines. One of the most world-famous Armenian products is fine cognac. Armenians trade for the products they need and are generally regarded by others as shrewd businesspeople.

Family life. Intermarriage between Armenians and other peoples is rare, and this practice of marrying among themselves has helped Armenians retain a distinct cultural identity. The family is strictly centered around the paternal head, and the behavior of women in the family is tightly defined. Anton Chekov described the Armenian husband as a military leader, a bishop, an artist, a grandfather, and an Othello. He typically married a lovely young woman, according to Chekov, whom the husband controlled with an absolute hand. This strong male-domination is seen in Yerevan, the capital of Soviet Armenia, where women are barred from public restaurants.

In the past, Armenians were proud of their accomplishments and distrustful of foreigners. With the changing family in an industrialized nation, however, the pride remains while distrust of others is waning. Young Armenians in the 1990s are neither boastful of their superiority, nor much aware of dangers from foreign sources.

Shelter and food. Large red-brick buildings are replacing the traditional mudbrick houses in Armenian cities. More traditional housing can be seen in the villages of the remote mountain regions. Village homes of stone and mud are built close together on the steep mountainsides, or are dug into the mountainsides to fend off the harsh climate.

An Armenian peddler carries his market goods. *Courtesy of the National Anthropological Archive of the Smithsonian Institution.*

Adjacent homes may provide shelter for an extended family of 30 to 40 people. Members of the family are related through the male line and include parents, unmarried daughters, and sons and their families. Also included are "milk relatives," foster parents from a poorer family who have become responsible for the rearing of a child of a richer family.

Traditional foods continue to prevail in the Armenian diet. They include seasoned pieces of roasted meat (*shish kebab*), rice, yogurt, bulgar, nut-filled pastries, and *aris*, a thick soup made with wheat and chicken. Popular breads include a large thin cracker known as *lahvash* and plump loaves of *peda.*

Religion. Armenians are a deeply religious people who believe in their own form of Christianity, as taught by the Armenian Apostolic Church. This independent offshoot of the Eastern Orthodox Church based on the teachings of the fourth-century apostles Bartholomew and Thaddaeus, broke with other Orthodox churches in A.D. 451. Every member of the culture automatically becomes a member of the Church upon birth and some join Roman Catholic or Protestant churches as well. Echmiadzin is regarded by the majority of Armenians as the world center of the Armenian Church and is financially supported by Armenians both inside and outside the country as well as in Armenia. Initially the Soviet regime confiscated all church property and persecuted church officials. Since 1941, church members have been divided over the issue of whether or not the headquarters of the church should be on Soviet soil. Some have felt that a safer headquarters might be based at Sis in Cilicia since much of the time in the Soviet Union was spent under circumstances that discouraged churches of any kind. After World War II, the Soviets relaxed their policy and attempted to use the Church to attract more Armenians to the Soviet Union. Armenians now are free to worship how and when they wish.

Language and arts. Many Armenians speak Russian but their native tongue is Armenian, a language in the same family of languages as Greek, but with liberal additions from the Iranian language. Armenian is a 38-letter language that is reputed to have been devised by St. Mesrop about A.D. 400. In the period from 481 to 484 Movses Khornenatsi began the literature in that language with his *History of the Armenians.*

Armenian arts include a heritage of literature by novelists such as Raffi, whose works were banned in the Soviet Union. The first Armenian novelist of note was Khachatur Abovean (1805-1848), who wrote *The Wounds of Armenia.* He wrote this volume after hearing that the few books available to students were in a classical Armenian unknown to them, and that the students were preferring Russian texts. Abovean started a literature using the common Armenian of the day. In the late 1800s favorite works of literature used common Armenian to romanticize the old feudal customs and their lords.

Known throughout history for their industrious attitudes, their stubborn adherence to principle, and their scholarliness, Armenian authors continued to study and write about the conditions of their people through the persecutions by the Turks, and later by the Soviet Union of Joseph Stalin. An example of Armenian writers who sought to call attention to the plight of peasants was Yervant Sermakeshkhanian (known as Yeroukhan; 1870–1915). Yeroukhan wrote strongly about the conditions of Armenian laborers, fishermen, washerwomen, exiles, and street venders, and was arrested for his stand. He was paraded through the city of Kharpert in chains, then murdered in a ditch outside of town.

Armenian architecture shows a great diversity of styles and reached its peak of creativity between the sixth and thirteenth centuries. The world-renowned Church of the Holy Cross is a stone polygon whose outside is covered with sculptured scenes from the Old Testament. Church manuscripts featured brightly painted animals and other images either displayed in the margins or attached to the capital letters in the style of the European illuminated books of that day. Until recently, Armenian artists were controlled by the Soviet policy of social realism, which calls for works that speak to the masses in an uncomplicated style to promote the collective life.

In the 1990s, Armenian authors, actors, and musicians work in all parts of the world and write and act in languages of the countries they inhabit. Akim Tamiroff (actor, United States), Charles Aznavour (composer, France) Arlene Francis (actor/author, United States), Hamo Bek-Nazarov (actor, Russia), Ana Aslar (doctor, Romania), and Artem Mikoyan (designer of MIG fighters, Russia) are but a few of the world-known professionals who were born in Armenia and practice their occupations in other countries and languages.

Holidays. As part of the Soviet Union, Armenia celebrated New Year's Day, January 1; International Women's Day, March 8; May Day (a labor day celebration), May 1; Victory Day, May 9; the October Revolution celebration, November 7–8; and Agricultural Workers Day in the third week of November.

Change. The Armenian Communist Party controls the government of Armenia. Persecution by the Turks had made Armenians receptive to Russian rule and some people appeared to be loyal to the Soviet Union while the political climate was split for and against communism. Today Armenians hold most positions of authority in their own local government and party organization. Armenians of the past, such as Mikoyan and Ktevosyan, have held high positions in the government of Moscow as well. With the breakup of the Soviet Union and while still recovering from the devastating earthquakes, Armenia faces an uncertain future in which its people must deal with serious disputes with the Azeris and old fears of the Turks.

For More Information

Armeni, English. *The Armenians.* New York: Rizzoli, 1986.

Baliozian, Ara. *The Armenians: Their History and Culture.* New York: Ararat Press, 1980.

Chaliand, Gérard. *The Armenians: From Genocide to Resistance.* London: Zed Press, 1983.

Walker, Christopher J. *The Armenians.* London: Minority Rights Group, 1991.

AZERI
(az er′ ee)

Turkic-speaking native people of Azerbaijan.

Population: 5,808,000 in Azerbaijan (1990 estimate); about 1,000,000 in Iran.
Location: Azerbaijan, between the Black and Caspian seas south of the Caucasus Mountains.
Language: Azerbaijani, a Turkic language; Russian.

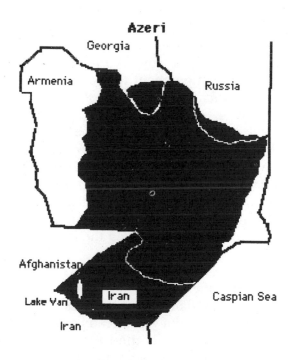

The Azeri live in Azerbaijan, Iran, Georgia, and Armenia.

Geographical Setting

South of Georgia and below the Caucasus Mountains, the land of the Azeri is a low, fertile, nearly treeless plateau through which the Kura River and its tributary, the Araks River, flow. These river valleys dominate Azerbaijan. The climate here ranges from very hot in the low, semiarid north and central lands, to subtropical conditions in the south. Fruits and vegetables grow in abundance in this fertile region. A prominent feature of Azerbaijan is a peninsula that juts into the Caspian Sea with the capital and principal city, Baku, located at its base. Oil discoveries on this peninsula have made the region most important to the surrounding countries. A pipeline carries petroleum from Baku to refineries in the country of Georgia.

Historical Background

The Azeri (or Azerbaijani) are spread across northern Iran and in a small region along the Caucasus Mountains. This Caucasus region was once one of the republics of the Soviet Union. To separate the Azeri of this region from those in Iran, Joseph Stalin ordered the altering of their written language—encouraging the Russian alphabet over the alphabet used by Iranian Azeri. This section deals mostly with the Azeri of the former Soviet Union, those in the country of Azerbaijan. For information about the Azeri of Iran, see Azerbaijani in *Peoples of the World: The Middle East.*

Under many rules. The homeland of the Azeri has long been of interest to other nations. It first came to Western attention when its people were conquered by Alexander the Great. Then from the seventh to the fifteenth centuries A.D. the land was invaded and controlled by Arabs, Turks, and Mongols. In the fifteenth century, the great Safvid family rose to power and gained control of all of the land of the Azeri, but the Safvid ruled the land under Persian suzerainty.

In the sixteenth century, Turkey, Persia, and, later, Russia all fought over control of the region. By 1723 the land had been divided among Persians and Russians, with the Russian Peter I claiming the peninsular area of Baku. Baku was already a thriving town and a key to Caspian Sea shipping. Shortly thereafter, the Persians pressed the Russians to withdraw north of the Arias River. The region south of the river became a Persian khanate.

Neglect. Little further attention was paid to the area until 1813. In that year Alexander of Russia annexed the Azeri land to Russia. However, the neglect of the region continued. No government was established to rule the people there until the Russians sought to consolidate their claim in 1905. Russia then began to establish a government in the region. The Azeri were not pleased with the arrangement, preferring self-government, and an unofficial Equality Party was founded in 1911 by Muhammad Emil Rasebzadi to press for independence. By this time, however, Russians had settled in large numbers in the principal city of Baku and its surroundings. Following World War I, this faction opposed independence for Azerbaijan. For a time the country was divided, with those seeking independence establishing a government at Elizavetpol, while the Communist leader, Stepan Shaumas, ruled at Baku.

Turkey and Great Britain. In 1918 Turkey joined the government at Elizabetpol in war against Baku. This brought the region to the attention of the British, whose shipping interests in the Caspian Sea were threatened. Britain sent 1,800 troops to Baku, the Turks withdrew, and a new Azeri government was formed. But unrest continued and the British returned to Baku to maintain peace.

The Soviet Union. In 1920 the victors of World War I recognized an independent Azeri government. However, an election that year put the Soviet-backed Communists in power. The government was formed under a Soviet pattern. So effectively had the Russians settled the country that the first Communist Secretary of Azerbaijan was a Russian, S. M. Kirov. Kirov ruled until 1925, during which time he sought to consolidate Soviet rule. Between 1921 and 1925, he had 120,000 Azeri, thought to be a threat to the government, sent to Siberian labor camps. In 1922 Azerbaijan officially joined the Union of Soviet Socialist Republics. The Union set about to increase the agricultural productivity of the area and also to exploit the oil resources of the Apsheron Peninsula, where Baku was located.

In Iran, during World War II, the issue of rule over Azerbaijan again arose. A party for independence and sympathetic to the Russians pressed for an independent Azerbaijan in the northwest of Iran. By 1945, this party had established an autonomous republic that was to endure only until 1947. In 1946 Iran invaded the republic, forcing the president to flee to Russia, and within a year the Azeri republic had disappeared.

Joining other southern Soviet republics, the Azerbaijan Soviet Socialist Republic elected to change its name to Azerbaijan Republic in 1990. This move was never approved by the Soviet government. When, in 1991, the Union was disbanded, the Azerbaijan Republic became independent and then joined the Commonwealth of Independent States.

Culture Today

The 1922 admission to the Soviet Union changed the face of Azerbaijan. Before that the Azeri had been devout Shi'ite Muslims who farmed the land as a livelihood and who were 90 percent illiterate. They were separated from their Iranian relatives by the high mountain range that divides the land of undulating plains, and also by their written language. The development of petroleum resources, however, changed that way of life. While some Azeri still farm the rich soil, many of them have moved to the cities and towns to work in industry. Here they find themselves occupying the lower-skilled jobs and taking direction from Russian managers.

In Iran, the Azeri followed the laws of inheritance set forth in the tenets of Islam until the land was in danger of being so fragmented that farmers could not earn a livelihood on their small plots. However, in the planned and partially carried-out land reforms of the 1960s, the laws of inheritance were modified to allow large enough plots for survival.

Economy. Grain, grapes, cattle, sheep, and goats are raised in abundance in the broad valleys of the Kura and Araks rivers. Vegetables, fruits, and some tea are also important farm products. However, about one-fourth of the population now lives in Baku. Here they have become factory workers in industries made possible by energy from oil and from water turned to electrical energy. Azerbaijan factories produce steel, iron, and mineral fertilizers from the raw materials of the country. Several factories have been set up to convert these materials to iron pipes, pump rods, refrigerators, and other products for markets principally in the countries of the former Soviet Union.

Clothing and housing. Having been exposed to British and Russian influences for some years, the Azeri have abandoned any older costumes for Western-style jeans, shirts, and dresses. Their housing has

In Azerbaijan a women tends her sheep. *From the Library of Congress.*

also changed as the people moved to towns and cities. The Soviet-style concrete apartment buildings now house many Azeri.

Language. The Azeri speak and write a Turkic dialect, Azerbaijani. However, the political maneuvering between Russia, Turkey, and Iran from the 1870s onward has divided the written language so that now the Azeri in Iran write using the Arabic alphabet, those in Turkey use the Latin alphabet, and those in Azerbaijan use the Cyrillic alphabet of their former Soviet overlords. All the Azeri speak a language that is Turkish, but with different accents than the language spoken in Turkey.

Arts and literature. The Azeri are world-famous for their beautiful wool carpets and rugs, woven in a number of geometrical designs. This craft has grown and been established in larger factories so that in 1989 nearly 3 million square miles of carpet were woven in Azerbaijan.

Almost totally illiterate before World War I, the Azeri produced few pieces of literature. The Soviet Union brought education and by 1946 there was a 90-percent literacy rate among the Azeri. This has produced a readership for more than 140 newspapers written in Azerbaijani and 55 periodicals in the language. An Azerbaijani encyclopedia has been developed, and book publishers print books about science, education, and fiction, as well as books for children. The use of Azerbaijani has grown in spite of the varied population of Azerbaijan, in which the dominant class is made of the 8 percent of the population that is Russian and another 8 percent that is Armenian. There are also some Arabs and Persians living in the country. Baku television and radio broadcasts in Russian, Azerbaijani, Arabic, Persian, and Turkish.

Education. By 1952, the Soviet Union had developed a school system of 3,121 schools, and had established a university at Baku. By 1990, the number of schools had grown to more than 4,500, and the University of Baku had become one of 17 institutions serving graduates of the secondary schools. There were more than 1,500,000 students in the schools. One million of these belonged to the Communist Union of Youth for the Progress of Azerbaijan.

Azeri in Iran are required to attend schools from ages 8 through 14, but this law is not fully implemented. Still, about one half of the Azeri in Iran who are under 15 years old, like one half of the Iranian population, can read and write.

Religion. The Azeri are almost all Muslims of the Shi'ite sect. Their lives are therefore ruled by the principles of the Shi'ite religion: *shahada* (the recitation of faith), *zakat* (alms giving), *namaz* (daily devotions), *sawm* (fasting during the month of Ramadan), *hajj* (a pilgrimage to Mecca), *jihad* (holy war in case a Muslim state is attacked), belief in "good thoughts, good words, and good deeds," and belief in the leadership of Ali, cousin of Muhammed. Among the Azeri, however, making a religious excursion to Mecca is of less importance than among Muslims elsewhere. The Azeri are more likely to look forward to an excursion to a local shrine such as those at Qom or Meshed.

For More Information

Nyrop, Richard F., editor. *Iran: A Country Study*. Washington, DC: American University, 1978.

Smith, Hedrick. *The New Russians*. New York: Avon Books, 1991.

BULGARIANS

(bul gar′ ee uns)

People of mixed Bulgar and Slavic ancestry now living mostly in
the country of Bulgaria.

Population: 9,000,000 (1988 estimate).
Location: Bulgaria, one of the Balkan states.
Language: Bulgarian, a western Slavic language.

Geographical Setting

Bulgarians

The Bulgarians inhabit a small region near the Black Sea surrounded by Turkey, Greece, Yugoslavia, and Romania. Some Bulgarians live in the Macedonian district of Yugoslavia, an area long claimed by both that country and Bulgaria. The Danube River separates Bulgaria from its northern neighbor, Romania. From there the land rises to a plateau and then to the Balkan Mountains, which divide the land north and south. In the west, these mountains extend southward to form the Rhodope Mountains.

Except for a plain near the Black Sea, the south of Bulgaria is mountainous. River drainage has deposited fertile soils over both the Danubian plateau and the southern plain, making the land rich for agriculture. The climate of the region is affected by the central Balkan range, which acts as a buffer. The Danubian basin endures extremes of heat and cold while other areas are more moderate. Rainfall varies from less than 24 inches annually at Sofia in the west, to 11 inches in the Maritsa Basin in the southeast and more than 35 inches in the Rhodope Mountains. Much of the plains regions and the mountain valleys are good agricultural land.

Historical Background

Beginning. Except for three periods of independence, the Bulgars have been dominated and influenced since their beginning by other peoples. About the fourth century A.D., Slavic people migrating from the region of the Volga River settled in what is now Bulgaria. Then, in the fifth century, Bulgars began to occupy the region of the Danube, and by the seventh century had organized a kingdom, merging with the Slavs, whom they had dominated. In 862, Boris I, the leader of this kingdom, adopted Christianity and also unified the people by declaring Slavic to be the national language, thus creating the first great Bulgarian dynasty.

Bulgar-Slav kingdom. The Bulgar-Slav kingdom reached its greatest strength under Simeon in the 900s, but his empire was broken into two parts as a result of religious feuds. The eastern half was conquered by the Byzantine emperor, John Zimisces. The western half was claimed by Emperor Basil II in 1018. By the middle of the century, revolters were proclaiming Bulgarian once again, but these revolts of 1040, 1072, and 1073 were unsuccessful. Finally, led by Ivan Asen, the country won independence and union again. From 1185 to 1396 the second Bulgarian dynasty flourished. Again the dynasty collapsed;

this time the Bulgarians became subjects of the expanding Ottoman Empire.

Turks. Bulgarians held to their own culture and nationalism during this period, aided greatly by the founding of nearly 50 Bulgarian schools. Champions of Bulgarian independence arose once more. In the eighteenth century, a Father Paisey wrote *A History of Bulgarian People, Czars, and Saints*, which revived Bulgarian national pride. Again in the early 1800s, Yuri Venelin (1802–1839) led a movement for Bulgarian nationalism. The Bulgarian nation was finally restored after the Russian-Turkish War of 1877–1878. With the Treaty of San Stefano (1878), Turkey recognized an independent Bulgarian state. From that time until 1894, Bulgaria was headed by a king, Ferdinand, but governed by a ruthlessly patriotic prime minister, Stefan Nikolov Stambolov.

Bulgarian monarchy. The monarchy that was established found it necessary to spend much of its energy in the next 40 years building an army to withstand Turkish threats. Nevertheless, independent rule remained in Bulgaria at the discretion of Russia. Not until 1908 did King Ferdinand declare total Bulgarian independence.

Balkan Wars. By 1912, Bulgaria was a sufficiently strong force that it could join Greece and Servia in the first of a series of Balkan Wars, at first against Turkey, then with Bulgaria in a war with Romania, Turkey, Greece, and Servia, and finally with Bulgaria and Servia again in a war with Turkey. These wars were over disputes for land and over the treatment of Bulgars, Greeks, and Serbs in Macedonia. Throughout them Bulgarians maintained their independence but with considerable adjustment to their national boundary, losing land to Romania and Servia. The boundary settlements left Bulgaria with a large Turkish minority.

World War I. Almost immediately Bulgaria was caught in another war, this time World War I, in which the nation was allied with Germany. Following the war, Bulgaria was forced to pay for its actions at high cost to its people. The country was then under the rule of King Boris III, who with his prime minister, Aleksandür Stambolyski, began to initiate reforms to aid the Bulgarian people. Their actions, however, were too slow for the Bulgarian peasants, whose political party Stambolyski served. The peasant revolt carried into

1923; Stambolyski was assassinated and Boris exerted his military power to subdue the peasants.

World War II. Again in 1939, Bulgarians sided with Germany in World War II, but by 1944 had wearied of battle and were ready to make peace with the Allies. At this point, Russia ignored the peace overtures and declared war on Bulgaria. In 1946 King Boris was forced to abdicate, the monarchy was abolished, and Bulgarians came firmly into the Soviet sphere under Georgi Dimitrov.

The Turks in Bulgaria. The Turkish minority in the south grew to be 10 percent of the Bulgarian population. In 1985, the Bulgarians ruled that the country should be one culture and that the Turks who wished to remain in the country should take Slavic names and cease worship of the Islamic faith. The ire of the Turks was further aggravated by the installation in 1987 of a national holiday to celebrate the 500th anniversary of the first Bulgarian liberation from the Turks. Demonstrations resulted in the deportation of at first 200 Turks, but this grew to 80,000. An alarmed Turkish government agreed to accept any Turks wishing to escape the oppression in Bulgaria. More than 300,000 Bulgarian Turks fled the country before Turkey was forced to close the border. Organizations throughout the world protested the Bulgarian action, and in 1990 the government announced its intention to reverse the 1985 ruling.

After socialism. Meanwhile, throughout the 1980s, groups opposed the Communist government headed by Todor Zhivkov and the Bulgarian Communist Party. They were joined by ecology groups protesting the industrial pollution of the country, and by the strong Agrarian Union that had been certified as an opposition party. In February 1990, 200,000 protesters marched in Sofia. The Bulgarian Communist Party suggested its interest in reform by changing its name to the Bulgarian Socialist Party and by denouncing its leader, Zhivkov, but to no avail. June and July saw student protests, and 880,000 workers conducted a general strike in November. Later that year, the Grand National Assembly, Bulgaria's parliament, changed the name of the country from the Bulgarian People's Republic to the Republic of Bulgaria and removed Communist symbols from the national flag. Immediately, Bulgaria began to make trade pacts with Western countries.

Culture Today

Religion. Throughout history, Bulgarians have clung to Christianity. Before 1949, about 85 percent of the people were members of the Bulgarian Orthodox Church. Approximately 13 percent were Muslims. The remainder were Roman Catholic, Protestant, and Jewish. Reflecting the major religions, the capital city of Sofia is dotted with great cathedrals and mosques. The Communist government has withdrawn support for the Orthodox Church and discontinued religious education in the schools. However, the clergy strives to maintain the religious life of the people.

Language. Bulgarians speak and write a form of Slavic language. Before 1855, the written language used in Bulgaria was the Greek of the Orthodox Church, but in that year a Greek priest named Cyril developed an alphabet for the Bulgarians and their literary tradition developed rapidly. In still another bond with Russia, this Cyrillic alphabet is common to both Bulgarian and Russian languages. In 40 years the Bulgarians had entered a "Golden Age" of their literature and art. A national literature grew and Bulgarian writers became preoccupied with the glories of the past and the difficulties of the present. Folk heroes such as Marko Krabjevic, who swept through the land on a magic horse and carried an invincible sword, were subjects of many stories, as were tales of the *haiduks*, earlier Bulgarian brigands. Perhaps the most powerful writer of the period after 1878 was Ivan Vazov. His book *Under the Yoke* was a documentation of Bulgarian oppression under the Turks. In the twentieth century Elin Pelin based his writings on the life of the Bulgarian peasant. The Soviet policy of socialist realism has affected Bulgarian writing since 1945; authors such as Dimitar Talev write about the acceptable themes of industrialization and the modernization of agriculture.

Arts. Although life under communism has changed in many ways, Bulgarians continue to spend their leisure time on music and dance. Many famous European opera singers are Bulgarian, and the people still enjoy the traditional circle dance called the *hora,* accompanied by music of the *gerdulka* (mandolin) and *kavel* (a kind of flute). Recent Bulgarian music has shown a decided Western influence. Folk music is mixed with jazz, young musical groups play rock music, and Bulgarian radio stations play music by popular Western artists.

Bulgarians have a long history of fine art and architecture that is influenced by their associations with Greeks, Romans, and Turks. Much of the artistic work involved religious themes and resulted in great murals and frescoes. In recent years, these themes have given way to Russian-influenced paintings and architecture emphasizing scenes of daily life and landscapes. Government buildings have taken on the grandiose forms of their Soviet counterparts. The greatness of Bulgarian architecture in the past, as well as the Russian influence, are to be seen today in structures like the great round-domed and ornate Alexander Nevski Cathedral in Sofia with the statue of Tsar Alexander II facing the church.

Since Soviet influence has come to the Bulgarians, writing and drama has turned to Soviet-style social realism. Popular authors and playwrights who have succeeded under the Soviet cultural guidelines are Orlin Vassilev and Kamen Zidarov.

Daily life. Today Bulgarian city-people work in industries and dress in Western-style clothing. Before communism, the extended family working on a small farm was the most important social unit. The extended family consisted of father, mother, and the sons and their families. In this traditional unit the father was authoritarian, and the mother was largely confined to the kitchen. Although communism has threatened the father's position by providing authoritarian figures

Bulgarian peasants gather to shop and gossip at the open market.
From the Library of Congress.

outside the family, the father still remains a strong family head. Young Communist leagues give children social as well as political guidance, and schools lead children into occupational specialities unknown to their parents. The government has also upset the customary role of women by requiring them to leave the kitchen for industry. The traditional small farms have been almost completely collectivized into about 300 large agro-industrial complexes.

Bulgarians' loyalty and gratefulness to their Russian liberators was reflected until recently in the shipping of most of the country's agricultural products to the Soviet Union. In exchange, Bulgaria depended on the Soviet Union for crude oil and raw materials for its growing industries.

Women. Industrialization demanded an expanding work force and, as a result, women began to find work outside the house and farm. With this came an expansion of women's rights, and in 1944 women were granted civil rights. Since then women have found success in many Bulgarian occupations. Binka Zheliazkova produced one of Bulgaria's few internationally successful motion pictures, *We Were Young,* in 1961.

Even with women taking many roles in the economy, Bulgaria is a country of worker shortages. So acute is the shortage that in 1980 early marriages were encouraged by taxes. Single workers under the age of 30 were required to pay an additional 5 percent income tax; those over 30 paid an additional 10 percent.

Food, clothing, and shelter. The homes of Bulgarians reflect the variety of influences of the past. As protection from the harsh winters of the Danubian plains, homes there are sometimes sunken so that only a low roof extends above ground level, and this roof is often covered with thick sod. Other homes are enclosed in walls and have curved, tile roofs, reflecting a Mediterranean influence. Still others appear to be oriental, with wood as the basic structure. As their country has become industrialized, more Bulgarians have found homes in cities, many living in concrete, high-rise apartments.

Still, the beauty of the countryside holds many Bulgarians to small villages and their collective farms. These large assemblies of what were once small, family farms raise such products as tobacco and wheat for export. Another important farm product is roses. Bulgarians produce 40 percent of the world's rose attar, which is used for perfumes.

Each farm family is allowed a garden of its own in which fruits and vegetables are grown for the family's use. It is unusual to find a farm home without a vineyard in which the family grows grapes to make its own wine. A typical farm village is a cluster of small mud-brick houses with tile roofs, shuttered windows, and whitewashed walls.

Farm women can still be seen wearing the traditional dress of dark skirt, light-colored blouse, vest, and possibly a sack-like back-pack used for carrying infants. Scarfs are often used to cover women's hair. The traditional male dress can now be seen only at ceremonial events. On these occasions, the men wear knitted hats along with embroidered pants, shirts, and vests. A sash completes this folk costume. Today, these costumes are being replaced by more plain Western-style dress. The ceremonies and festivals that feature such traditional clothes are part of a growing tourist industry in Bulgaria.

Bulgarian farms yield an abundance of vegetables and these form the basis for most Bulgarian meals. A most common dish is *ciorba*, a vegetable soup that may be enhanced with tripe, meat, or chicken. Rabbit and pork are the meats most widely eaten. Minced meat is an ingredient of many dishes, such as *mousaka*. Although Bulgarians raise many sheep, using the wool to produce clothing, lamb and mutton are delicacies in Bulgaria. Most of the sheep meat is shipped to Arab countries or to the republics of the former Soviet Union to pay for energy sources and raw materials needed by the new economy.

Economy. Until the communist government was organized, Bulgarians depended mostly on agriculture. The land produced wheat, maize, beets, barley, and tobacco crops which supported the population and provided an early base for international trade. Beginning in 1950, the communist government implemented a series of five-year plans that industrialized the Bulgarians and expanded their efforts into industries other than the small, long-standing trade in textiles. Many Bulgarians now work in metal and petroleum industries. In the five years from 1946 to 1951, the labor force involved in agriculture dropped from nearly half of all workers to less than one-fourth of the work force. At the same time, the number of people in industry rose to 32 percent of the Bulgarian work force. This movement from agriculture to industry has changed in succeeding five-year plan periods. For example, from 1976 through 1980, industrial work rose by 35 percent. At the same time fewer farmworkers using more effective methods increased agricultural productivity by 20 per-

Girls often serve as shepherdesses in Bulgaria. *From the Library of Congress.*

cent. To support this move to industrialization and improved agri-culture, the Soviet Union supported the construction of highways, creating a vastly improved transportation system in a country that had traditionally depended on wagon trails and hiking paths.

In many places in Bulgaria, wagon carts and walking are still the most reliable modes of transportation. New highways have brought truck and bus transportation to even the smallest villages, but few Bulgarians can afford to own automobiles. Wages are generally low, interest rates on savings even lower, and wages in the 1980s have not kept pace with industrial productivity. This productivity has been achieved in some areas at great cost to the environment. Outdated production equipment and disregard for any standard other than productivity has resulted in heavy pollution. Still, many products are in short supply in Bulgaria, a country always struggling to balance import and export monies.

Holidays. Bulgarians celebrate their own national holidays—New Year's Day, January 1; Labor Days, May 1–2; Education Day, May

24; and National Days, September 8–9. The people also celebrate the anniversary of the beginning of the Russian Revolution, November 7.

Long an established country and relatively unified people, and always an independent satellite of the Soviet Union, the 1991 changes in that Union will affect Bulgaria as a buyer and seller of goods. With its economy shaken by the recent changes, Bulgarians face an uncertain near-future.

For More Information

Bulgaria, A Country Study. Washington, DC: American University Press, 1980.

Bell, J. D. "Post Communist Bulgaria." *Current History*, vol. 89, December 1990, pp. 417–420.

Brown, J. A. "Bulgaria Awakening." *America,* vol. 164, June 1, 1991, pp. 596–598.

Gibbons, Boyd. "The Bulgarians." *National Geographic*, vol. 158, July 1980, pp. 91–111.

BYELARUSSIANS

(byel uh rush′ uns)

A Slavic people of the former western Soviet Union, who early escaped oppressive rule by the Mongols.

Population: 10,590,000 (1990).
Location: Byelarus, bounded by Russia, Lithuania, Ukraine, and Poland.
Language: Byelarussian (a dialect of Russian).

Geographical Setting

Byelarussians

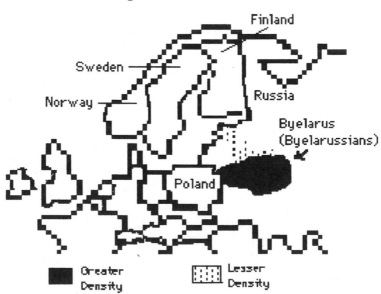

Byelarus occupies a roughly pentagonal area, almost exactly equal in size to Kansas in the United States, and bordered by Ukraine, Russia, Latvia, Lithuania, and the Baltic Sea. Much of the country is low-lying marsh and forest. Soil quality is generally poor, the result of ancient glacial deposits of clay, sands, and rock. There is some remaining forest mostly in the north. The better-drained central region is now largely cleared, and contains most of the land's people, industry, and agriculture. The Pripet Marshes dominate the south, and extend into Ukraine. Byelarus has more than 3,000 rivers and 10,000 lakes. Several of the larger river systems have provided important communication and trade networks.

The climate of Byelarus is temperate and wet, owing to the nearness of the Baltic Sea. Winters are cold, but not as cold as those farther inland. Though the entire country is farther north than the continental United States, winter temperatures rarely drop below −10° Fahrenheit. Summer days are usually around 70°, but seem hotter because of the high humidity. Annual rainfall averages about 25 to 30 inches, making Byelarus one of the wettest parts of the former Soviet Union.

Historical Background

Early Slavic states. Like Russians and Ukrainians (see separate entries), Byelarussians are descended from the eastern Slavic tribes. From about A.D. 900 to 1240 the eastern Slavs formed the loose confederation of states known as Kievan Rus. The most powerful of the principalities in the confederation (in what is now Byelarus) was Polotsk; like the other states it owed informal allegiance to the princes of Kiev (hence the name Kievan Rus). In about 988 the Kievan prince Vladimir I adopted the Orthodox Christianity of the Greek Byzantine Empire, thus establishing the eastern Slavs' religious heritage. Following the invasions of the Mongols in the 1200s, Kievan Rus broke up, with the ancestors of the Russians and Ukrainians coming under Mongol rule. Byelarus remained free; the name, meaning White Russia, seems to have appeared at this time, and apparently refers to the parts of Kievan Rus not under Mongol domination.

Alliance with Lithuania. The Byelarussians turned west for protection, to the powerful princes of non-Slavic Lithuania. A union of the two peoples joined Lithuanian military strength with the language, civilization, and Orthodox Christianity of the Byelarussians. The new state, called the Grand Duchy of Lithuania, existed from the mid-1200s to the mid-1500s, eventually including territory from the Baltic to the Black seas.

Polish influence. In the 1300s, the duchy began to fall under the increasing political and cultural influence of nearby Poland. The two states were driven together by threats from the Teutonic Knights of Germany on the one hand, and the growing power of Moscow on the other. The Union of Lublin (1569) formalized Poland's influence in the former Grand Duchy of Lithuania. Poland was strongly Roman Catholic, however, and many Lithuanian, Ukrainian, and Byelarussian nobles gave up their Orthodox faith for that of the greater power. Those who did not stood to lose land and privileges to Polish colonists. In 1596, the Poles forced the Byelarussians to accept union with the Catholic Church and imposed Polish as the official language of the former duchy. Most Byelarussian nobles became Polish in religion, culture, and language. In contrast with the nobles, the peasants who worked the land generally retained their Orthodoxy, as well as their traditional customs and language.

Imperial Russia. Moscow under the tsars became an imperial power in the 1500s. As Moscow's power grew, that of Poland's shrunk, partly because of ethnic disunity. Between 1773 and 1795, Poland was divided among growing neighboring powers, with the final result being that Russian gained all Byelarussian territory. During the 1800s, Polish Catholic forces clashed with Russian Orthodox strength over Byelarus. However, to the peasant forced to labor for little reward, it made no difference if the land was owned by Russian or Polish landlords.

Rise of national identity. In the 1860s a wave of unrest swept Russian-dominated Lithuania, Poland, Byelarus, and Ukraine. In 1863, as many as 75,000 peasants took part in a Byelarussian uprising. The leader, Kastus Kalinouski, demanded land reform, social equality, and political independence for Byelarus. The uprising was put down, however, and Kalinouski was captured and hanged. Still, the 1863 revolt marks the beginning of modern Byelarussians' sense of their own cultural and national identity.

Soviet communism. After the 1917 Russian Revolution, the new communist government, at the urging of Byelarussian communists, established the Byelarussian Soviet Socialist Republic (BSSR). Thus, Byelarus became one of the republics comprising the Union of Soviet Socialist Republics. At first, the central government in Moscow encouraged Byelarussians to emphasize their ethnic identity. Holding important posts in the BSSR's government, Byelarussian officials supported books, journals, and artworks that reflected this policy of Byelarussianization. The Byelarussian language was used in government and in universities until Joseph Stalin reversed this policy in 1929, attempting to Russianize Byelarussia and the other republics. During his "Great Terror" of the 1930s, perhaps 2,200,000 Byelarussians were executed or sent to a slow death in Siberian prison camps.

Wartime devastation. Hitler invaded Russia through Byelarus in 1941, occupying the region until being driven back in 1945. Byelarus was the scene of intense battles and harsh repression. In addition to the casualties of Stalin's policy, another 2,200,000 Byelarussians are said to have died during World War II. Over three-fourths of all Byelarussian towns and cities were virtually destroyed in battles.

Recovery and reawakening. As daily life slowly improved in the postwar reconstruction period, Moscow continued its policy of Russianization. Economic benefits came from central rule; by the 1980s, Byelarussians enjoyed one of the highest rates of urban and industrial growth in the Soviet Union. In return, however, they were discouraged from speaking their own language and from carrying on daily life in traditional ways. Still, the old ways survived until, in the Gorbachev era, Byelarussians were again able to promote their nationality. With the abandoning of communism by the Soviet Union and its dismemberment in 1991, Byelarussian independence came to the fore. In September 1991, Byelarus declared independence, as did most other former Soviet republics and autonomous regions. Byelarus changed the name of the country, although only slightly, from Byelarussia to Byelarus.

Culture Today

The Byelarussians are traditionally a rural and agricultural people. Early in their history, much of the west-central land of the country was marsh and swamp, the very large Pripet Marshes. Through time, much of this land was reclaimed and restored to farmland while the country as a whole turned to industry. By the mid-1980s about half

Representatives of the peasants frequently met to discuss problems of their collective farm under the old Soviet Union. *Courtesy of the National Anthropological Archive of the Smithsonian Institution.*

the population lived in cities, such as Minsk, the republic's capital. For those who continued to work the land, the estates of the land-owners were replaced in the 1930s by the large, collective farms of Soviet communism. Because of poor soil quality, agriculture has never been an easy enterprise in Byelarus. Still, Byelarussians grow significant amounts of potatoes, flax, and grain, and in 1970 held about 6 percent of the Soviet Union's cows and pigs.

About a fourth of Byelarus is forestland, and much Byelarussian industry has been developed around this product. Mostly destroyed in the two world wars, Byelarussian industry was encouraged under the Soviet Union. Hydroelectric plants were constructed to provide energy for lumber mills, woodpulp processors, food-processing factories, textile mills, and a growing chemical industry. It is the renewed industry that has brought a migration to the towns and cities.

Food, clothing, and shelter. The Byelarussian diet is similar to that of their eastern neighbors, the Russians. Meat or spiced sausages are enjoyed when available, as are fresh vegetables. Also popular are dairy products, in particular milk, sour cream, and various cheeses. Those who work on collective farms have been allowed to cultivate small private plots for their own food purposes, and, as elsewhere, these plots have proven more productive than the communal ones.

Amounting to three percent of the land, private plots produce almost 30 percent of the food. Each farmer tends his plot after finishing a day's work, grows potatoes, cabbage, strawberries, and vegetables, keeps livestock of his own, and cultivates flowers or keeps beehives for honey. Much of these harvests are used at home or traded for other farm products grown by neighbors. Some are sold as surplus in special farmers' markets. Cereals, hemp, fruits, vegetables, and fodder for cattle and pigs are principal crops of the cooperative farms.

Clothing is simple. White is the traditional color, causing some to suggest that it was the peasants' costumes that led to the name Byelarus (although it is more commonly believed that the name came at the time that Mongols were overrunning neighboring societies while leaving Byelarus relatively unscathed). Until Western clothing began to be the daily costume, men wore white jackets, shirts, and linen belts; women wore white skirts, aprons, and kerchiefs. Today, however, as with other Soviet citizens, old dress habits have given way to cheaper, mass-produced clothing.

Lumbering has been a source of income, comparable in value to agriculture. In a land of abundant forests, houses were traditionally built of logs and roofed with shingles or straw. The structures were small, dark, and ventilated by a small window or two. Small settlements of such households may survive in the more isolated areas. However, on collective farms, families live in modest wooden cottages, while most city-dwellers occupy modern, concrete apartment blocks.

Family life. As in other Slavic cultures, and indeed among many peoples, the earlier Byelarussian family was a large, communal group. Incorporating distant relatives or even strangers, the family was held together by the work each contributed to the farm rather than by blood relationships. A stranger (*zdolnik*) might join a family for life or for an agreed period; he and his heirs were accorded equal status with other members. Most often the father or grandfather acted as family head. He assigned the men jobs and acted as trustee for the family property, which was collectively owned. In modern times, such families have become rare, but some of the family leader's authority remains. At family gatherings, for example, the head sits in the place of honor, with the other men grouped by rank around him. Women sit at the other end of the table. The family head blesses the meal and serves himself first.

The sexes are also divided with respect to the jobs each performs. Washing clothes or preparing food, for example, are traditionally considered women's work, and no man would consider doing these tasks. Women also enjoy financial independence, within the limitations of family obligations. Like the men, for example, they keep the money made from the sale of surplus vegetables. The women have unquestioned authority in the household, with complete responsibility for children younger than 14 years. As the male head of the household supervises the men, his wife directs the work of women within the parameters of the farm community. Byelarussian women have long been respected for their willingness and ability to work.

Religion. Western Byelarussians, who came under the strongest Polish influence, are primarily Roman Catholic or Uniate in religion. (Uniate denotes a part of the Orthodox Church that has adopted Roman Catholic rituals and beliefs.) Eastern Byelarussians are mostly Russian Orthodox. In the past, religion, rather than language or origin, has determined whether citizens were counted as Polish, Byelarussian, or Lithuanian.

Language. The Byelarussian language is closely related to other Slavic languages, sharing elements with Russian and Ukrainian as well as Polish. Depending on which border they are closest to, Byelarussian dialects have tended to be heavily influenced by neighboring languages. The written language reflects this tendency. Byelarussian is sometimes written in the Latin alphabet, like Polish, and sometimes in the Cyrillic alphabet of Russia. The Latin version, called *lacinka*, was used in western Byelarus when the territory was under Polish control, between World War I and World War II. It continues to be used by some Byelarussian groups outside the former Soviet republics. The Russian or Cyrillic alphabet, called *hrazdanka,* became standard in Byelarus while it was a republic of the Soviet Union.

The language originated in the isolation of Byelarus following the Mongol invasions of the 1200s. During the period of alliance with Lithuania, Byelarussian was used in official and diplomatic documents, in private letters, and in local and national courts. Later, it was gradually overthrown in public use first by Poles and then by Russians. Byelarussians began to study and write their language again in the late 1800s, taking pride in its ancient history. Byelarussian remains a crucial element of national identity. Beginning in 1989,

Byelarussian language courses have been required for students from grade-school to university.

Literature and arts. Before the sixteenth century, growing Byelarus nationalism resulted in a beginning literature in that language. *The Battle of Mamay* and *Chronicle of Avraanka* were written in the 1400s. About this same time, Frantzisk Skorina printed the first books in Byelarussian. But as the Russian tsars took control of the land and discouraged the use of a language they considered inferior, Byelarussian literature became scant and remained so until the late 1800s. Then in 1906, a literary movement arose around a magazine called *Naša Niva* ("Our Field"). Until 1915, the magazine printed stories, poems, and articles by Byelarussian authors. More Byelarussian literature arose in the early days of communism, when conditions were more favorable for national cultures than under the tsars. Two poets in particular, Yakub Kolas and Janka Kupala, created works that came to be regarded as the classics of Byelarussian literature. As Joseph Stalin gained power, he again discouraged writing—except for that which furthered the socialist objectives.

Recent artistic activity has centered around political issues, primarily resistance to Soviet rule. Filmmaker Arkady Ruderman has made several documentary films critical of the regime, one of which includes a videotape of the beating of peaceful protesters by police in Minsk, Byelarus's capital.

For More Information

Aspects of Contemporary Byelarus. New Haven: Human Relations Area Files, 1955.

Lubachko, Ivan S. *Belorussia under Soviet Rule 1917-1957.* Lexington: University Press of Kentucky, 1972.

Vakar, Nicholas P. *Belorussia: The Making of a Nation.* Cambridge: Harvard University Press, 1956.

Zaprudnik, Jan. "Belorussian Reawakening." *Problems in Communism*, July-August 1989, pp. 36–52.

CROATS

(krow′ ats)

People of the former Yugoslavia who adopted Roman Christianity in the seventh century.

Population: 5,000,000 (1991 estimate).
Location: Croatia, formerly a northern province of Yugoslavia, and the Adriatic coast.
Language: Serbo-Croatian.

Geographical Setting

Croatia, the Croats' homeland, stretches in the shape of a huge arch across the north of the land that was, until 1991, Yugoslavia. The second-largest of the six Yugoslavian republics, Croatia has historically been divided into two regions. Pannonian Croatia comprises the broader, inland arm of the arch. This eastern half of the nation borders Slovenia in the northwest and Hungary in the northeast. Dalmatian Croatia, the arch's thinner arm, lies to the west, along the Adriatic coast. Dalmatia's rocky Dinaric Alps run parallel to the coast close to the shore. These rugged mountains have acted as a barrier between the coast and the interior. The Dalmatian coast has over 900 islands of various sizes, as well as numerous gulfs, bays, and channels. By contrast, inland Croatia is dominated by the fertile Pannonian Plains, which also extend south into the republic of Bosnia-Herzegovina. The plains also extend north into Hungary. Approximately 1,000,000 Croats live in Bosnia-Herzegovina, much of which in the past has been under Croatian rule.

Croatia's most important two rivers are the Sava and the Drava, both of which run on a southeastern angle to join the Danube near Belgrade, the Yugoslavian capital. The Sava flows through north-

Croats

Poland
Ukraine
Austria / Hungary
Slovenia
Romania
Croatia
Bosnia
Yugoslavia
Bulgaria
Herzegovnia
Italy
Armenia
Turkey
Macedonia
Greece

Greater
Density

Lesser
Density

Smaller type indicates breakaway states of the former Yugoslavia.

central Croatia from Slovenia, through the Croatian capital of Zagreb. The Drava runs parallel to it, to the north, and forms part of the border between Croatia and Hungary. Coastal Dalmatian Croatia enjoys a Mediterranean climate, with mild winters and warm, dry summers. Summers are hot in the mountainous interior, except for the highest elevations, and winters are long and severe. The plains are warm in summer and often very cold in winter, with strong winds and snow.

Historical Background

Western influence. Croatian tribes migrated from southern Ukraine and Poland in the seventh century, settling what is now Croatia. In 803, they accepted the rule of the Frankish (French) emperor, Charlemagne, and soon adopted Roman Catholicism, the Western form of Christianity. Frankish control was firmer in Pannonian Croatia; along the coast the Frankish rulers competed for influence with the still powerful Greek Empire of Byzantium to the east, and with the growing strength of Venice.

Feudal kingdom. In 924, Tomislav the *župan* (or tribal leader) united the Pannonian and Dalmatian Croatians to form a single kingdom, throwing off Frankish and Byzantine rule. Croatia remained independent for nearly 200 years, developing a feudal society in which nobles owned the land and the peasants became serfs. The nobles eventually grew strong enough to undermine the power of the king. In 1102, a lengthy struggle over the throne led the nobles to offer the crown to the king of Hungary. Croatia's association with Hungary lasted until 1918. During this time, however, much Croatian territory fell into other hands, as the Croats became pawns in centuries of strife between powerful states.

Turks, Austrians, and Venetians. In the late fourteenth century, the Ottoman Turks began their conquest of the northern Balkans (see SERBS). By the early sixteenth century the Turks had conquered most of Pannonian Croatia south of the Sava and occupied Hungary. In 1526, the Croatian nobles offered control of what remained to the Austrian emperor, Ferdinand of Habsburg, who became King of Croatia. For nearly 200 years, Pannonian Croatia was the front line in the struggle between the Christian Habsburgs and the Muslim Turks.

In Dalmatia, meanwhile, the growing commercial empire of the Venetians vied with Hungary, and then Turkey, for control of the seafaring coastal cities. Venice gradually won the upper hand, and from the fifteenth to the eighteenth centuries much of Dalmatian Croatia, when at peace, enjoyed commercial prosperity. Aside from trade, Venetians brought the artistic and intellectual vitality of the Italian Renaissance, which the Croats combined with Slavic culture. The result was a unique flowering of architecture, painting, sculpture, and literature, especially in the city-state of Ragusa (modern Dubrovnik). Ragusa remained mainly independent, becoming an important power in its own right.

Yugoslav movement. By the eighteenth century, both Venice and Turkey had passed into decline, and during the next century most of Croatia again came under the Austro-Hungarian empire. In the late nineteenth century, Croatian nationalists increasingly began to support the "Yugoslav idea." This doctrine held that the Yugoslavs (or "southern Slavs," meaning Croats, Serbs and Slovenes) should establish their own state, independent of the Austro-Hungarian and Turkish rulers (see YUGOSLAVS). The Croat who came to embody the idea was Bishop Josif Strossmeyer, who envisioned a Yugoslavia in which Croats and Serbs lived together and respected each other's cultures. Other Croatian leaders, such as Ante Starčević, promoted hostility towards Serbs while calling for an independent Croatian state.

With the collapse of the Turkish Empire in the mid-1800s and the breakup of Austria-Hungary following World War I, the southern Slavs formed the Kingdom of Serbs, Croats, and Slovenes, renamed the Kingdom of Yugoslavia in 1929. During World War II, this region fell to the Germans and, under fascist rule, was independent from 1941 to 1944. After the German and Italian occupation of the region was broken, Yugoslavia came under communist rule. Under their leader Josip Tito, a Croat, the communists had been largely responsible for resisting the Germans. Tito's own version of Strossmeyer's idea would hold the state together; after his death in 1980, ideas like Starčević's would work to tear it apart.

Culture Today

Civil war. As this entry is written, Yugoslavia has endured months of civil war, beginning in June 1991. The issues involved in this conflict, in which the Serbian-controlled federal army has attacked Croatian and Bosnian territory, are too complex to be discussed here (for a summary of them, see YUGOSLAVS). Much of the fighting in 1991 took place in Croatia, and it is not clear what effect the war has had on Croatian society. Several Croatian cities, besieged by the Serbs, have been heavily damaged by bombs and artillery shells, including Vukovar and Osijek in Pannonian Croatia, and Dubrovnik in Dalmatia. Nevertheless, in early 1992 Croatians declared independence and separated themselves from the rest of Yugoslavia.

Dalmatian coast. Because of their isolation, the Croats and others who live on the Dalmatian coast have always relied on the sea. It has supplied them with food and with an easy route for trade and communication among themselves and outsiders. Their greater exposure to the outside world has made Dalmatians worldly, tolerant, and outgoing. Dalmatia's historical interest and its great natural beauty have turned the coast into a major international tourist attraction. It is a loss for the world as well as for Yugoslavia that Dubrovnik's medieval town, previously well-preserved, was so badly damaged in the recent war. Its red-tiled roofs, great stone walls and ancient churches led it to be called the "pearl of Dalmatia."

Food, clothing and shelter. Croatian diet varies by region. Along the coast, where fishing fleets bring in catches of sardines and tuna, Mediterranean dishes such as fried squid are popular. Farther inland, the diet is closer to that of other peoples in the region. Sheep, lamb and chicken are popular meats, often grilled or included in soup. Like other Yugoslavs, Croats enjoy coffee, wine, and the national drink, a plum brandy called *sljovica.*

The Croats' traditional costumes, colorful like those of their neighbors, are distinguished by their intricate embroidery. Women wear long linen dresses—often white—covered by a colored apron and shawl over the shoulders. They usually cover their heads with a kerchief. Croatian men's white shirts are topped with a colored vest or jacket. Their pants are often dark linen or wool, worn with high leather boots or knee-socks. The outer garments are embroidered in red or gold with geometric designs or images such as birds or flowers. Today, however, such costumes are worn only on holidays or special occasions.

In modern cities such as bustling Zagreb, glass-and-concrete apartment buildings provide housing for most of the people, but in other areas, older buildings of stone or wood are lovingly preserved. Wood is the traditional material for Croatian houses, since most areas of Croatia are heavily forested. A typical dwelling is the *brvnera*, made of logs and sometimes having two or three wings. Large stone houses are more common in rocky Dalmatia.

Family life. Croats are one of the Slavic peoples that in the past utilized the *zadruga*, or extended family. In the zadruga, siblings, cousins and in-laws would live under the same roof, with the oldest male usually acting as head of the family group. Today, as young people seek the advantages of town- or city-life, family sizes have become smaller. Yet Croats preserve a strong sense of family loyalty. Aged parents, for example, almost always live with their children, taking an active role in raising the young and looking after the household. The larger family, even if dispersed, remains close and gathers for holidays and events such as weddings. Many Croatian folk songs and poems celebrate the joys and rewards of family life.

Religion. Their Roman Catholicism has meant that Croats share a common religious heritage with the West. Religious observation has tended to be strict. As recently as the 1940s, for example, the Croatian *sabor*, or parliament, passed laws against blasphemy and cursing. Religion has been a strong element in Croats' nationalism—indeed, it is the root cause of their historical enmity with the Orthodox Serbs. It also contributed to one of the most fascist *ustaše* during World War II. This extremist group came to power by collaborating with the German occupiers of Croatia and Serbia. The ustase's policy was to convert or deport two-thirds of the Serbs under their control. The rest were to be "eliminated." Thousands were killed, mostly Serbs. The genocidal policy has since been a source of great shame for the Croats.

Language. Religion also affected the Croats' language. Before their adoption of Christianity, the Slavs had no alphabet. Those converted by the Roman Catholics took the Latin alphabet (used also in English); those converted by the Greek Orthodox Church took a modified form of the Greek alphabet. Thus, though the Croats and Serbs share a common language (called Serbo-Croatian), they use different letters to write it. The alphabets themselves inspire intense national feeling. For example, during their rule the ustase outlawed road signs in the Serbian alphabet.

Literature. The church was responsible for keeping Croatian (as the written language is called) alive in the earliest years. Secular writers in Dalmatia in the fourteenth and fifteenth centuries, though Croatian, were often educated abroad. Though these scholars wrote mostly in Latin or Italian, one of them, Marko Marulić, is generally regarded as the first to write literature in Croatian. His epic poem *Judita* ("Judith") was written in 1501. Croatian literature developed into a rich one, often utilizing folktales or themes taken from them. In the nineteenth century, a number of poets wrote passionate pieces advocating Croatian independence.

The best-known Croatian writer of this century is Miroslav Krleža. Born in Zagreb in 1893, Krleža wrote over 20 books, including short stories and plays. Krleža's *The Croatian God Mars* examines the corrupting effect of war on human values. After World War II, he became a leading cultural and political figure in Yugoslavia, and was a close friend of Tito.

The arts. Croatians pride themselves on their artistic heritage and intellectual sophistication. Earliest works were religious, whether in music, sculpture, architecture, or painting. Churches from as early as the ninth century survive, and frescoes (wall paintings done on wet plaster) survive from the eleventh. From the thirteenth to the eighteenth centuries, Dalmatian architects created beautiful churches and cathedrals that became internationally famous. Like the architects, Croatian sculptors who decorated the churches combined Romanesque, Byzantine, and Renaissance techniques, displaying styles that reflected their own distinctive touches.

The best-loved artist of modern times is perhaps the sculptor Ivan Meštrović, born in 1883, who worked in many styles and materials, including wood, stone, and bronze. His figures are powerful and muscular, using large sweeps rather than close detail. When Meštrović emigrated to the United States after World War II, he left behind an entire generation of Yugoslav painters and sculptors indebted to his artistic leadership. In the United States, he became well-known for his huge sculptures of Native Americans (one of these sculptures can be seen in Chicago). Meštrović died in Indiana in 1962.

Politics. The biggest question facing Croatian and other Yugoslav politicians concerns the reorganization of the former Yugoslavian territories. In April 1990, Croats elected Franjo Tudjman president of the Croatian Republic. Tudjman, a senior officer under Tito in the Partisan Army that defeated the Germans, quarreled with Tito in the 1960s over Croatian political rights. Tito expelled him from the Communist party and imprisoned him twice. However, Tudjman held to his beliefs—that Croats, Western in outlook, can never live happily with the Serbs. It was his resolve that Croatia secede from Yugoslavia, which prompted the Serbs to attack Croatia. Another Croat, Ante Marković, serving as Yugoslavia's prime minister, argued that the country should attempt to patch up its complicated territorial disputes. Only by remaining united could Yugoslavia compete with the economic might of Western Europe, Marković claimed. Yet his position was unpopular with both Serbs and Croats. When the Serbian-dominated federal army invaded Croatia in 1991, even though he was by law its commander-in-chief, he was unable to stop it.

By the beginning of 1992, the former Yugoslavia had begun to break up into smaller, more cohesive states. Slovenia and Croatia had achieved recognition as separate nations by the middle of the year, and Bosnia-Herzegovina (the home of many Croats) had declared its intention to break away from the Serb-dominated Yugoslavia.

For More Information

Danforth, Kenneth C. "Yugoslavia: A House Much Divided." *National Geographic,* August 1990, pp. 92–123.

Doder, Dusko. *The Yugoslavs.* New York: Random House, 1978.

Eterovich, Francis H., and Christopher Spalatin. *Croatia: Land, People, Culture.* Volume I. Toronto: University of Toronto Press, 1964.

Jordan, Robert. "Yugoslavia: Six Republics in One." *National Geographic*, May 1970, pp. 589–633.

Singleton, Fred. *A Short History of the Yugoslav Peoples.* Cambridge, England: Cambridge University Press, 1985.

Viorst, Milton. "A Reporter at Large: The Yugoslav Idea," *New Yorker*, March 18, 1991, pp. 58–79.

CZECHS
(checks)

Slavic people of western and central Czechoslovakia.

Population: 9,880,290 (1990 estimate of Czechs in the Czech and Slovak Republic).
Location: Northwestern Czechoslovakia.
Language: Czech.

Geographical Setting

Czechs

Czechoslovakia (the Czech and Slovak Federative Republic) lies south of Poland and southeast of Germany. The land is divided geographically into three parts: Bohemia, Moravia, and Slovakia. The Czech people live predominantly in Bohemia, a mountain-ringed bowl in the northwest, and in Moravia, the mountainous central portion of Czechoslovakia. In Bohemia, tributaries of the Elbe River flow from the low mountains toward the North Sea. The Czech people are gathered in towns and cities along the streams, lakes, gorges, and valleys of the northern mountains. Moravia, the central part of the country is marked by hills and low mountains crossing north to south across the land and dividing the land of the Czechs from that of the Slovaks.

Historical Background

Origin. The Czechs originated from Slavic groups of the Vistula River basin northeast of the Carpathian Mountains. Before the sixth century A.D., these Slavic groups migrated to a mountainous region of Central Europe that the Romans had named Bohemia after the Boii Celts who had settled there. By the time the Slavs arrived, Germanic tribes had also begun to settle the region. Over the centuries, a distinct group with its own language, a blend of old Slavic and Germanic words, was identified by the local area they inhabited, Čechy.

Early history. The earliest Czechs were loosely organized into many separate tribes. When the Asian Avars raided the region periodically from A.D. 550 to 795, these tribes were easily dominated. Eventually, however, the Avars were defeated by the Franks and their king, Charlemagne. In the ninth century, the great Moravian Empire grew out of one small local dynasty. For a century, this empire endured as an association of landholding nobles who quarreled among themselves as frequently as they banded together to repel other Germanic tribes. It was in the period of the Moravian Empire that Byzantine missionaries came to Moravia and converted both Czechs and Slovaks to Christianity.

Magyars from the powerful Hungarian kingdom included the Slovaks in their rule, but were not able to defeat the Bohemian princes who remained independent in the face of Magyars and Germanic tribes attempting to enter the area from east and north. During the ninth and tenth centuries, princes from the house of Přemyslid held thrones in Prague and were recognized in Europe as kings of Bohemia.

St. Wenceslas built the cathedral of St. Vitus in A.D. **930.** *Courtesy of Cedok Czechoslovak Travel Bureau.*

These kings were loosely connected with the Holy Roman Empire and to Western Europe in general. Eventually, the Bohemian-Moravian state became a part of the German political system and expanded its territories into present-day Poland and Austria. Throughout the German domination, however, Czechs maintained their cultural independence.

A European power. When the last Premyslid king was murdered in 1306, there was great competition among powerful Europeans to take the throne. Four years later John of Luxembourg finally acceded to the throne. Two years later his father became the Holy Roman Emperor and the Czech state gained an important position in Europe as a whole. John's reign was followed by Charles I, who, in 1355, became Holy Roman Emperor. His election made Prague the foremost city of the empire.

During the reign of Charles I, Prague, in addition to its political importance, became a cultural center of Europe. At that time, artists and architects designed many of the grand buildings that mark Prague today. Under Charles I a code of laws was developed, and the formalizing of a new language for the Czechs was encouraged. (Writers had written in a Czech dialect since the 900s.) The first central Eu-

Statues of saints line the famous Charles Bridge over the Elbe River.
Courtesy of Cedok Czechoslovak Travel Bureau.

ropean university was founded at Prague, making the city a center for intellectual activity. This creativity would continue for centuries, producing such giants as Jan Comenius (1592–1670), considered to be one of the originators of modern educational systems.

The Hussite reform movement. Greatly influenced by the British John Wycliffe, Jan Hus, a Bohemian, led a movement attacking the Church and papal abuses. After Hus was burned at the stake as a heretic in 1415, many Czechs continued to fight for reform in the Roman Catholic Church and were attacked by the church advocates. The next 20 years, a period known as the Hussite Wars, were characterized not only by a polarization of Catholics and Protestants, but also of peasants (who clung to the church) and landlords (who were advocates of church reform). The issues and the struggles of the Hussite reform movement would be carried on by Martin Luther as he led the sixteenth-century Reformation movement that swept through much of Europe.

House of Habsburg. In 1526, Ferdinand I of Austria began his reign as King of Bohemia (and soon after, of Hungary) and the Habsburg rule of Central Europe grew. Founded by Count Rudolph, King of Germany in 1273, the Habsburg dynasty eventually controlled most of Europe. In favor of religious reform as well as individual liberties, Czech armies fought against the Habsburgs for decades before losing to them at the Battle of White Mountain outside of Prague. From that date until the end of World War I, the Czech people were never politically independent. During this period, the Czech language was replaced by German as the official language of the land, and for hundreds of years Czech women were banned from teaching their children the Czech language. During this period, the Czechs lost more and more of their sense of national identity. Prague became a German-speaking city, and one of the greatest centers of learning was the Prague German University. However, the Czechs under Austria built one of the strongest industrial complexes of Europe, and accounted for nearly 75 percent of the industrial production of Austria.

World War I. Under Austrian rule, Czech nationalist movements had begun to revive Czech culture in the wake of the 1848 revolutions in France and Germany, and again with the Young Czech Movement in the 1870s. But it was not until after World War I that Professor Tomáš Masaryk and his student, Dr. Edvard Beneš, working from

**Ancient statues stand by live guards at
the entrance to Czechoslovakia's
government offices.** *Courtesy of Cedok
Czechoslovak Travel Bureau.*

London and Paris, successfully led a campaign for independence,
which relieved the Czechs and Slovaks from the Austro-Hungarian
yoke. Under these leaders, a constitution modeled on those of France
and the United States—calling for a bicameral parliament—was rat-
ified and Czechoslovakia became a democratic republic. Czechs and
Slovaks joined in this union to escape management by other nations
even though there were significant differences between the two cultures. These differences were enhanced as the greater population of
Czechs took control of a government that directed Czechs, Germans,
Slovaks, Hungarians, Ruthenians, Jews, Poles, and Gypsies. Even

though the only democratic government in Central Europe between the two world wars attempted to provide representation for the Slovaks, ethnic friction was to bother the Czech government from that time on.

World War II. Having played such a significant role under Habsburg rule, Germans in Czechoslovakia were particularly dissatisfied with their subordinate role in the Czech government. At the same time, Slovaks in the east were in fear of invasion by Poland and Hungary. This discontent was reflected in the pleas of such Slovak leaders as Josip Tito for German intervention (intensified by Germany's threat to leave the Slovaks to Hungary). Slovak dissociation with the Prague government also aided Germans under Hitler in their takeover of Czechoslovakia in 1939.

However, many Czech problems in World War II were external. England's prime minister, Neville Chamberlain, believed that the way to deal with Nazism was by appeasement. In 1938, England, France, Germany, and Italy signed a Munich Agreement declaring German rights to the German-populated Sudetenland in western Czechslovakia. Using the excuse that 3,000,000 Germans on Czech soil gave them the right to enter the country, Germany invaded Czechoslovakia at the beginning of World War II. Having been let down by France and England, and refusing help from the Soviet Union as too distant and too unprepared, Czechoslovakia was taken over with little overt opposition by the Germans. Czech exiles formed a provisional government led by Tomáš Masaryk, Josef Dürich, Edvard Beneš, and Milan Štefánik (the lone Slovak representative) that was recognized first by the Soviet Union and then by France, Great Britain, and the United States. Following the German defeat, President Beneš was reinstated and formed a new Czechoslovak government. The Czechoslovak Republic became a democratic government ruled by a parliamentary government in Prague, and with separate Czech and Slovak state governments in Prague and Bratislava. World War II restored Czechoslovak land taken by Germany, Poland, and Hungary, but ceded the former Czechoslovak region of Ruthenia to Russia. In the new democracy, the communists formed one party and began local organizations, an effort that grew stronger in 1945 and 1946.

Soviet domination. In order to secure a treaty of friendship and mutual assistance with the Soviet Union, which the Czechs felt necessary as protection against the Germans, President Beneš agreed to political compromises favoring communism. The two nations agreed to exchange minority populations. In the elections of 1946, the Communist party won 38 percent of the vote, and the party leader Klement Gottwald became prime minister. As early as 1947, Communists in the Czech government had come under severe public scrutiny as they rejected an invitation to participate in the United States-sponsored Marshall Plan. By that time, however, members of Communist-controlled action committees had formed in towns, factories, trade unions, and schools. These committees joined the police in demonstrations in the streets of Prague and other cities. The strength of the Communist party was inflated in successful media propaganda. On February 25, 1948, the resignation of representatives of other parties placed Czechoslovakia completely under Communist control and Soviet domination.

Soon purged of anti-Communists, Czechoslovakia became a satellite of the Soviet Union. Upper classes were denied access to education in order to de-emphasize the power of property and wealth. Production was nationalized and agriculture was collectivized. When the resulting poor quality of Czech goods could no longer compete on the international markets, the country's reliance on imports upset the balance and resulted in shortages of almost all kinds of goods. Discontent and near-economic collapse swept the country.

The "Prague Spring." Alexander Dubček, a Slovak, became Communist Party Secretary in 1968. He began to implement policies that restricted the comprehensive control the Communist party had over all political and economic considerations, and granted greater individual rights and more independence to local governments. However, Secretary Dubček and the Czech people were too early with their reforms in the eyes of their Soviet overlords. Under the Soviets, an army of 500,000 soldiers from all the nations who had joined in the Communist Warsaw Pact of 1955, except Romania, invaded Prague and other major cities. Czechs and Slovaks fought courageously with their homemade weapons, but these were not enough to compete with tanks in the streets. In the end, the Soviet Union regained control and restored the central-government control of most sectors of daily life.

The Velvet Revolution. In 1989, the same year that saw liberation in Bulgaria, East Germany, Hungary, and Poland, Czechoslovaks

Graffiti, Prague, Czechoslovakia style. *Courtesy of Leah M. Cadavona.*

successfully asserted their right to an identity separate from the Soviet Union. Welcomed by crowds of half a million people, many of whom had been demonstrating for ten days, Dubček reiterated his 20-year-old motto: "The ideal of socialism with a human face lives on in the new generation." This was, however, no longer the Czech goal. The old Communist rulers resigned, admitting that they had failed to bring about adequate democratic reforms. Eventually a new party, the Civic Forum, came to power. The new republic was a federated state, with independent Czech and Slovak diets exerting more power than in the past.

Since 1989, the events of 1968 are no longer viewed as a glaring victory for the government, but as a heroic act on the parts of all who risked their lives for freedom to choose. All five Warsaw-Pact countries who participated in the invasion have since condemned their own actions. In 1991, the people's celebration of Prague Spring was a particularly momentous occasion as it coincided with the Soviet people's defeat of the hard-line Communist coup attempt.

Culture Today

Early in his career, Adolf Hitler warned his countrymen of the industrious nature of the Czechs. As a student in Vienna, he observed Czechs whom he described as arriving empty-handed and dragging their worn shoes over the streets of the city only to install themselves in prominent positions soon afterward.

Government. The Czechs of Bohemia and Moravia are citizens of the Czech and Slovak Republic with its government at Prague. However, the country is divided further into sections, with Slovaks dominating the east and Czechs holding a majority in the west. Bohemia, the area of greatest Czech population has a regional capital at Prague, while the eastern Slovak region has a capital at Bratislava. Internal matters are dealt with by regional councils while foreign affairs, defense, transportation, and communication are administered by the Federal Assembly. So independent are the regional governments that until recently there were no direct rail lines between Prague and Bratislava. In part, this independence is a result of Czech and Slovak distrust. The Slovak people have, since the founding of the new country in 1918, felt that they were not well-represented in the national government, and have long campaigned for independence.

Education. Although private and religious schools were legalized in 1990, most schools are public and education is free and compulsory between the ages of six and 16. Almost all children, however, attend kindergarten from the age of three. Sixteen-year-olds who plan to attend a university may go either to secondary grammar school, where they continue with a general curriculum, or to working people's secondary schools, particularly if they are interested in economics or administration. Vocational schools also exist for young people who wish to learn particular job skills.

Food, clothing, and shelter. As in most of Europe, dress in Bohemia and Moravia is very much like that in other parts of the Western world. Traditional Czech dress, characterized by a great deal of white lace as well as embroidered materials, is worn on special occasions. For men, a holiday costume might consist of a white shirt with wide sleeves gathered at the wrists, and white trousers. Both shirt and pants are frequently highly decorated with embroidery. A brightly colored vest decorated with embroidery and buttons is worn over the shirt. Women wear gathered skirts and blouses made of simple materials such as linen and cotton. These clothes are embroidered, however, giving them a very rich appearance. To complete this costume, an apron, again heavily embroidered, can be worn. Both men and women complete their festive costumes with boots. In rural parts of

Street musicians are common sights in Prague, Czechoslovakia. *Courtesy of Leah M. Cadavona.*

southern Bohemia and southeastern Moravia, folk costumes are still worn, consisting for women of calf-length, dark, gathered skirts, plain blouses, boots, and scarfs.

Industrialization has resulted in mass movements to the cities, where housing is extremely limited. Here many Czechs live in tall apartment buildings of concrete brick or cement, in great contrast to the ornate buildings of the past. Other city and town dwellers live in block houses similar to those in other European countries, or in single stucco and tile-roofed homes. Rural homes are small, often wood houses sometimes decorated with colorful, hand-carved designs.

In the cities, especially, nightlife and student life are centered around cafes, wine cellars, and beer halls where food can be purchased as well as drinks. Czechs are well-known as brewers of some of the best beers in the world, including Budvar and Pilsner Urquell, the latter coming from the town of Pilsen (*Plzeň*). Beer is often the beverage served with meals.

Czech food specialities include *zeleninová*, a vegetable-and-cream soup, and many pork dishes. Salads are frequently vinegar-based with onions and tomatoes. Salamis and sausages are common, as are fruit-filled dumplings and creamy pastries. A favorite dish consists of roast pork, dumplings, and sauerkraut, while carp is the traditional Christmas food.

The Elbe River is a major waterway in Czechoslovakia. *Courtesy of Cedok Czechoslovak Travel Bureau.*

Family life. While extended families were at one time the central organizing unit of society, industrialization and urbanization have changed families significantly. Children rely less on parents and older siblings as almost all children attend school from a young age. Industry has provided jobs away from home and lessened young persons' reliance on their fathers. However, the nuclear family—parents, children, and sometimes grandparents—is still important. Today both parents most often work outside the home. Nevertheless, women are still largely responsible for most of the work of maintaining a home and caring for the children.

Religion. Most Czechs are Christian, both Catholic and Protestant. Many Czechs turned to Protestantism following Jan Hus's campaign to reform the Roman Catholic Church in the fifteenth century. There are also people of the Jewish faith in Bohemia. Before World War II, about 250,000 Jews lived in Czechoslovakia, but both persecution by the Germans during the war and fear of persecution after it, forced many thousands of Jews to leave the country.

Language. Although Czech has existed as a literary language since the thirteenth century and the first books in the language date to the ninth century, it has not always been the official language of Bohemia and Moravia. Because languages tend to reflect political and religious movements, German was, for many years, taught as the primary language in the schools. Today, both Czech and Slovak are official languages. The two languages are similar in that they are both derived from the old Slavic language and both use the Roman alphabet. Proximity to other languages and the long separation of the country under different foreign rules has resulted, however, in differences. Czech became sprinkled with German terms and Slovak was influenced by Hungarian, Russian, and Polish.

Literature. The important role of writers and intellectuals in Czech society is particularly well-illustrated by the leadership of the 1989 revolution. The human rights movement was led by Vaclav Havel, a playwright who was joined by other writers and students. In 1990, Havel was elected president of the country and enlisted the aid of other artists to build the government. Perhaps the most well-known Czech fiction writer is Milan Kundera. The 1988 motion picture adaptation of *The Unbearable Lightness of Being* stirred international interest in Kundera's work. Czech literary tradition emphasizes poetry. In fact, the earliest known document in the language is a hymn written in 973. Poetry began its dominant role in Czech literature as early as the thirteenth century.

Much of the literature of the twentieth century deals with the difficulties of living under Soviet domination, as illustrated in this excerpt from "A Village Story" by Jan Drda (Nemcová 1967, p.151):

> In the afternoon, the Gestapo had arrived in the village with a squad car. They had found the Russian at the Bernats' in a cupboard. He had a high fever and his leg had been chafed to the bone on the frozen snow. They took Bernat and his wife, their seventeen-year-old son Tonda, and the hired man. Without coats and in wooden clogs, they were herded into the car with rifle-butts.

But just as often the writing is fanciful, as reflected in "One Brief Moment" by Jaroslava Blazkova (Nemcová 1967, p.267):

> There was a little mouse
> Who had a little house,
> She saw a cat named Mighty Mite
> With yellow eyes and teeth that bite.

The arts. Cities such as Prague display examples of medieval, Byzantine, baroque, Gothic, renaissance, and rococo architectural styles. During the nineteenth century, painters and sculptors were involved in a national movement aimed at reviving Czech traditions and themes in both architecture and other art forms. Paintings and sculptures depicted daily life, historical events, the roles of peasants, and Czech landscapes. Thus, the art history of the Czechs is documented in its architecture and sculpture.

In the twentieth century, travel and communication have made artists everywhere more aware of the art of other countries. A well-known leader of German expressionism, Oskar Kokoschka, was actually half-Czech and half-Austrian, worked in Switzerland, and became a British citizen. Psychological portraits and lyrical landscapes were his specialties. Mikulaš Medek, on the other hand, produced many colorful abstract and semiabstract paintings.

Under Communist rule, all of the arts were promoted, though art projects had to meet with government approval. As a result, public art abounds in Bohemia and includes sculptures done in metal, glass, and concrete as well as art in other media. Rene Roubicek is acclaimed for his glass creations, especially lighting fixtures such as those that lighted the Czech pavilions at the Brussels, Montreal, and Osaka World's Fairs. Now painting on glass, Jan Cihla is an abstract painter from southern Bohemia.

Embroidery, crochet, and needlework continue to be popular crafts among the women of Czechoslovakia, although today fewer young women are learning these skills.

Music. Czechs are well-known for their interest in music and for their musical contributions. Libor Peske, a conductor, has begun the Mozartian Foundation in order to bring the best productions of Mozart to Prague every year. Although not a Czech, Mozart composed both *Don Giovanni* and *The Marriage of Figaro* in Prague in the eighteenth century. Václav Tômasek is an internationally regarded Czech classical composer.

A rich tradition of folk songs and dances in Bohemia and Moravia continues to bring Czechs together today. Famous composers, in-

Wenceslas Square, Prague, Czechoslovakia. *Courtesy of the Simon Wiesenthal Center for Holocaust Studies.*

cluding Antonín Dvorák, Bed, and Leos Janá are known for operas, ballet scores, and choral works often based on the folk music. Two great festivals—the annual Prague Spring Music Festival, and the International Jazz Festival Prague—draw audiences from around the world.

Other accomplishments. Prague has long been a center of intellectual activity with its great university, but because of Czechoslovakia's long history of persecution, many of its most famous citizens have either worked outside of the Czech land or have not acknowledged their Czech heritage. Sigmund Freud developed much of his psychological theory in Vienna, but was born in Příbor, Moravia. Gregor Mendel first read the studies that made him the father of modern genetics in Brno, Moravia. Bernardo Bolzano, a leader of modern mathematics, was born in Prague. Franz Kafka wrote realistically and critically about America even though he had never traveled there. Thus Czech science, medicine, literature, and arts have had global influence. It is not surprising, then, that a scholar such as Tomáš Masaryk or Edvard Beneš, professors of literature, should be chosen to lead the Czech people in times of greatest stress.

For More Information

Blunden, Godfrey. *Eastern Europe: Czechoslovakia, Hungary, Poland.* New York: Time Incorporated Life World Library, 1965.

"Czechoslovakia." *Europa World Year Book*, Volume I. London: Europa Publications, 1991, pp. 655–858.

Czechoslovak Life. A monthly magazine published in English, German, and French.

Kundera, Milan. "The Unbearable Lightness of Being." *Time.* December 1989, pp. 20–24.

Mastny, Vojtech. *The Czechs Under Nazi Rule.* New York: Columbia University Press, 1971.

EASTERN EUROPEAN JEWS
(ee' stern yoor' eh pee' en joos)

Jews of Eastern European republics and the former Soviet Union; third-largest community of world Jewry.

Population: 1,500,000 to 1,600,000 (1989).
Location: Czechoslovakia, Poland, Hungary, Romania, Bulgaria and the post-Soviet republics.
Languages: Czech, Polish, Hungarian, Romanian, Bulgarian, Russian, Ukrainian, and Ladino; also Yiddish and Hebrew.

Geographical Setting

Once 75 percent of world Jewry lived in Eastern Europe, mainly in Poland. Shifting eastward in Poland as the centuries passed, most Jews had migrated toward Lithuania, Byelarus, and the Ukraine by the early 1700s. This region would remain the heartland of East European Jewry for the next two centuries.

By the twentieth century, three types of Jewish communities had appeared in East-Central Europe. Jews at the western end (present-day Czechoslovakia and Hungary) blended somewhat with surrounding peoples, speaking local languages and participating in national politics. Jews of the southeast (Bulgaria, Serbia) spoke Ladino, a Spanish dialect, and lived peaceably apart from the main population. Most of Polish Jewry, the third grouping, lived not so peaceably apart from surrounding Poles. Speaking Yiddish, this largest group developed a distinct community life, which was shattered by events of the twentieth century, giving way to the most recent shift in population, as shown in Table 1. After World War II, most of the area's Jews moved eastward once again to the Soviet Union, mainly to the Russian and Ukrainian Soviet Socialist Republics. Polish Jewry dwin-

Eastern European Jews

Jews are scattered throughout Eastern Europe and Western Asia. More than half of the Jews live in large cities.

dled, its survivors resettling in cities like Warsaw and Kraków, or in Silesia, where their saga began some ten centuries ago.

1989 Population Estimates of Eastern European Jewry			
Bulgaria	3,000	Romania	20,000
Czechoslovakia	5,000	USSR	1,449,167*
Hungary	70,000	Yugoslavia	6,000
Poland	7,000		
*(includes Asian regions)			

Historical Background

Origins. Archaeologists have uncovered in East-Central Europe gravestones written in Hebrew from the fourth century. Traders note the arrival of Jews in Prague as early as 961 and in Poland around 1098. From the tenth to the thirteenth centuries, the group played a key economic role in the region, facilitating long-distance trade: metals, furs, grain, and wine from Western Europe; money, crafts, textiles, spices, and agricultural products from Arab lands, and slave labor and raw materials from Eastern Europe. The Jewish traders settled here and there in Poland's southwest region, Silesia, until the thirteenth century. Afterwards, a great influx of Jews, persecuted during the Crusades, Reformation, and Counter-Reformation, arrived from Germany.

After the ravages of invasions in the 1240s, both Jews and German merchants were invited by Polish rulers to settle their lands in the interest of developing an urban life. The Poland these newcomers entered was a collection of local communities and private towns ruled by kings and nobles. Soon the German merchants ruled towns too. Beneath them were shopkeepers, artisans and a great mass of peasants.

A charter by Prince Boļeslav the Pious in 1264 isolated the Jews, putting them under the king's authority and exempting them from the laws of the German merchants. New statutes in 1334, 1364, and 1367 by King Kazimierz III broadened this charter to cover the whole kingdom of Poland. Polish towns granted the Jews "privileges"—that is, rights and obligations that were a matter of record. The privileges permitted them a wide range of economic activities and the right to practice Judaism without interference. They had their own judicial system, appointed their own rabbinical judges, and enforced their own decisions. The privileges also spelled out obligations on Jews. In exchange for rights, they had to fulfill a host of duties from working on a lord's manor, to paying rent, to observing restrictions on their behavior. Jews were not allowed to own land but could manage it: non-Jewish nobles, who owned large tracts in remote areas such as the Ukraine, would lease their estates to Jews, engaging them as middlemen over non-Jewish peasants. In some towns, Jews were not allowed to own houses on main streets. These communities had separate "Jewish streets"; in others, Jews were the majority. They became entrenched in villages and small towns, working as innkeepers, estate managers, artisans, and the like, identified in the minds of the non-Jewish peasants with the nobles who exploited them.

Polish shtetl. Flocking together to preserve their traditions, Jews built a vigorous communal life in the small towns in which they formed a majority of the population. The shtetl, or small town, consisted of a mass of poor folk and a smaller group of craftsmen, shopkeepers, and estate stewards. Shtetl dwellers made ends meet any way they could. So common was the pursuit of some trades that they became

The Jewish street in Lubin, Poland. *Courtesy of the Simon Wiesenthal Center for Holocaust Studies.*

identified with the group: Jewish tailors, cobblers, blacksmiths, coachmen, and water carriers. Besides cutting hair, barbers circumcised male newborns. Once a week on market day, stalls were set up in the town square, and women sold wares crafted by their husbands. Costermongers (traveling merchants) drove their ware-laden wagons to different shtetls throughout the week (market day differed in each town). Other Jews, *luftmenshen*, served irregularly as agents or brokers, seeming to live on thin air.

Some occupations serviced only the Jewish community. The key functionary, the rabbi, presided over marriages, divorces, the rabbinical court, and the learning academy, meanwhile resolving an endless stream of everyday questions. In the synagogue, the chanting was led by the cantor, a singer who represented the congregants in prayer to God. Other functionaries made it possible to observe religious law: the synagogue caretaker (*shamus*), ritual slaughterer (*shochet*), kosher butcher, bathhouse (*mikvah*) attendant, matchmaker (*shadchen*), and scribe (*soifer*). Finally, there was the body of Jews who did nothing but study religious law.

Most boys began *cheder* (meaning "room") at age three, usually in a room of the teacher's house. Otherwise they went to Talmud Torah, a public school. From three to 13 they completed their compulsory education, which included training in the Hebrew alphabet, prayers, Yiddish, arithmetic, the Five Books of Moses and rabbinic law as set down in the Talmud. Those who pursued their studies after 13 entered an academy, or *yeshiva*. Girls had less education, learning to read (mainly Yiddish; sometimes Hebrew too), write, and compute from age seven. At 13, they were typically apprenticed to seamstresses.

Mainstream religion. At first, community religious life was scant. Not until the fourteenth century did rabbis appear in Silesia. They came even later (in the fifteenth century) to the frontier, where there were Jews unable to read the Hebrew Bible as late as the 1600s. Meanwhile, back in more developed Silesia, Jewish commentators were already applying religious law to everyday life in Poland.

Aside from the Ten Commandments, the religion as practiced by most Jews in Poland included the oral law—regulations believed to have been passed down verbally from Moses to spiritual leaders, then written down in the Talmud. Above all, studying Talmud was the most laudable profession in the shtetl. Wives would take responsibility for the family livelihood, convinced that a husband's preoccupation with Talmud paved both his and her way into heaven after death. The academic ability of a penniless youth might win him the daughter (and dowry) of a rich family, while the opinions of Jewish scholars carried weight at community meetings. Supporting its scholars, the shtetl would give them a weekly allowance and daily meals in different houses.

All this effort bore fruit. Beginning in the late fifteenth century, Polish Jewry produced an outstanding series of commentators on rabbinic law. Their ability to apply it to everyday life would make Poland one of the foremost centers of intellectual activity in Jewish history. An earlier center of activity, Spain, had written a digest of Jewish law that was easy for the average person to follow. Called the *Shulhan Arukh*, the digest was tailored to the Sephardim, or Spanish Jews. Central- and East-European Jews, known as Ashkenazim, practiced the faith differently from Sephardim. Tailoring the Sephardim's *Shulhan Arukh* to the needs of the average Ashkenazi, the Polish rabbi Moses Isserles (1520–1572) gave the group a digest of their own. Rabbi Isserles wrote also on secular subjects like astronomy.

His concern for secular learning was echoed in the next century by Elijah ben Solomon Zalman (1720–1797), called the Vilna *Gaon* ("rabbinic excellence"). The Gaon studied music, astronomy, physics, mathematics, and philosophy as well as religion. Within Judaism, he rejected the tendency to overanalyze. Scholars of his time were preoccupied with the skills of arguing to make subtle points (*pilpul* and *hilluk*). Instead the Gaon favored exact, common sense interpretations of Jewish law, even if they conflicted with ancient opinions. The Gaon, in this way, infused new energy into traditional Judaism. As generations passed, Poland-Lithuania's Talmudic colleges (especially Vilna's) attracted students from Germany, Bohemia, Hungary, even Italy.

Hasidism. Dissident religious movements appeared in the shtetl. From a Ukrainian village, Jacob Frank (1726–1791) proclaimed himself the Messiah, who would usher in the kingdom of heaven on Earth. Frankism, which encouraged people to commit sin, never took root, but it was succeeded by Hasidism. Rooted in the teachings of the Baal Shem Tov, Hasidism exists today in Israel and in the Americas as well as in Europe.

Eleazaer Baal Shem Tov (1700–1760), a folk healer from the Carpathian Mountains, taught that Jews should not be preoccupied with guilt for their sins. They should instead lose themselves in the joy of worship. Humankind was meant to laugh, sing, dance, and perform simple acts of loving kindness in cheerful devotion to God. When their minds wandered during prayer, the Hasids would try to drive out all other thoughts with strange sounds, jumping, and gestures to restore their concentration on God. Doing good, believed the Hasids, meant more than strict observance of Jewish law. They produced a new religious leadership based on the spiritually superior individual (called the *zaddik*, or *rebbe*) who, it was believed, could pass on people's petitions to God. Dynasties developed. Great rebbes attracted huge followings, then passed on authority to their children. By the 1780s, a bitter feud had erupted with more traditional rabbinic leaders, the Mitnagdim. In Vilna they denounced the Hasidim to the Russian government and some rebbes went to jail for a time. Later, the feud faded and the two sides moved closer together, the Hasids influencing the mainstream religion of the Mitnagdim. The Mitnagdim had believed in inflicting hardships on the body to perfect the spirit. Instead they came to emphasize ethical behavior and the joy of the spiritual connection.

Anti-Semitism. From the mid-1500s to the mid-1700s, a type of national Jewish parliament, the Council of Four Lands (Great Poland, Little Poland, Lithuania, the Ukraine) administered Jewish affairs. It negotiated with the crown the level of Jewish taxation, then divided the tax burden among provinces and communities. The Polish kings of the period had a consistently positive policy toward the Jews.

Kingly power was fading fast, however, and with it the favorable standing of the Jews. Beginning in 1648, Polish society experienced two decades of almost continuous warfare. In the Ukraine, a Cossack chief, Bogdan Chmielnicki, led a peasant revolt that spread northward to Byelarus and Lithuania. Then came war with Sweden. About 20 percent of the Jewish population died in these two decades, often violently and in the company of Polish Catholics. As one account (Weinryb 1972, p. 188) describes,

> Some were skinned alive . . . some had their hands and limbs chopped off, . . . others were buried alive. Jews were given rifles and ordered to kill each other.

The special status of the Jews deteriorated rapidly. In 1764, the Jewish "parliament," the Council of Four Lands, was abolished. Poland was partitioned several times by Prussia, Austria, and Russia (1772, 1793, and 1794), despite a revolt led by Tadeusz Kościuszko and fought by Catholics and Jews. Poland had disappeared from the map by 1795. Some Jews resided in Prussia's share of it and more fell into Austria's, but most of Polish Jewry lived in Russia's share for the next century-and-a-half. Intolerance grew. In 1804, Russia moved to keep Jews out of its interior, confining them to the Pale of Settlement, a stretch from the Ukraine northward to what is now eastern Poland, Byelarus, and Lithuania. Jews could no longer lease land, sell liquor, or run inns. Furthermore, the tsar ordered an end to customary clothing, burned Jewish books, and stripped Jewish community councils of their power.

Russian army conscripts served a 25-year stint. In 1827, Tsar Nicholas I ordered that Jews be conscripted for an additional six years, from age 12 rather than age 18; the additional six years were designed to convert Jewish boys to Christianity. A youth would be made to kneel on the floor all night or be served salted fish without anything to drink until he consented to baptism. Some were whipped to death.

From where did all the hatred come? A long-standing negative image of Jews had spread through Russia and Poland. Medieval anti-

Semitism fed on wild, religious rumors. The Jews, went one accusation, used the blood of Christian children to bake their unleavened bread, or matzahs. Called a *blood libel*, this unfounded charge crops up repeatedly in Jewish history (1367 in Poznań, 1407 in Kraków, 1698 in Sandomir, and 1747 in Zaslav).

Generally, the Jews were pictured as an evil people with strange accents who corrupted non-Jewish peasants with drink. In the seventeenth century, the Polish scholar Sebastian Petrycy defamed Jews as a group that bribed judges, hoarded gold, demoralized women, and lured Christians away from the Church. Some prominent outsiders held the Jews in high esteem but this view was the exception, not the rule. The Polish poet Adam Mickiewicz (1798–1855) praised the Jews in his verse; the Russian author Fyodor Dostoyevsky (1821–1881), however, depicted them as moneylenders who drained the poor, an old stereotype formed during pre-Poland days, when lending was one of the few occupations a Jew was allowed to pursue.

Outside Poland and Russia. Elsewhere, in areas such as Bohemia (present-day Czechoslovakia), more a part of Western than Eastern European culture, the Jews fared better during these years. In 1781, Bohemia's government issued a *Toleranzpatent* for Jews and Protestants, an edict that opened all forms of trade and commerce to them. Joseph II invited the Jews to set up government schools of their own with instruction in math, geography, and morality. As time passed, conditions that encouraged assimilation mounted. The Ordinance of 1786 made marriage licenses depend on attending a *Normalschule* (modern elementary school). Bohemia's Jews stopped using Hebrew and Yiddish in their business records.

In contrast, most of Poland's Jews continued to speak Yiddish and to live in separate communities, where the children and older students attended strictly Jewish schools. Relations with the non-Jews varied with the generations, growing strongest around the mid-1800s under Russian rule. Friendship between the Polish Catholics, who were generally anti-Russian, and Polish Jews reached an all-time high in 1863. The Jews joined the Catholics in an insurrection that ended in freedom for the serfs. Conditions improved briefly, then deteriorated drastically with the onset of pogroms.

Pogroms. A *pogrom* was an organized and officially tolerated massacre of the Jews. Already in Polish history there had been anti-Semitic outbursts (for example, a 1464 pogrom in Poznań) but these were isolated incidents in a mostly harmonious environment. The late 1800s ushered in almost a century of massive anti-Jewish violence. Scores of savage pogroms erupted in Eastern Europe in 1881–82, 1903, 1905–07 and 1918–20. They outdid earlier incidents in degradation and deadly horror. Officials would organize a pogrom to channel social discontent, then look the other way as Jews were attacked, their homes burned, their bodies raped and mutilated. Anti-Semitism actually seemed to escalate during the interwar period; as many as 2,000 pogroms erupted in Jewish communities scattered through the Ukraine.

With the industrial revolution came the growth of Jewish organizations such as the Bund, the national labor group that fought for the rights of its members as workers and as Jews. The Bund, a socialist, anti-Communist organization, stressed social justice and supported cultural independence for Jews in the large, multiethnic cities. Another organization, the Zionists, was largely inspired by Leon Pinsker (1821–1891), a physician from Odessa in the Ukraine, and Theodor Herzl (1869–1904), a Viennese intellectual. The two men, who did not know each other, prescribed a Jewish homeland as the antidote for anti-Jewish violence, with Pinsker publishing his reasons in *Autoemancipation* and Herzel publishing his in *The State of the Jews*. There were other voices too: Jewish Communists rejected the cry for a homeland or separate Jewish culture; Orthodox rabbis formed Agudat Israel (League of Israel), which fought modernization; assimilationists, calling themselves Poles of the Mosaic Faith, favored ties with other Poles over ties with other Jews. It was a vigorous and divisive period; each group opened schools to promote its viewpoint: socialist, Zionist, or Orthodox.

Interwar contrasts. The assimilationists were never a very large group in Poland, but other areas saw a growing trend among Jews to adopt many national customs. Czechoslovakia was a bulwark of democracy during the interwar period, the only country in which Jews actually sent delegates to parliament. Led by President Tomáš Masaryk, the government supported a Hebrew school system that produced a new generation of youth who took pride in their Jewish and Czech heritage. There were individual incidents of anti-Semitism, such as young students being ridiculed or spit at because of their Jewishness. Yet the atmosphere in such areas was considerably more favorable than in Poland.

Official anti-Semitism mounted in Poland, fanned by the flames of Nazi Germany. The year 1937 saw Polish authorities tolerating pogrom after pogrom (in Mazowiecki, Zetochowa, Brest, and Przytyk). A Polish political party, the National Democrats, spread anti-Jewish rhetoric. While they frowned on pogroms, several church leaders (for example, Archbishop Sapieha) approved of economic boycotts against Jewish businesses. Signs appeared: "Jews, Go to Palestine"; "Beat Up a Jew"; and in some Warsaw coffeehouses, "No Jews Allowed." At universities, there were *numerus clausus* (Jewish quotas) and anti-Jewish riots. Thousands of Jews chose to emigrate during this period. Then came World War II.

Ghettos. "Liquidate the Jews, or the Jews will liquidate you," said the Nazis. Their attempt went through three stages: 1) isolation in ghettos; 2) breakup of ghettos and deportation to death camps; 3) murder by gas or hard labor.

After Hitler's victory in Poland in September 1939, the move to segregate Jews was immediate. From December 1, Jews had to wear a special badge, the Star of David armband. Then the Nazis herded them into ghettos in the large cities. Caravans of Jews were forced to trek to the cities, their sledges piled high with furniture and other belongings. Around the ghetto in Warsaw the Nazis erected a 19-foot wall topped with broken glass and barbed wire. Locked within were 500,000 people, about 13 people per room at the peak. The per-person food allotment was 184 calories a day, on which adults were made to labor for the German war effort. With overcrowding and malnutrition came typhoid and death. The bodies lay in gutters and on sidewalks. Over 100,000 had perished by 1943, when the Warsaw ghetto dwellers revolted. From April 19 through May 8, 1943, 50,000 young Jews staged an uprising led by Mordecai Anieliewicz. Their weapons—hand grenades, pistols, dynamite—had been dismantled and smuggled into the ghetto at night, piece by piece through holes in the walls. The rebels had also built an elaborate maze of underground corridors and shelters for self-defense. The uprising was at first successful but ultimately defeated by German fire power. Combat flared up here and there until autumn 1943, though most of the rebels had perished earlier.

Death camps. Other ghettos saw their inmates deported to concentration camps until the ghettos had been liquidated. Traveling in cattle cars, the victims had no idea where they were going. A cattle

Odd Nansen, deported to Sachsenhause, painted this picture of Nazi prisoners at hard labor. *Courtesy of the Simon Wiesenthal Center for Holocaust Studies.*

car held from 75 to 100 Jews, their bundled belongings, a few loaves of bread, and two buckets, one with water, the other for excrement. Children were tossed atop the bundles, the doors locked and barred. Invariably, passengers died along the way.

Whole communities were deported at once. From Czechoslovakia, Martin Weiss, then 14, recalls the arrival of his family at Auschwitz (Cohen 1989, pp. 31–35):

> The story they [the Germans] gave us was that we (the men) will work. The women and children will be taken care of . . . Cecilia and Hannah [sisters], both were spared at that time. But Hannah died in camp.

> We smelled flesh burning. Still, we didn't know what was going on. By the next day we knew. . . And from there on, it was the question of survival. Your mind works on a different level.

> A lot of people will give you different motives for different things, but the truth is that nobody was very smart and nobody was very brave. You learned to survive.

> Sometimes I gave some food to my father. At other times he gave food to me. We didn't lose our compassion.

"The Jew's Last Road" was painted with watercolor in Auschwitz Prison Camp, 1943, by Waldemar Nowakowski. *From the Jaworska Collection, Warsaw. Courtesy of the Simon Wiesenthal Center for Holocaust Studies.*

In the end, Martin Weiss did lose his father, mother, three sisters, and a brother in the camps; hundreds of thousands of other Jewish families suffered similarly devastating losses.

There were earlier mass killings, with guns. September 29–30, 1941, saw the massacre of 33,771 Jews at Babi Yar near Kiev, capital of the Ukraine. From 1941 to 1944, the pits of another wooded area, Ponar, near Vilna, became a burial site for 80,000 more Jews massacred by gunfire. The systematic gassings began in 1942. All six death

Nazi Death Camps

o Cities   • Death Camps

camps (see map) sat on Polish soil: Auschwitz (1,000,000 killed); Belzec (550,000 killed); Chelmno (150,000 killed); Majdanek (50,000 killed); Sobibor (200,000 killed); and Treblinka (800,000 killed).

The death camps resembled each other in layout. Assembly areas and barracks were surrounded by guard towers and electrified barbed wire. At Auschwitz, the subcamp Birkenau was equipped with four crematoriums for Jews. Upon arrival, the sick, the old, the pregnant, and babies went straight to the gas chambers, under the pretense that they were being led into a shower room. About 6,000 bodies could be gassed at once at Birkenau. After 20 minutes the gas had done its work, the Nazis knew, because the screaming had stopped. They then had the gold removed from teeth and the bodies transported to ovens or open spaces for burning.

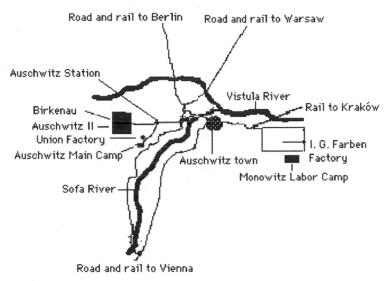

Auschwitz Labor and Death Camp

Other Jews were temporarily spared for hard labor. First they underwent quarantine (two to eight weeks of terrorizing drills on smaller rations than in camp), then worked to either maintain the camp or assist the German war effort. Conditions varied among camps, but generally the prisoners slept in barracks or "blocks." The inmates lay on straw on the floor at first, later on multi-story bunk beds, as many as eight inmates per bunk. Men wore thin tunics and trousers, and women wore thin dresses. Later, there were too few uniforms, so the clothing of dead civilians was used. The starvation diet consisted of about a pint of coffee or tea for breakfast, roughly a quart of soup (potato, turnip, carrot, or cabbage) at noon, and for supper coffee or tea and one slice of bread with an ounce of sausage, cheese, margarine, or jam. The mounting calorie deficiency, coupled with hard labor, brought disease and death.

Harnessed to pull wagons, inmates had to build roads. They were also made to construct barracks and gas chambers, sort and disinfect possessions of the dead, and work in chemical, cement, and airplane salvage plants. Wakened at 4:30 A.M., they endured morning roll call, an agonizing process—even the dying were carried out to be counted. The nightmarish day proceeded: standing in line for a meal, leaving

The ovens used for incinerating Jewish bodies at Auschwitz.
Courtesy of the Simon Wiesenthal Center for Holocaust Studies.

camp to the music of the ashen-faced, inmate orchestra; performing hard labor; returning with the dead on stretchers; and surviving evening roll call. The average life span of the laborers was a few months. In the end, most of almost three million Polish and one million other Jews perished either by gas or hard labor in the camps. Estimates of all Jews exterminated during the war range from four to six million. The most widely accepted figure is 5,721,800.

Resistance. There were repeated cases of resistance, both physical and spiritual. Over 10,000 Jews were killed daily at Treblinka, where Dr. Leichert, once a captain in the Polish army, led a suicidal revolt on August 2, 1943. The rebels, fighting with hand grenades, machine guns, and pistols stolen from the German arsenal, were massacred after six hours, but their revolt prompted the Germans to blow up Treblinka altogether. At Auschwitz, prisoners formed the *Kampfgruppe Auschwitz* (Auschwitz Fighting Group), locating medicine and food, organizing escapes, documenting Nazi crimes, and staging an uprising on October 7, 1944. Led by Roza Robota, Jewish women from a labor camp on the premises (Monowitz) smuggled in firearms and blew up Crematorium IV. Afterwards, Roza and three other women were executed.

Most escapes failed, but some succeeded. Alfred Wetzler and Walter Rosenberg escaped Auschwitz on April 7, 1944. Reaching Bratislava in Czechoslovakia, they wrote a detailed report on Auschwitz, which they smuggled to the free world. Less fortunately, Mala Zimetbaum and Edward Galinski were caught and executed in front of others on September 15, 1944.

Operating outside the camps were the Jewish partisans (guerrillas). Young women transported messages, food, medicine, and weapons to different ghettos while the ghettos lasted. Caught by the Nazis, Sonia Madeisker (1913–1944), a partisan of Vilna, shot seven of her captors as they seized her, then tried to kill herself but failed. Later they tortured Sonia for information, which she never divulged.

The Jews mustered continuous spiritual resistance as well. In the ghettos, they established schools, published newspapers, performed concerts and plays, and held religious services despite the threat of death. In the camps, poems and songs helped make life endurable. The conductor Martin Rosenberg formed a secret chorus and reworded "Tsen Brider" ("Ten Brothers"), an old Yiddish folk song, to capture the truth of the death camps (Kalisch 1985, p. 57).

Yidle with the fiddle,
Moyshe with the bass,
Play for us a little,
The gas chamber we face.

Ten brothers were we together—
We hurt no one and did no wrong.

The conductor, Rosenberg, died in Auschwitz.

Exodus. Though the Nazi's "Final Solution" to the presence of Jews in East-Central Europe ultimately failed, it drastically reduced their population in almost every area, by close to three million in Poland, one million in the Soviet Union, 250,000 each in Czechoslovakia and Romania, 200,000 in Hungary, 60,000 in Yugoslavia, and 5,000 in Bulgaria.

Some 200,000 survivors resettled in Poland after the war, about 84 women for every 100 men and almost no children. Of the Jewish organizations that resurfaced after the war, the Zionists (in favor of a Jewish homeland) were strongest. Over the next two decades, emigration, mostly to Palestine and the United States, reduced Poland's Jewish population drastically.

Jews who remained in Poland faced postwar anti-Semitism. Jewish property had passed into the hands of non-Jews during the war and there was opposition to returning it. Also, Jews were unwelcome competitors for factory jobs. The stereotype of the time was that all Jews were Communists. Poles boycotted Jewish stores, and about 1,500 Jews died in violent incidents from 1945 to mid-1947. Some Poles staged a pogrom in Kielce on July 4, 1946, which killed 41 Jews. The pogrom prompted thousands to emigrate, although nine rioters were sentenced to death for it. Fleeing for their lives, about 150,000 Jews left Poland in 1946 alone, usually by way of the Bricha, an underground railroad for illegal emigrants.

Poland's Jewish population continued to dwindle and the center of Eastern European Jewry shifted eastward to the Soviet Union. Some Jews gave their loyalty to the Communists, who promised them safety and equal rights. The friendliness was short-lived, though. In 1949, all Jewish cultural institutions in the Soviet Union were closed. Publications in Yiddish ceased. Tens of thousands were arrested. The stereotype of the Jew as Communist was abandoned for the stereotype of the Jew as capitalist who aimed to overthrow communism for the West. In 1952, Rudolf Slánský was put on trial in Soviet-dominated Czechoslovakia for his role in an alleged worldwide Zionist conspiracy. A purge of Jews in the Communist party followed. Under Nikita Khrushchev every trace of Jewishness was suppressed. More anti-Semitic incidents erupted in 1967, after the Arab-Israeli war. Again Jews left—25,000 Soviet Jews emigrated from 1971 to 1980. Restrictions on emigration were lifted in 1989 and by 1992 another 400,000 Jews had left. The pace has since slackened. Over a million Jews are expected to remain behind in the post-Soviet republics.

The remainder. The 1980s included positive and negative times for Jews in the Soviet Union and its satellites. Authorities apologized for misdeeds of the past and allowed new freedoms. Though no longer alive, Jewish members who had been expelled in the purge of the Communist party were publicly reinstated. Catholic bishops announced their regret (December 1990) for anti-Semitic incidents that had occurred on Polish soil. Soviet Jews were allowed to form a national coordinating body, *Vaad*, to aid emigrants and to promote Jewish culture and religion in the Soviet Union. Yiddish language courses and theater appeared. In Lithuania, the government allowed monthly Yiddish radio broadcasts and restored Jewish street names. Meanwhile, negative incidents spanned the decade. Soviet journals printed anti-Semitic articles to oppose Polish liberals (the Solidarity

Party) in 1981; in 1989, leaflets that blamed the Jews for the country's economic problems were distributed in Kraków, Poland.

Culture Today

The cultural heritage of today's Eastern European Jews is the shtetl lifestyle, which had already begun to change with the movement to big cities and the Industrial Revolution that preceded the world wars. The trend in dress, language, and schooling was to adopt customs from the surrounding culture and develop an urban, middle-class lifestyle. This occurred to an extreme under Communist rule. In the decades after the Holocaust, many of the region's Jews assimilated and lost touch with the language, history, and religious practices that had enriched Jewish identity. The years of anti-Semitism left mixed feelings in the people themselves, including shame about their heritage. Now, a more liberal atmosphere is producing a new generation with a different outlook. Unlike their parents, the young show a desire to be fully Jewish.

Food, clothing, and shelter. Though proponents of Jewish culture teach the Yiddish language, their intent is not to recreate the past. The aim instead is to use the distinctively Jewish tools to keep the heritage alive in the present. Long an urban people, Jews in the former

The "Sepinker" rabbi arriving at Upper Viseul, Romania. *Courtesy of the Simon Wiesenthal Center for Holocaust Studies.*

Soviet republics reside mostly in large cities, such as Moscow, Minsk, and Kiev. Their daily habits are those of the majority population in their regions (see BYELARUSSIANS, RUSSIANS, and UKRAINIANS), but the Jews throughout these areas share the unique heritage of shtetl customs. No longer do they wear the clothing or live in the homes of the past, but customary foods still enter the daily diet.

Everyday wear for a man of the shtetl was a black long caftan over black pants, a white shirt and a shawl with *tzitzis*, or fringed corners, to recall the Commandments. In Poland, men also wore the rock (a jacket) and a sleeveless overcape. A fur or velvet hat covered the man's *yarmulke* (skull cap). The yarmulke was never removed, even at bedtime. Besides a beard, men had long, curled sidelocks. Some men were already combing these sidelocks behind their ears by World War I, and wearing shorter caftans or suits. Most women wore fashions of the day, but observed the biblical ban against mixing linen and wool. If married, a woman cut off her hair and wore a wig to reduce her appeal to other men, a custom that had begun to fade by World War I.

In some shtetls, houses were attached to one another with perhaps 15 in a row. They ranged from the two-story brick structure with a balcony, to the small wood-frame house with clay-and-straw walls under a thatched roof. A *mezuzah*, a parchment scroll (with quotations from the Bible), was attached to the doorpost. Inside were prayer vessels and books and a charity box for Jews in Palestine.

Meals included a few staples and various specialities. Among the staples were borscht, a beet soup, and *krupnik*, a thick soup of barley or groats with potatoes. Potatoes and herring were standard fare. On the Sabbath or a holiday, the family ate meat and specialties: noodle pudding, potato pancakes, chopped goose-liver, chicken soup, carp, sour cucumbers, or baked apples, and always *challah*, a light bread, usually twisted in celebration of the holiday.

Family life. Today's Eastern European Jews live in small, nuclear families, but before World War I the large Jewish family (eight children or more) was common. Rituals marked stages in the Jewish life cycle, beginning with circumcision for the entrance of a newborn male into the covenant between Abraham and God. Bar mitzvahs (ceremonial passage into manhood) were a matter of course in the shtetl. The occasion was a quiet, simple affair. A boy read in the synagogue, his father said "I am no longer responsible for his sins," and the boy received gifts from his parents. Given new religious freedom in the post-Soviet republics, some men have chosen to undergo circumcision now as adults and to become bar mitzvah, a rite usually performed at age 13.

As in general society, strict rules governed male-female behavior in the shtetl before World War I. Girls were chided for loose behavior, for example, if they wore short sleeves. At 18, a young man was marriageable. The age for girls was once 12 to 14. Arranged by a matchmaker, the decision of whom to marry depended largely on the fathers. Marriage, it was believed, came first; love followed. Sometimes the betrothed were complete strangers who first laid eyes on each other at their own wedding. After the bride immersed herself in the ritual bath, the rabbi read the marriage contract (*ktubah*) and the couple was married under a wedding canopy (*chuppah*). The groom placed a ring on the bride's finger, said, "Thou art consecrated unto me," and the wine was blessed. Making the groom dizzy, the bride circled him seven times, then tried to step on his foot so she might be the dominant one. He stepped on a glass in a rite traditionally understood to recall world suffering even in this hour of happiness. If the marriage was unhappy, a religious divorce was possible, but it required the consent of both husband and wife.

Shtetls had burial associations to take care of deaths. For a week, family members mourned at home; for a year, they abstained from pleasures like hearing music. This is a heritage with which the present-day Jews of Eastern Europe are becoming reacquainted.

Education. The educational pendulum has swung from predominantly Jewish studies before World War I to almost wholly secular studies after World War II to a resurgence of Jewish studies in the post-Soviet republics. Called the National Jewish School, a Jewish day school that spans ten grades has recently opened in Moscow. Education is free, with secular studies paid for by the Russian government; Jewish organizations pay for the Judaic studies. After World War II, Soviet Jews continued to pursue secular education—one of the few avenues open to them for advancement in Soviet society—with the ardor they had shown before the war. The Jews concentrated in the exact sciences, biology, and medicine. By the mid-1960s nearly 25 percent of the educated wage earners were physicians. Few became attorneys, since Soviet bureaucrats rarely employed Jewish lawyers.

Religion today. A rabbinical college sits in Budapest, Hungary, and a few rabbis are scattered throughout the countries of the region. In

1991, the first rabbi in Poland since the 1950s, Menachem Joskowicz, came to the Warsaw synagogue. His Sabbath services attract 70 or so congregants. In its heyday (1878–1939), the High Synagogue in Warsaw was famous for its choir of over 100 singers. Non-Jewish musicians sought invitations to hear not only the choir but also renowned cantors, such as Gershon Sirota (1877–1943), a masterful tenor who was burned in his flat during the Warsaw Ghetto uprising. At that time one of the few centers of Reform Judaism in Eastern Europe, the High Synagogue played organ music, which was foreign to houses of prayer that observed traditional, Orthodox customs.

Arts. A summary of the creative outpouring of Jews born in the region can name only a few in an army of artists and scholars, from psychoanalyst Sigmund Freud (1856–1939) to author Franz Kafka (1883–1924), whose stories about guilt, power, and truth described the modern human condition.

Early literature was religious or practical, including the Five Books of Moses, as well as a guide with hints for daily life—the Yiddish *Ze'enah Ur'enah* ("Come and See") by Jacob Ashkenazi. Literary masterpieces appeared in the nineteenth century: short stories by Mendele, the Wandering Bookseller (Shalom Abramovitsch, 1836–1917), who comically yet lovingly portrayed Jews as matchmakers and the like; bitter satire by Isaac Peretz (1851–1915) and the poem "Monish," about a Jewish boy's love for a Christian girl; tales of shtetl life by Shalom Aleichem (Solomon Rabinowitz, 1859–1916) featuring characters like Tevye, the dairyman, and his daughters. In the twentieth century, I. J. Singer (1893–1944) wrote *The Brothers Ashkenazi*, a novel about sibling rivalry in turn-of-the-century Poland, and Isaac Babel (1894–1941) spun tales on the Ukrainian Jewish experience. Isaac Bashevis Singer (1904–1991) wrote stories such as "Yentl the Yeshiva Boy," a melancholy piece about the limits of male-female roles in the shtetl. There were oral tales, too, including humorous anecdotes about how the so-called "ignorant" Jews managed to outsmart bigoted non-Jews.

Wandering organ grinders and folksingers visited the shtetl. First appearing in the sixteenth century, *klezmerim* (folk bands) performed in the inns. Self-taught, the musicians knew no notes but played so masterfully that, for example, Josef Michal Gusikof (1806–1837) performed in palaces on the *strohfiedel*, a variation of today's xylophone. In Russia, pianist Anton Rubinstein (1821–1894) and violinist Henryk Wieniawski (1834–1880) became the tsar's soloists. The twentieth century produced pianist Arthur Rubinstein (1887–1982) and violinist Yasha Heifetz (1901–1987).

Once thought inferior because he worked with his hands, Mark Antokolsky (1843–1902) became a renowned Russian sculptor. Isaak Levitan (1860–1900) was called the father of Russian landscape painting and Samuel Hirszenberg (1865–1908) achieved worldwide fame with paintings such as "Golus," which portrays a village of Jews fleeing a pogrom, their rabbi in front with the Torah in his arms. Other painters include Chaim Soutine (1894–1943), who used thick brushwork on subjects such as choirboys and hanging sides of beef. Beside his paintings, Marc Chagall (1887–1985) earned high esteem for his etchings, theater sets, and stained-glass windows.

Called the father of Jewish theater, Abraham Goldfaden (1840–1909) set up a company in 1886 to perform his plays in southwest Russia and Romania. Other theater groups followed, featuring fine actresses such as Ida Kaminska (1899–1980). Today in Russia, the Jewish Chamber Musical Theater carries on the tradition in a modern-day context with plays like *A Lady from Odessa*, about the trauma of emigration.

For More Information

Cohen, Marcia, ed. *The Moss–Weiss Families Survive World War II and Immigrate to America.* Unpublished manuscript, 1989.

Kalisch, Shoshana, and Barbara Meister. *Yes, We Sang!: Songs of the Ghettos and Concentration Camps.* New York: Harper and Row, 1985.

Niezabitowska, Malgorzata. *Remnants: The Last Jews of Poland.* New York: Friendly Press, 1986.

Reitlinger, Gerald. *The Final Solution: The Attempt to Exterminate the Jews of Europe 1939–1945.* Northvale, NJ: Jason Aronson, 1987.

Weinryb, Bernard D. *A Social and Economic History of the Jewish Community in Poland from 1100–1800.* New York: Jewish Publication Society of America, 1972.

ESTONIANS

(est own′ ee uns)

A Siberian people who settled on the Baltic Sea coast across a
narrow neck of the sea from Finland.

Population: 968,000 (1990 estimate).
Location: Estonia, North of Russia on the Baltic Sea and the Gulf
of Finland.
Languages: Estonian, a Baltic-Finnic language; Russian.

Geographical Setting

Estonia is essentially a peninsula like its Scandinavian neighbors to the north, surrounded by three bodies of waters: the Gulf of Finland to the north, Lake Peipus and the Narda River to the east, and the Baltic Sea to the west. Estonian history and culture is interwoven with its southern bordering republics, Latvia and Russia. A relatively small country, Estonia has an area of 17,400 square miles, consisting of a mainland and some 800 islands which make up 9 percent of Estonia. The largest of these islands are Saaremaa (1,048 square miles) and Hiiumaa (373 square miles).

The relief of Estonia is generally undulating with small hills, and numerous rivers, lakes, and forests. Throughout the country, the land has left traces of the glacial activity of its geological past. In the south, hills were once formed of glacial deposits and, along the northern coast, extensive sandy areas mark the ancient glacier's edge. Along the coast, sheer cliffs stretch around the Gulf of Finland and the Baltic Sea. Throughout Estonia, numerous rivers carry their waters to sea and to Lake Peipus. The largest rivers are the Parnu (88 miles) and the Pedja (81 miles). About 5 percent of Estonia is comprised of lakes. Lake Peipus, the largest lake, has a surface area of 1,370 square miles. Vast peat bogs cover some regions of the lower lands and are used extensively to provide energy for the Estonian people. Unlike many parts of Russia at the same latitude, the climate of Estonia is temperate and humid. In the winter months, the mean temperature is 23 to 43 degrees Fahrenheit. In the summer, temperatures average in the low 60 degrees Fahrenheit. With an annual precipitation of 24 to 28 inches, the Estonian climate is generally favorable for agriculture.

Historical Background

Along with Latvia and Lithuania, Estonia is one of three republics (countries) known historically as the Baltic States. Due to their strategic position linking western and central Europe, these Baltic countries share a common history marked by invasions and rule from the neighboring countries of Russia, Germany, Sweden, and Denmark. The countries, however, are culturally and linguistically diverse. As residents of the northernmost Baltic State, less than 70 miles from Finland, the Estonian people are descendants of the Finno-Urgic people.

Ancient origins. The majority of the people of Estonia are descendants of Finno-Urgic peoples, related to Hungarians and Finns, who may have migrated from southern Siberia to the shores of the Baltic by the third century B.C. and then settling in Scandinavia. They moved into an area that had been inhabited long before their arrival; archaeological records suggest that Estonia has been inhabited since 6000 B.C. During the Roman Iron Age, Estonians developed commercial relationships with the countries to the south and began an intensive sea trade with the Goths of eastern Germany. Estonia became the portal for important trade routes and served as a link between the West and North-Eastern Europe. In the later Iron Age (A.D. 800–1200), it became one of the most prosperous nations of the region. At the dawn of written history, Estonia was divided into eight independent states headed by one or more "elders," who were sometimes designated as kings. There was no central government for the people, although the states often formed allegiances in wartime, as evident in their maritime expeditions to Sweden and Denmark, and their successful defense against Russian invaders.

The conquest of Estonia. The loss of Estonian independence came with Christianity. In the eleventh and twelfth centuries, Danes and Swedes tried to Christianize the Estonians without success, although many of the northern islands came under Danish rule. In the twelfth century as part of the Crusades, Teutonic (German) missionaries came to Latvia and Estonia to convert the peoples of these countries. The unsuccessful experience of the first two bishops (Meinhard and Bertold) demonstrated that the Estonians and Latvians were not willing to voluntarily embrace the Christian faith nor the rule of the Church. However, the missionaries' successors, Bishop Albert of Buxhoevden and his Knights of the Sword, were able to subjugate Latvia and Estonia in 1227. Estonian resistance was fierce and successful in places but unable to defend the Estonians as a whole. In 1237, the Knights of the Sword merged with the Order of Teutonic Knights and, in 1346, the Danish crown sold its sovereignty over the northern islands to the Teutonic Order. The Estonian people were brought under a feudal system, with the knights replacing local lords, who subjected the peasants to taxes and forced their allegiance. For 300 years Estonians served in this feudal system in the region known then as Livonia.

Swedish period. By the end of the fifteenth century, as the Teutonic Order was disintegrating, three major powers were emerging around Latvia and Estonia. The alliance of Poland and Lithuania to the south, the Russian Empire to the east, and the Swedes to the north all became involved in a struggle over Estonian and Latvian territory. In 1558, northern Estonia fell to the King of Sweden. In 1561, Poland took over all of Livonia (part of today's southern Estonia and northern Latvia), and in 1558 the forces of Russian tsar Ivan IV (the Terrible) penetrated deeply into Estonia, to be expelled in 1561 by the Swedes. With the Truce of Altmark (1629), which ended the first Polish-Swedish War, Poland surrendered most of Livonia to the Swedes, who had also gained sovereignty over all of Estonia.

The Swedish kings initiated a number of reforms which improved the status of Estonian peasantry. King Gustavus Adolphus established a special court to hear the complaints of the peasants against the nobility and founded a number of schools, including the University of Tartu. The decree of the Stockholm Diet of 1680 called for a reduction of fiefs held by nobility. Through this law about two-fifths of the land of northern Estonia and five-sixths of southern Estonia were taken from resistant landlords and transferred to crown lands. The work of the peasants was reduced and many schools were opened for them. Due to the reforms, this period in Estonian history is often called "the good Swedish times."

The Russian conquest. Swedish rule ended with the Great Northern War, which brought the Baltic provinces under the empire of Peter I (the Great). With the defeat of Charles XII of Sweden in 1709, the Russian armies seized Livonia, extending the Russian territories to the long-coveted strategic Baltic Sea. Sweden relinquished its reign over Estonia, which became annexed to Russia under the Treaty of Nystad (1721). Many of the reforms that were initiated by the Swedes were reversed as the peasantry was officially recognized as the property of the landowners, the Baltic-German nobility. In 1804, however, Alexander I set forth the "Livonian Peasant Law," which gave peasants the right to private property and inheritance. Open peasant revolts brought more change that led to sharing the production of the land through tenant farming. In 1849, 1856, and 1860 laws were introduced that gave peasants the right to lease and buy land. Although the rights of the peasants remained inferior to the nobility, by 1900 peasants had been able to buy about 40 percent of the privately owned lands of the country. The improvement in the lot of peasants created a background for the economic progress of the Estonian people, which led to an Estonian renaissance. During the long rule by the Russian tsars, Estonians had been forbidden to write or study in their own language.

Estonian renaissance and independence. The economic progress caused by the reforms coincided with the growth of urban centers and industrialization. The first Estonian newspaper made its appearance in the mid-1800s and chronicled the rise in national consciousness. While the pressure for Russification became even stronger, Estonian nationalist movements began to spread through cooperatives, farmers' societies, literature, and the press.

Russian Revolution. By 1905, Russian tensions to overcome serfdom under the tsars had spread to Estonia and the other Baltic States. In this atmosphere, Estonia was prepared to take advantage of the Russian Revolution of March 1917. The Estonian National Council (later called the *Diet Maapaev*) appointed a provisional government which declared its separation from the Russian government and, on July 14, 1917, independence. This declaration went recognized in the struggle for power created by World War I; the Communist Red Army remained in Estonia until it was forced to flee by the advancing German army. Through the Treaty of Brest-Litovsk in March 1918, Germany momentarily gained sovereignty over the Baltic countries. The Germans were, however, shortly ousted by the Red Army and the Allied European forces. By February of 1919, Estonian territory was completely freed with the help of the Estonian Army. On June 15, 1920, an elected assembly was formed which voted a new constitution for a single-chamber parliament (*Riigikogu*). Immediately, Estonians began to reinstate their own language in the country. For 19 difficult years, through the worldwide economic depression and attempted Communist takeovers, Estonia remained independent under such political leaders as Konstatin Pats, who served as president for several terms and attempted many constitutional reforms.

Loss of independence and Russian occupation. In 1939, the fate of Estonia and the other Baltic States was decided through a non-aggression treaty between Nazi Germany and the USSR. This secret agreement assigned the Baltic States to the Soviet Union. The Soviet government set up military bases in Estonia which were later used to occupy all of Estonia. On August 6, 1940, the Supreme Soviet voted to incorporate Estonia into the USSR and Estonia's independence was officially lost—but not without resistance. In the first 12 months alone, more than 60,000 people were killed or deported. For the following eight years, Soviet power over Estonia was challenged by periods of German occupation and war. During this time, many Estonians fled abroad and massive deportations moved Estonians from their homeland to isolated parts of Russia. From 1944 to 1990, Estonia, like the other Baltic countries was subject to "Russification," the intense indoctrination of Russian Communist ideology, language, and culture. Collectivization of agricultural lands, control of property and education and the persecution of religion were changes brought about by the Communists. Through the later years of this regime, Estonians pressed for independence and held tightly to their own language and culture even though thousands of Russians were imported to staff government agencies and the new industries (see ESTONIA).

As the Soviet Union became more liberal under Mikhail Gorbachev, Estonia and its Baltic neighbors took advantage to declare, once again, their independence. In 1991, Gorbachev agreed that the three small countries could become independent, a status long recognized by some other countries. Since then, Estonia, Latvia, and Lithuania have refused to enter into any treaty agreements with Russia, the Soviet Union, or its successor, the Commonwealth of Independent States. However, the impact of Russia's dominance in the past will continue to affect the Estonians. Of the people of Estonia, 60 percent are Estonians, and nearly 40 percent are Russians, Ukrainians, and Byelarussians who moved to Estonia as it became more industrialized.

Culture Today

Estonian culture today is comprised of various influences of the past and present, traditional and modern. While older traditions, both universal and regional, have remained, Russian influence has had a great impact on urbanization, industrialization, and socialism. While under Russian domination, the folk culture was an important force in maintaining a unique Estonian cultural identity for less than 2,000,000 people. Today Estonian intellectuals, artists, writers, and politicians have actively created new aspects of Estonian culture in the world. Estonia has developed into a prosperous nation of 310 state-owned cooperative farms and was one of the most highly industrialized republics of the former Soviet Union. Estonians grudgingly accepted communism and turned it to their own interests—

making a success of a new system by the spirit to do well whatever is required. This spirit is instilled in them by their artists, intellectuals, educators, and government officers. However, theirs is an economy that succeeds in a topsy-turvy style and with a large black market. Because they have access to foreign currency, waiters, taxi drivers, and other workers in the services earn more money than do teachers, engineers, and doctors.

Estonia is unique among the Baltic States because of its own energy supply. The land is rich in shale, which bears oil and gas to operate Estonia's industries, and much of the land is forested, providing wood fuel for many rural homes.

Religion. Christianity was first brought to Estonia in the middle of the twelfth century by Danes, who were followed by the crusading Teutonic Knights. Under Russian rule in the 1800s, the Russian Orthodox Church also gained prominence. However, while most Christian denominations are represented in Estonia, the majority of Estonians belong to the Evangelical Lutheran Church established during the Swedish rule of Estonia in the sixteenth century. Under Russian Communist rule (1940–1990), which disfavored organized religion, the church, its clergy, and congregations suffered many losses and restrictions. Much church property was taken over by the Russian government and many of the clergy were deported from Estonia. Estonians in exile formed Estonian Evangelical Lutheran churches in Australia, Belgium, Canada, Germany, Great Britain, New Zealand, Sweden, South America, and the United States.

Estonian language. The Estonian language belongs to the Finno-Urgic family of languages and is spoken by the Estonians of Estonia and other parts of the former USSR. Closely related to the Finnish spoken in neighboring Finland, the Estonian language has two major dialects, northern and southern. In the past Estonians did not refer to themselves as *eestlased* (eastern people) nor did they refer to their language as *eesti keel* (Estonian tongue). The northern Estonians called themselves *maarahvas,* and their language, *maakeel.* The name *eesti* (Estonia) was borrowed into the Estonian language from Swedish and came into general use in literature written in Estonia after the middle of the ninth century. Before its appearance in written form, Estonian was the spoken language of the farmers that survived and was enriched through the oral tradition. In 1637 the first Estonian grammar was published, but because the Estonians were always under the rule of others who preferred that the people use another language, the language was first taught at the University of Tartu only in 1803. With Estonian independence in 1917, the Estonian language was declared the national language. It became the language of instruction in schools and in the university until the new Russian period, in which Estonians were encouraged to replace their language with Russian. Still, more than 80 fiction books are published each year in the Estonian language.

Family life. Once the Estonian people were farmers of small plots carved from the Estonian forests. Fiercely independent, each farm family maintained its own management and distanced itself from others. It has been said that these Estonian families were comfortable only when they could not see their neighbor's house for the forest. The cold winters helped to further isolate families. For much of Estonia outside the cities, winter travel was and is restricted to horse-drawn sleighs.

As in other countries that were once part of the Soviet Union, industrialization has brought migrations of workers to the cities and created severe housing shortages. City-workers sign up to buy apartments that are in large, rectangular blocks.

During Soviet rule, family life was also impacted by industrialization, collectivization of farming, and government-sponsored housing and schools. Fathers and their land no longer dominated the lives of their children, who often moved away to work in the cities. Exiled Estonians, like political refugees from other parts of the world, have had to adapt to the culture of their country of residence while setting up Estonian organizations to maintain their culture.

Food and agriculture. Farming is difficult due to large glacial stones which need to be removed from the fields. However, extensive meadows and forests encourage herding animals, so the Estonian diet is comprised primarily of meat and dairy products. Cattle, pigs, and fodder crops account for most of the agricultural efforts; rye, wheat, other grains, and vegetables are also grown. A typical lunch might consist of black bread, cheese, and a variety of fruits and berries. A soft fermented rye bread is an Estonian staple at meals. Potatoes are a major crop; Estonia was once known as the "potato republic." As part of the Soviet Union beginning in 1940, all of the Estonian lands and forests were nationalized and 120,000 small farms were converted to collectives and state farms. Collective farms or *kolkhozes* were a dominant part of Soviet policy. Estonian farmers were forced to join collective farms or face deportation. Long marginally sufficient for the food needs of the people, production in collective farms, based on quotas, fell. By the 1960s, however, farm production had regained its 1939 level. In addition, the population swelled as Russian soldiers were imported to maintain rule and Russian workers came to manage government and to work in the new factories. Estonia found a need to import more and more grain. The often supply-short government stores were supplemented by markets such as the open market in Tallinn. At such markets, Estonians can buy fruits and vegetables from private entrepreneurs—at prices somewhat higher than those in the official stores—when the products are available.

Clothing. In 1979, Estonia hosted part of the Olympic Games and was invaded by foreigners. These visitors, along with the Finnish television and radio that is heard in many parts of the country, have made Estonians aware of Western fashions. Blue jeans became the style. Estonians today dress in Western clothes for everyday affairs, while folk costumes reflecting Estonian heritage are worn for holidays, festivals, and special occasions. These costumes are also worn by the performance ensembles of folk dancers and musicians. A typical traditional women's costume is composed of a tunic shirt, a full colorful skirt, and an embroidered apron. The headdress worn by women distinguishes the different regions and villages of Estonia. In the southern part of Estonia, the traditional headdress for a married woman is a long, linen, embroidered kerchief worn around the head and down the back. In northern Estonia, small, intricately designed coifs (hats) adorn women's folk costumes. Heavy necklaces often supplement this costume. Men's costumes are generally wide-legged pants gathered at the knee, with loose-fitting shirts. The principal headdress is a high, stiff felt hat or a fur cap with earflaps that is worn in the winter. Both men and women's folk costumes include a decorative broach to fasten the shirts and blouses.

Winter temperatures cause the Baltic Sea to freeze, so many Estonians wear high felt boots, *valenka*, to protect against the cold.

Education. As in other sections that were once part of the Soviet Union, education is free to all Estonians who desire it, and is compulsory for elementary students. Not all Estonians embrace higher education, since the inverted economy, which is dependent to some extent on foreign currency, pays higher salaries to some occupations that do not demand college education. (Estonian waiters, cab drivers, and bell hops, for example, earn better than average incomes often paid in foreign currencies.) Still, Estonians' pride in doing things well and their zeal to preserve their own language and culture encourages scholarship. There is a sound encyclopedia written in the Estonian language, and the nation of 1,500,000 people supports six major universities. Also, 70 percent of the students at the University of Tartu receive a monthly stipend that pays about half their expenses.

Literature and arts. The folk music, dance, and song of the Estonians are distinctive parts of Estonian heritage. Two types of Estonian folk songs are sung today. The older *runo* melodies derive from Estonian folklore cultivated throughout the feudal age of Estonia. Runo songs, noted for their improvisation, are often stories of agricultural life and its hardships. In the past century, new folk song styles have been created from Swedish, Latvian, and German influences. The Setu area of southern Estonia is particularly noted for its number of folk songs and their richness. Estonian folk songs are played to various traditional instruments: bagpipes, bowed harps, fiddles, various types of flutes, concertinas, and zithers (a stringed instrument).

Estonian folk-dance consists mostly of group dances performed in the round and in chains that break off periodically into couples. Many of the circle dances are based upon older ceremonials and continue to be danced today at weddings, on religious holidays, and during local and national festivals. The waltz, polka, quadrille, and other European dances introduced in the 1800s have also influenced the development of Estonian folk dance. Throughout the twentieth century, folk dances have been collected and documented by folklorists for the benefit of future generations. Folk-dance evenings, festivals, and theater performances are a part of Estonian culture today.

Since the mid-1800s Estonian song festivals have become one of the principal expressions of Estonian national and cultural consciousness. Music comes to the fore every five years at the great festival of Laulupidu. Organized in 1869 in Tartu to demonstrate that Estonian culture survived its conquerors, the spirit of the festival survives today. More than 30,000 musicians gather to perform at the concert shell in the city of Pirita, and hundreds of thousands come to listen and renew their vows to preserve Estonian culture. Since 1923, the festivals have been held nationally at the capital, Tallinn, bringing participants and audiences of more than 100,000 people. Each of the hundreds of town and country choirs, along with music and dance groups, compete within their locality for many years before joining the song festival. The unique aspect of the song festivals is the joining of the groups to form choirs of up to 15,000 people. Estonia's first composers received their training and inspiration through the song festivals.

Estonian literature did not flower until the nineteenth century with the development of an Estonian national epic poem. Based upon oral tradition, this poem, the *Kalevi Poëg*, was written by Dr. F. R. Kreutzwald from 1857 to 1861. The poem, containing some 2,000 Estonian legends, had a tremendous effect upon the national consciousness of the people and inspired several new generations of poets and novelists. Folktales continue to be a major part of Estonian literature. One folktale relates growth, city development and the Estonian respect for the sea. In this story, a powerful figure appears in the outskirts of Tallinn annually and inquires if the city has been completed. An Estonian must reply that it is not finished, for when it is completed, the powerful visitor will destroy it by flood.

Realistic novels, depicting the depressing social reality of the Estonian people in the simple, everyday language began to emerge with the writings of Eduard Vilde, Peterson-Sargava, and Juhan Liiv. At the turn of the century, much of the literary activities were focused upon modernizing the Estonian language. During World War I, a group of young lyrical writers formed a movement known as the "Siuru"—groups, which produced passionate works about contemporary Estonia. H. Visnapuu is a well-known innovator of the "Siuru" group. In 1926, A. H. Tammsaare published a monumental novel, *Truth and Righteousness*, describing the social life of Estonia from the last quarter of the nineteenth century to the 1930s. After World War II, many Estonian writers were forced into exile, during which time literature continued to be produced around the common themes of wartime experiences, Estonian independence, and the difficulties of adjusting to new countries. Meanwhile, world literature, such as Shakespearean plays, have been translated into the Estonian language.

Shelter and architecture. Many of the older, small farm dwellings in Estonia were lost in war, in the seizure of property by the Soviet government, or as a result of increasing urban populations. Estonian architecture is characterized by the medieval appearance of its towns, with large sections of Gothic-style houses, buildings, and churches. The capital, Tallinn, has the best-preserved Gothic architecture on the Baltic Sea. Some of the towns still have protective walls, left over from the thirteenth and fourteenth centuries, surrounding the inner city. In the countryside, unique barn dwellings with thatch-covered roofing provide examples of the housing of Esth peasants over the centuries. Most of the twentieth-century architecture in the urban areas reflects modern, Western building designs.

Challenge. In 1991, Estonia faced the challenge of managing its own affairs, including an industrialization supported by contributions from the central Soviet government. This industrialization created a demand for workers that could not be filled by the few Estonians. About 40 percent of the Estonian labor force is made up of migrants from Russia and other republics. What to do with these migrants, who have been looked on as less than full citizens of the country, is a major issue for Estonians.

For More Information

Gimbutas, Marija. *The Balts.* New York: Frederick A. Praeger, 1963.

Pullerits, Albert. *Estonia: Population, Cultural and Economic Life.* Tallinn, Estonia: Tallinn Press, 1935.

Raud, V., editor. *Estonia: A Reference Book.* New York: The Nordic Press, Inc., 1953.

Uustalu, Evald, editor. *Aspects of Estonian Culture.* London: Boreas Publishing Company, 1961.

GEORGIANS

(jor′ jans)

People of the land bridge between the Black and Caspian seas.

Population: 3,748,000 (1989 census).
Location: Republic of Georgia.
Language: Georgian.

Geographical Setting

The land of the Georgian people is highly varied. While some of the highest mountain peaks in Europe appear in the north, southward the country flattens into a plain that is broken by another mountain range stretching wedgelike from the Black Sea toward neighboring Azerbaijan and the Caspian Sea. The land is triangular, with a broader coastline on the Black Sea and arching borders with Ukraine, Armenia, and Azerbaijan. The mountains and their deep valleys have varied climates related to their altitudes. In contrast, the coastlines have a more Mediterranean climate and vegetation. The Black Sea coast has become a major resort region for the people in the countries of the former Soviet Union. Georgia has also become a major industrial center. The major city, Tbilisi, is the capital, home to Georgians and a number of other peoples.

Historical Background

Perhaps because of the mountainous region in which they live, and which separates their land from the larger Russia, the Georgians have developed a language and culture that is different from those of other peoples who made up the Communist Soviet Union from 1920 to 1990. However, even with their own language and customs, Georgians were one of the most influential groups in the former USSR.

Origin. The beginnings of a Georgian people can be traced to migrants from Asia Minor who settled in the region just south of the Caucasus Mountains between the twelfth and seventh centuries B.C., and over the years united into the state of Colchis and the kingdom of Iberia. Both were conquered by the Romans and became part of their empire in the first century A.D. From headquarters in neighboring Turkey, the Roman rulers guided the lives of the Georgians. By A.D. 500, Georgians had adopted Christianity, the religion of the empire.

Arabs and independence. The new religion spread throughout Georgia until Arab armies overran the region between A.D. 500 and 600, and attempted to spread their Muslim religion in the area. However, by A.D. 900 Arab domination had come to an end. Georgia became a self-governing territory from 1080 to 1120. It was then conquered by the Turks, to become self-governing again from 1120 to 1235. During this last period of independence, Georgia itself grew into a flourishing empire of trade, science, and philosophy.

Mongol rule. Genghis Khan and his Mongol armies invaded the area in 1235 and began a century of rule over the Georgians. Arab invasions followed from 1385 to 1453 and divided the land and people between the Persians and Turks. This condition endured until the eighteenth century.

Georgia and Russia. Russia defeated Turkey in the struggle for control of the area and began incorporating Georgian lands into the Russian Empire; Georgia became part of the empire in 1801. Russians and Georgians joined efforts to expand the area's economy and further develop the cultural and intellectual growth of the region in the nineteenth century. Poetry, journalism, literary movements (which often took political positions), and a Marxist political movement had developed by 1900. Under Russian rule at that time, the Georgians were barred from political activities, but managed to maintain a political interest and dialogue through three literary groups until they were allowed political participation in 1905. Georgians were active participants in the Russian Revolution of 1917 and their area was recognized as an independent nation by other countries of the world. The Soviet Union signed a treaty with Georgia in 1920 that promised not to interfere with its government. Later, under the leadership of Joseph Stalin, the USSR reversed this policy, forcing Georgia to become a Soviet Republic on February 25, 1921. Stalin himself came from Georgia and, beginning in the 1930s, the area continuously provided Communist party officials. In the 1900s, Georgia became highly industrialized and improved its electrical power and transportation system tenfold to become a strong influence in the Soviet Union. The principal city, Tbilisi, produces machinery, engines, automobiles, textiles, ironwork, and is a major food-processing center.

Not all the people of Georgia are of the old Georgian ancestry. About a third of the population is Russian, Armenian, Abkhaz, and Osset. Since the collapse of the Soviet Union, and even though it has had ties with Russia for nearly two centuries, Georgia refused to align itself with other former Soviet states in a Commonwealth of Independent States. Georgians have pursued their own course under clouds of civil war.

Culture Today

Variety. Sixty-seven percent of the region's population is Georgian, a people made up of many different subgroups. Among them are the

Svanians in western Georgia, the Khevsurs and Kakhetians in eastern Georgia, the Karthians in central Georgia, and the Meskhians in southern Georgia. Their communities range from agricultural towns to mountain villages to industrial cities, where they produce automobiles, textiles, cement, and steel. Long a kindgom that survived by paying homage to Turks, Greeks, Persians, and others, this region is a mix of European and Asian cultures. The capital city, Tbiliśi, for example, has fine new factories and apartments, old cathedrals and palaces that date to the fifth century A.D., residential sections of old wooden buildings, and oriental markets and bazaars.

Political units. The people of the country of Georgia are a mixture of Georgians with three other ethnic or religious groups, who are represented by three self-governing states within the Georgian Republic. One is occupied by Georgians who practice the Muslim religion and are known as the Adjar peoples. The other two republics are occupied by groups of non-Georgians, the Abkhaz and the Osset peoples. Political leadership for the republic as a whole resided, until the 1990s, in the Georgian Communist Party. Since the land has been inhabited for thousands of years and has been ruled by Mongols, Persians, Turks, Russians, and others, the mixture of ethnic groups in Georgia is one of the most complex in the region.

Much of Georgia is male dominated. Still, the role of women improved under the Soviet regime as they assumed industrial and administrative positions.

History of subservience. Georgians have long experienced domination by others. They have learned to be subservient while maintaining their own lifestyles. This is reflected in the work of current artists, who under Soviet rule were forced to paint realistic works with social messages. The "realistic" art takes many forms in Georgia, and many bright colors enhance the realism. On the whole, the Georgians are cheerful and confident, and possess the Middle Eastern reputation for friendliness.

Agriculture. Georgians grow grains, sugar beets, sunflower seed, potatoes, grapes, and tea on the land around agricultural villages. They also raise pigs, cattle, and poultry, using their livestock to produce meat and dairy products. Some produce is grown on collective farms under government direction. However, nearly half of it is produced by farmers working small plots of land for themselves. Their inde-

**This painting of a Georgian man is
typical of the social realism
encouraged by the former Soviet Union.**
From the Library of Congress.

pendently grown produce is sold in open-air markets in most cities.
One of the largest markets is in Tbilisi, where buyers sometimes shop
for fruits and vegetables to resell in Moscow and other northern cities.

Food, clothing, and shelter. Sour milk and cheese are standard fare
in many meals in all seasons and contribute largely to the protein
content of the diet. The milk products are supplemented by vegetables, meat, and fruit, which are produced in abundance in the deep
valleys. Bread is the main carbohydrate. Along with locally grown

tea, wine made from the grapes of household vineyards is a common beverage.

Most Georgians in the cities and large towns dress in European-style clothes, sometimes accompanied by fur or cloth hats. In the mountains, shepherds and farmers dress in more conservative colors, but still with European shirts and trousers over which a vest or coat is worn. Rural women wear blouses and long skirts as is common throughout the area.

Houses in Georgia are as varied as the people. Some city-dwellers live in stone or brick houses. Most of the older homes and those in the villages are wooden homes. The birthplace of Joseph Stalin, who was born of peasant parents, is an example. It is a wood-frame home on a stone foundation. A wooden porch spans the front of the house, with the wood-shingled roof covering the porch.

Religion. Although the Adjar practice the Muslim religion, the majority of religious Georgians are Christians. Some Georgians (the Khevsurs) are animists who believe in spirits of nature, and there are also Georgian Jews. In the 1930s, the Soviet Union confiscated church property and attempted to discredit Georgia's religions, but the religious bodies are officially recognized.

Arts. Georgians have remained comparatively free from direct control from Moscow, while a rich national folk literature has reminded

Georgian art in the time of the Soviet Union was often planned to beautify industrialization. *From the Library of Congress.*

them of their ethnic independence. Native tales such as *The Man in the Tiger's Skin,* by Shota Rustaveli, recall traditional personality traits and reinforce the Georgian reputation for being an amusing, humorous, and clever people. Many parts of Georgian folklore build on the devotion of children to parents in the Georgian family.

In spite of the repressive nature of collectivism and other Soviet government policies, several Georgian poets and authors have created works of world interest. In the first half of the 1800s, writers divided themselves between those who longed for Georgian independence and those who favored a larger union. During this time, Nikolos Baratashvili wrote "Fate of Georgia," a poem about liberty. Later in that century, a number of writers became famous for their descriptions of life in the Caucasus Mountains. More recently, Giorgi Leonidze and Galaktian Tabridze have exercised considerable freedom of expression in well-acclaimed poetry. Konstantine Gamsakhurdia wrote his novel *Hand of the Great Master* in 1951.

Georgian dancers accompanied by music on the balalaika or accordion commonly provide entertainment for vacationers who are attracted by the beaches and the hot spas in and around Tbilisi. A popular music used by singers is the *chastushka*, songs in which short verses are sung alternately by a man and a woman. In some Georgian villages the chastushka cannot be performed in this manner, however, because women are forbidden to take part in public singing and dancing. The Balanchivadze (written in other countries, Balanchine) family has produced leaders in music and ballet, both at home (Andira) and in the United States (George).

Recreation. Much of Georgia allows travel from warm waterfront to permanent snow within an hour or so. In this environment, music and dance compete with winter and water sports as major recreational activities. In addition, the volcanic activity of the region has produced a number of hot springs around which resorts have been built. Tbilisi, on the Kura River, is famous for its hot springs and for the people, such as Josef Stalin, who have visited them.

Education and aging. All elementary-age children are required to attend school. In a growing population in which births outnumber deaths by two to one, 890,000 children attend secondary school.

An old story tells how God set about to distribute land to all the different peoples of the world. Finally, arriving in Georgia and asked by the people for their portion of land, God was chagrined that the only land left was that reserved for His own use. In their typically congenial style, the people forgave this oversight and invited God for a drink. After some sociability, God gave his own land to the people. That it is somehow a blessed land is reflected in the long lives of some of the people. The substantial numbers of old people in families of Georgia has brought their lifestyle under scientific study. The aged are particularly numerous in the Caucasus mountain area, where a number of people claim to be well over 100 years old.

For More Information

Horlin, Pierre. *The Soviet People and Their Society.* New York: Frederick A. Praeger, 1969.

Kort, Michael. *The Soviet Colossus: A History of the USSR.* New York: Scribners, 1985.

Rywkin, Michael. *Soviet Society Today.* Armonk, New York: M. E. Sharpe, 1989.

Shanon, Donald R. *Soviet Europe.* New York: Harper and Row, 1975.

GYPSIES
(jip′ sees)

Wanderers of Europe and Asia who call themselves Romani or Rom.

Population: 1,000,000 (1990 estimate).
Location: Europe, North America, South America, Asia, Oceania.
Languages: Romany and other European languages.

Geographical Setting

Having no land of their own, Gypsies have scattered throughout Europe and western Asia, and across the ocean to the Americas. They are most densely populated in Romania, Bulgaria, European Turkey, and Hungary. They are a seminomadic, non-urban people who are gradually, and mostly reluctantly, being absorbed into the industrial economies of the countries they inhabit.

Historical Background

Origin. The most widely held theory of the origin of the nomadic people known as Gypsies is that they were originally of India. Some claim them to be low-caste people of India related to the Dome, a caste of musicians and ropemakers. The evidence for an Indian origin is primarily that the Gypsy language, Romany, is related to the ancient language of India, Sanskrit. Some words of languages used in India today are readily understood by Romany-speaking Gypsies.

Dispersal. In the second century A.D. the Gypsy people seem to have left northwest India, probably driven out by Mongol invaders. First moving into Persia, the Gypsy bands had spread to Greece by the

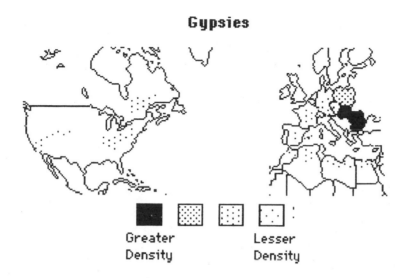

Gypsies

Greater Density

Lesser Density

The greatest concentration of Gypsies is in northeastern Europe. However, Gypsies have spread across Europe, North Africa, and North America.

fourteenth century. Forced out of Greece by the Turks, the Gypsies scattered in small groups throughout Europe. Bands of Gypsies reached into Romania, Austria, and Hungary by 1400, arrived in Germany in 1417, in Spain by 1422, and in France by 1427. The nomadic Gypsies earned their living as musicians or metalworkers. By 1496, they had become skilled as "shotmakers" for Hungarian soldiers, and had been granted freedom to come and go in that country. The Gypsies had reached England, Russia and Sweden by 1500.

Gypsy persecution. Few in number and with no central organization, the Gypsies adopted the languages of the people whose land they visited. At the same time they maintained the Romany language that is understood by Gypsies throughout Europe, parts of Asia, and northern Africa. Everywhere, small bands lived as entertainers and potmakers. They were not prepared to defend themselves when an anti-Gypsy movement swept across Europe and England from 1555 to 1780. Almost nowhere in Central and Western Europe were these immigrants treated kindly. In Moldavia and Bulgaria, Gypsies were owned by the lords on whose land they lived, or were property of the state if they were skilled gold washers or bear trainers. Even the clergy took Gypsies as slaves, a practice that persisted into the 1800s. As described in 1852, slaves owned by lords endured a pitiful existence. Their clothing included a coarse, threadbare shirt. Rain generally did the job of washing the clothing. In the morning, the lord's bailiff, wearing furs and holding a whip, would assign the Gypsies tasks. The gaunt, thinly clad group gathered for the assignments, coming from the stables, kitchens, and open sheds. At times the bailiff used his whip. Such was the fate of Gypsies belonging to some lords.

Life in Hungary was a bit better for the Gypsies, who were, nevertheless, slaves as early as the fifteenth century. Here they belonged to the ruler of the country. One account describes how Ladislas VI demanded that a group of Gypsy blacksmiths make instruments of torture to be used to punish the leaders of a rebellion, then had the blacksmiths impaled alive. In 1761, Maria Theresa, Queen of Hungary and Bohemia tried to denomadize the Gypsies by banning sleeping in tents, horse dealing, using their own language, or selecting their own chiefs. The men were pressed into military service.

Although Catherine the Great of Russia made Gypsies slaves, they received better treatment in Russia than in some other areas. However, in 1759, the tide turned here also and Gypsies were not allowed to enter the capital city of St. Petersburg. Meanwhile, at first accepted in Germany, Gypsies soon came to be thought of as creatures of the devil, and were chased away from many parts of the country.

Again in the early 1900s, prejudice against the Gypsies grew. Nowhere were they called by the name they prefer, Rom. Instead, countries adopted derogatory titles for the Gypsies implying less intelligence or lower moral standards. Early in the century, anti-Gypsy feeling grew so that there was a movement to imprison all European Gypsies and send them to an island home to be isolated from the rest of humanity. The Gypsies have long countered these feelings by requesting a European homeland of their own, Romany. However, even though the proposal has been carried to such authorities as the United Nations, Gypsies lack the political power and organization to succeed in their request.

A Gypsy kingdom. Although Gypsy people were brutalized nearly everywhere during that period, they did little to organize until the

1900s. Then Michael Kwick of Poland declared a kingdom of Gypsies and named himself king. In 1928, Michael I abdicated in favor of a son, Michael II. Two of Michael II's brothers contended for the throne of the landless kingdom, forcing Michael to flee from Poland to Czechoslovakia. There, he died in 1935. He was replaced in 1937 by his brother Basil and then by Januz, another brother, who declared himself King Januz I. Despite all this controversy for the throne, only a limited number of Gypsies recognized the right of any of these leaders to be king.

World War II. During World War II, Germans under the guidance of Adolf Hitler established a policy of extermination of the Gypsies.

A gypsy woman and child in typical dress in Romania. *Courtesy of the National Anthropological Archive of the Smithsonian Institution.*

The success of this policy is evidenced by the reduction in the number of Gypsies in German-occupied Poland—18,000 before the war and only 4,500 after the German defeat.

Division. Gypsies now live throughout Europe and have scattered to other continents of the world. They share customs and traditions that have kept them distinct for ages, but their lifestyle is changing. Today they are split into two groups: settled Gypsies who have found homes in villages and cities and a smaller number who still travel in the nomadic lifestyle of the past. Those who have settled near cities live in houses made of wattle. In the villages Gypsies live in one-room brick or wooden homes.

Culture Today

Economy. Since Gypsies have been forced to earn a living however possible, they generally perform menial tasks. In the past they may have been horse traders, peddlers, metalsmiths, musicians, or fortune tellers. Today many of the settled Gypsies work as auto mechanics and in factories. Those who have held to the nomadic lifestyle, live in tents or in caravan wagons and earn their livelihood in traditional ways: metalworking, horse trading, and providing music, dance, and divination.

Language. Most Gypsies are at least bilingual, speaking the language of the country in which they live and Romany, the Gypsy language related to languages of India. This language has been altered through the centuries with the addition of words and sounds from Persian, Greek, Armenian, and other languages. It has also been broken into dialects as the Gypsy people have been scattered throughout the world. Among themselves, Gypsies are also said to use a sort of sign language, *patrin*—marks meaningful to their own people but unintelligible to others. They seemingly used these symbols to describe conditions of camps for future campers, as well as to provide information about people in the area that might be useful for those practicing the Gypsy vocation of fortune telling.

Literature and arts. Even in music the Gypsies have adopted the melodies of surrounding peoples and lack a distinct identity. The Gypsy language, Romany, is a simple one with many dialects and borrowed words of which little more than 1,000 words are in common use. In Gypsy history, only nine books are known to have been written in the language. Many Gypsies do have excellent abilities as fiddlers and cymbalists, however, and these people quickly adapt the folk music of any region they inhabit to their own playing style. The Gypsy interest and skill in music, along with their habit of adopting the language of their neighbors, may have led to the greatest contribution of Gypsies to global society. Gypsies are quick to learn folk music from their neighbors, and perpetuate this music in their own street acts. Some of these folk songs, which might otherwise have disappeared, have been the bases for more revered classical music.

Religion. Gypsies were slow to accept an organized religion, preferring to follow their ancient beliefs in charms, spirits, and curses. However, the Gypsies have become masters of adjustment to other cultures, so they frequently adopt the religions of surrounding peoples and blend these religions with more ancient beliefs. Most often this adopted religion is Roman Catholicism, which the Gypsies espouse while identifying with the Gypsy saint, Sara. Beyond these organized religions, the Gypsies have their own strong set of beliefs and traditions. Their religion holds that there is but one god, o Del, but this god is variously believed to be the creator of the earth and the god of an earth that preceded the god. Appearing with this god in the beginning was o Bengh, the devil. Gypsies continue to believe in a wide array of spirits and in magical powers. The positions of the sun and moon play important roles in the superstitions and magic of the Gypsies.

Gypsy religion and mythology includes demons and witches. To be a witch is honorable among these people; Gypsy witches can evoke good or evil through their magical powers.

Food, clothing, and shelter. In the forests of Transylvania, one of the regions in which the greatest concentration of Gypsies live, day-to-day existence is drab and uncertain. Gypsies improve their lives with music, dance, and bright colors. Those who cling to traditional lives paint the caravan wagons in brilliant reds and yellows. The same bright colors appear in the traditional clothing, such as dresses with full skirts, or baggy pants with colorful loose-fitting shirts for the men. A scarf often adorns a woman's hair or is used as a cummerbund by the men.

However, Gypsy clothing varies with the country in which they live and work. A Gypsy chief in France, for example, might be seen in suit and tie, and a worker in jeans, while a Gypsy man in Romania still clings to the old peasant dress of the country with a fuzzy, conical cap that tops the long hair of men of the woods.

Poorly paid or living from meal to meal, Gypsies have developed a diet based mainly on whatever vegetables are available. The staple has been a thick soup or stew.

In the days of the Ottoman Empire, Gypsies moved from camp to camp, sometimes rapidly to avoid persecution. In those days, the typical Gypsy home was a tent rapidly pitched wherever there was work to do. Much of this work was some form of entertainment—playing the ancient Indian stringed instrument, the *cithara*, or zither, performing in circus acts, or directing trained animals, particularly bears. Another form of housing was a heavy-wheeled, covered wagon. Those Gypsies who opted for city life often found shelter in small houses or shanties fabricated from abandoned metal or wood. The covered wagon was later replaced by the caravan van, a brightly colored, horse- or ox-drawn, wooden room on wheels. All these shelters are still in use among the various Gypsy groups who have not succumbed to the enticements of industry throughout Europe.

Social life and changes. The Gypsies are divided into several different groups or clans depending on their chief means of livelihood, or the region in which they live. There are Kalderash Gypsies, who are metalsmiths by trade, Gitanos, who live in Spain, Portugal, and southern France, and Manush, the traditional "bohemians" of Central Europe.

Gypsy social life has long been determined by seasonal changes. Regular seasonal gatherings are times of celebration and matchmaking. The gatherings are times when extended families gather—a good time to seal the common and preferred marriages between cousins. These events are also often the best times for Gypsy weddings, but Gypsy marriages can be arranged by this mutual consent, by abduction, or by purchase. Women who marry outside their clan are held in contempt, and their husbands find it difficult to be accepted in the woman's family group.

The strongest form of social control among the Gypsies has been *kris*, a code of customary law and values. The law is an oral tradition that includes a complete basis of beliefs that prescribe order for even the smallest actions. Gypsies are reminded of this law in the stories they tell in the evenings, stories often reinforced by their ending, *Chapité*, "It is true."

The kris code. Among the Gypsy values are readiness to help fellow band members and to pay what is owed. The kris code reflects a high regard for loyalty to the band and provides for the settlement of disputes and breaches of the code, ultimately by excommunication. An International Gypsy Committee has been created with headquarters in Paris, but active government is a function of the band. The political leader of a Gypsy band is a chieftain who is elected for life. Another leading figure is the treasurer, who in the past decided where the band would migrate and acted as its spokesperson to local authorities at that location. The band itself is governed by a council of elders, who habitually consult a senior woman of the band. Her influence is great due to the higher earning power of Gypsy women.

Women. Although men are dominant in Gypsy families, women have been the steady earners of income for the household. Families consists of a husband, wife, unmarried children, and married sons and their families. The members of this extended family generally live together and cooperate economically. The household is centered around a group of women who work as a team, each woman's earnings being added to a common fund that is managed by the oldest among them. Bands are formed from groups of extended families that shared a common ancestor.

Change. Settled Gypsies have adopted the ways of their neighbors, abandoning their horse-drawn caravans for house trailers, and sending their children to school to learn local languages. The cities and industrialized societies in which many of them now live have exposed them to different ways. The lifestyle of these twentieth-century Gypsies has changed, but their traditions of loyalty to family and ethnic origins have been retained.

For More Information

Puxon, Gratton. *Roma, Europe's Gypsies*. London: Minority Rights Group, 1980.

Wilson, Robert Charles. *Gypsies*. New York: Doubleday, 1989.

Yoors, Jan. *The Gypsies*. New York: Simon and Schuster, 1967.

KAZAKHS
(kay' zaks)

People of both Mongol and Turkish origin now living in Kazakhstan and neighboring members of the Commonwealth of Independent States.

Population: 7,930,000 (1990 estimate).
Location: Kazakhstan, Uzbekistan, Turkmenistan.
Language: Kazakh, a Turkic language.

Geographical Setting

Kazakhstan, the home of nearly 8,000,000 Kazakhs, is second only to Russia in size among the republics that made up the Soviet Union before 1991. It is a vast steppe (grassland with scattered trees) that rises in the north to a high mountain range. These steppes extend to the mountains of Afghanistan and China. The climate in the steppes is extreme—very cold in winter, very hot in summer. Here Kazakhs were content to lead a nomadic herding life for centuries, with some eventually becoming more settled farmers. The land was sparsely settled until serious shortages of grain in the Soviet Union led the government to experiment with grain farming in large plots of Kazakh land. As many as 2,000,000 Soviets from more populated areas such as the Ukraine were transplanted to Kazakhstan in the 1960s to attempt farming on the steppes. Fifty-eight percent of the people of Kazakhstan are nineteenth and twentieth century settlers from Russia and Ukraine.

Historical Background

Beginnings. In the thirteenth century, Genghis Khan led the Mongols in a successful invasion and settling of central Asia. His followers

Kazakhs

The Kazakhs are Mongol-Muslim people who are related to the Kyrgyz and were once part of the empire known as Turkestan.

dominated the area but, by the middle of the fourteenth century, the Mongol rulers had been greatly influenced by the Turkic lifestyle of the inhabitants of the area. These earlier inhabitants and their Mongol invaders intermarried and gave birth to the Kazakh people in the fifteenth century. Physically, the Kazakhs were a combination of Mongol and Caucasian peoples, and exhibit a wide variety of physical characteristics. They were and are united by a common language and the Muslim religion.

Turkic rule. From the fifteenth to the seventeenth century, Kazakhs enjoyed some autonomy under the Turkish-directed Kazakh Khanate. The whole region was to remain uneasily under the rule of Ottoman Muslim dynasties until Russians began to settle the area in 1830. The Russian tsar took military control of the area, bringing peace to the war-torn region and changes in the lifestyle of the people. Fearing Russian rule, many Kazakhs fled to the Sinkiang province of China or to Afghanistan, where nearly a million Kazakhs still live nomadic lives. Under the Russians, Kazakhs became settled farmers as well as herders. In addition, railroads, factories, and highways were built on their lands. Otherwise, the Kazakh continued living in traditional ways until the collapse of the tsarist government and the Russian Revolution of 1917.

Soviet Revolution. By the time of the revolution, the Kazakhs had already begun a nationalist movement against the tsar's rule. From 1917 to 1921, they fought against both the White Russians (tsarist armies) and the Communists. The Communists prevailed and many Kazakhs responded by fleeing to China. Approximately one million Kazakhs died of starvation in the winter of 1921. Others who rebelled against the Soviets were deported to forced-labor camps. Those who remained were collectivized on Soviet farms through the 1930s. Their land became part of the union as the Kazakh Soviet Socialist Republic on December 5, 1936. Thereafter, the Kazakh people experienced rapid economic growth and an improvement in health and living standards. There were also, however, restrictions in religion, art, and their manner of herding. The republic became a launch-site for Soviet spacecraft in the 1950s; today, the Kazakh settlement of Baikonur is used for this purpose.

With the dismantling of the Soviet Union in 1991, the Kazakh Soviet Socialist Republic became Kazakhstan, an independent nation and one of the former Soviet Republics to join in the formation of the Commonwealth of Independent States.

Culture Today

Food and shelter. Changes in the Kazakh economy have brought rapid economic growth. Traditionally the Kazakh were nomads whose herds consisted mainly of horses and sheep. Kazakh herders were known for their fondness of the small, but strong and spirited, horses they bred. The horses were raised for sale, for use in warfare, for horse racing and for the status they brought their owners. Sheep provided mutton, yogurt and cheese for food. Sheep hides were used for clothing and as coverings for tents. Wealthy Kazakhs kept herds of camels as well for wool, meat and milk. With Russian encouragement, cattle were added to the Kazakh herds and today are the most important livestock in the Kazakh economy.

Until they were encouraged by the Russians to abandon their nomadic lifestyle, the Kazakhs lived in tents (yurts) that were easily

**The memory of the once-common
nomadic dwelling, the yurt, is kept in
this cultural park in Kazakhstan.**
Courtesy of Intourist.

dismantled and moved. The tents were formed of a lightweight
wooden frame that rose four or five feet above the ground and was
arranged in a circle. A pole supported a wooden ring in the center
of this circle, somewhat above the level of the wooden frame, and
the ring was attached to the outside frame by wooden slats. Over all
this, felt mats were fastened to form a secure tent. Depending on the
wealth of the owner, these tents, called *yurts*, were decorated outside
with fringes or with double wooden doors. Inside, the floor was
pounded hard and covered with mats and the walls were often decorated with tapestries.

Fewer Kazakhs live now in the white, felt-covered, dome-shaped
Kazakh tents, and construction of new prefabricated concrete housing
has become a major occupation for the Kazakhs. However, the Kazakhs still base their economy on raising and herding animals, though
now the Kazakh herders are grouped on collective farms and have
become specialists in looking after only one kind of animal. The
Kazakhs fiercely resisted the collective lifestyle encouraged by the
former Soviet Union. Nevertheless, their farms have been productive.
Kazakh herds provided much of the meat, wool, and cotton for the
rest of the Soviet Union. Three-fourths of the agricultural land is
devoted to pastures. On one-fourth of the arable land, the Kazakhs

grow grain and have provided an important source of wheat for the nation. They have been brought into wheat-growing by Ukrainian farmers who were relocated to Kazakhstan in a massive experiment to turn the steppe into productive farmland. Today, more modern equipment has made farming less labor intensive and a minority of Kazakhs, not needed on the farms, are employed in heavy industry, producing lead, electricity, petroleum, coal, copper, or tin. Kazakh lands yield more than 90 minerals that are important raw materials for Kazakhstan and Russian factories.

Family life. The family life of the Kazakhs has not been disrupted by the collective lifestyle. Often the members of a single enterprise are also members of a single clan so that family ties remain intact and may even be strengthened. On the collective farm, hundreds of families share in the use of land, animals, equipment, schools, hospitals, and libraries—in regions where they had previously wandered as nomads. Some Kazakhs still live in *yurts*, but today most live in small wood-framed houses with metal roofs. At one time there was a yurt for each wife in a family. The family might include two to three wives, and the status of the woman was lower than that of the man. The Russian government had forbidden both marriage to more than one wife and payment for wives, and had attempted to raise the status of women by providing them with jobs in education and government.

Government. The Kazakhs were once politically organized into clans that were grouped into three main hordes: the Great Zhuz in the east, the Middle Zhuz in the center, and the Little Zhuz in the west. Each horde had its own khan, or ruler. He and those around him acquired great wealth while the masses of Kazakhs remained poor. The system imposed by the Communist regime has closed the gap between rich and poor Kazakhs. The tribes and hordes as governmental entities no longer exist. Officially the political leadership of the people has been transferred to the Kazakh Communist party.

Language and literature. The Khazakh language is an ancient Turkic language of the Kipchak group, which also includes the language of the Kyrgyz. This language was once written using Latin characters, but in the late 1930s the Soviet Union required the use of the Cyrillic alphabet of Russian. By 1992, there was a growing number of publications in the new script, including a Kazakh encyclopedia, books on natural sciences and art, as well as popular fiction books. Kazakh literature is traced to the tenth-century author of science, mathematics, and philosophy works, Abü Nasr Al Favali. In the 1990s Jambul Jabayev is the most well-known poet, while Mukhtar Auezov has produced widely accepted plays.

Education. By 1992, 3,000,000 Kazakhs were attending schools and being taught in the Kazakh language. Education is now compulsory from ages seven to 17. There is a state university and a teachers' college, along with many technical training institutes. The Kazakhs are strongly Shi'ite Muslim, and many of the school-age students attend Muslim schools that parallel the public ones.

Arts and recreation. Kazakh artists are world-famous for their weaving of fine rugs. In various degrees of coarse weaves—all of wool— bright and intricate designs are woven using rectangles, stars, and latch-hook patterns. In the Kazakhstan of 1992, there are several art and drama schools, and a fine picture gallery displays Kazakh paintings in Alma Ata.

Kazhaks are fond of horse racing, perhaps their most popular recreational activity. However, a close second to racing is wrestling. Wrestlers, performing on mats in large arenas and dressed in wraparound skirts or robes entertain large crowds of onlookers.

Religion. At first the Russian government attempted to eliminate all traces of religion among the Kazakhs. Their traditional religion was Islam combined with the pre-Islamic practices of shamans, or religious leaders. The shamans claimed the ability to communicate with spirits who controlled forces such as illness, weather, and the fertility of the soil. Under Soviet dominance, the government officially recognized the existence of Islam but discouraged its practice. Its forces crushed a strongly religious movement of Muslim Kazakhs in the twentieth century and the people have abandoned many of the Muslim traditions.

For More Information

Gregory, James S. *Russian Land, Soviet People.* New York: Pegasus Press, 1968.

Olcott, Martha Brill. *Kazakhs*. Palo Alto, CA: Hoover Institute Press, 1987.

Stewart, John Massey. *Across the Russias*. Chicago: Rand McNally and Company, 1969.

KYRGYZ
(kir′ geez)

Pastoral people, also known as the Black Kyrgyz, who inhabit the Tien Shan Mountains.

Population: 2,209,900 in Kyrgyzstan (1989 census).
Location: Kyrgyzstan and China.
Language: Kyrgyzian, a Turkic dialect.

Kyrgyz

Related to the Kazakhs of Kazakhstan, the Kyrgyz of Kyrgyzstan prefer to live in the mountainous regions of the Chinese border.

Geographical Setting

The land of the Kyrgyz is dominated by the Tien Shan Mountains, which rise from high plateaus to Mount Pobeda (24,409 feet high). In the midst of the mountain ranges is a high (about 10,000 feet) plateau that is 120 miles across. This plateau and river valleys of the mountains provide meadows of heavy grass and flowers, and the valley bottoms are sometimes strewn with evergreen trees—the only trees in the region. In the north and east the mountains drop to the vast steppes of central Asia. Far from the oceans, this land does not experience abundant rainfall. Pishpek, the capital of the Kyrgyzstan, has an annual rainfall of about 15 inches. However, the high mountains gather abundant snow (the highest two mountains have permanent glaciers) which runs off in many streams. In turn, these streams have cut deep valleys that shape the mountains into fingers running into the steppes. These valleys provide fertile areas for some agriculture, but the Kyrgyz prefer to use them as pasturelands, once moving up and down the valleys with the seasons. In the northeast, Lake Issyk-Kul is one of the deepest bodies of fresh water in the world.

Historical Background

The early Kyrgyz. Some historians trace the Kyrgyz to be part of the hordes of Asians who swept across the steppes long before the Mongol hordes of Genghis Khan. About 99 B.C., Chinese armies were battling with the Huns and penetrating into Hun territory in the north. One commander, Li Ling, was captured by the Huns and joined them. He was given a rule called Khyagas. Li Ling and his followers settled along the Yenisey River. Although the Kyrgyz, as these followers came to be called, migrated west and south from this setting and blended with other peoples in the process, their chiefs claim descent from Li Ling.

Along the Yenisey River, the ancestors of the Kyrgyz built bark-covered tents and settled to farm the land, raising millet, barley, and wheat. Here the aristocracy began to give up agricultural life to raise great herds of animals.

Pushed along with the great hordes of the Huns, some of these early people migrated to the region of the Tien Shan Mountains where they were at different times ruled by Turkic khans and Uygur khans from China. Freed from these rulers by the ninth century A.D., the

Kyrgyz turned to raiding others and to herding as a way of life. Some established trade routes through the mountains with Arabs, Tibetans, and Chinese. The early Kyrgyz exported musk and fur. A Chinese chronicle of the period from 618 to 917, *T'ang-shu*, described Kyrgyz life. Apparently, sable and fox fur were valuable clothing. In winter the chief wore a sable hat, and in summer he wore a hat with a gold rim, a cone-shaped top and a curved bottom. Others dressed in white felt hats. Typically, they carried a whetstone in their belts. The garb of the lower classes was sheepskin clothing and no hats. Women's clothing was made of woolen and silk. For food, the people consumed meat and mare's milk, never eating fruit or vegetables. They kept camels, sheep, and numerous cows.

By religion, the early Kyrgyz were shamanists. Their greatest possession was the horse. Commoners were buried with their horses, aristocrats with horses, fine jewelry, and household equipment. These ancestors of today's Kyrgyz possessed a written, runic language.

A Kara-Kyrgyz man of 48 years. The Kara (black) Kyrgyz are so named because of the traditional color of their tents. *Courtesy of the National Anthropological Archive of the Smithsonian Institution.*

Chinese rule. By the tenth century the Kyrgyz had been conquered by people of northern China, the Kidamans, and lived under them as tributaries until 1207, when the Kyrgyz rulers voted to join the forces of Genghis Khan. Under the Mongols, some of the Kyrgyz of the steppes turned again to farming, raising wheat for the Mongol hordes. The role of the mountain dwellers under the Mongol rulers was to mine iron and mold weapons.

Black Kyrgyz. The mountain people continued to be nomadic herders, and became well-known for their black felt houses from which they eventually were given the name Kara-Kyrgyz, or Black Kyrgyz, to distinguish them from the Kazakh-Kyrgyz of the steppes. By 1615, about 1,000 Kyrgyz were living in various tribes in the Tien Shan Mountains.

Russian rule. In 1822, Russian frontiersmen entered Kyrgyz territory and claimed the land for the tsar. At first, Kyrgyz resistance was strong and it was some time before the Russians could claim even a loose control over the native people. By 1860 Russia and China had settled boundaries, and by 1868 Russians had built two forts on the steppes north of the Kyrgyz city of Pishpek. Still, the Kyrgyz resisted both Russian rule and the intrusion of Russian farmers on the lower lands they had traditionally used as pasture. They staged a minor revolt in 1898 and, following intensified Russian settlement beginning in 1905, a second one in 1916. Russians responded to this second revolt with violence. Kyrgyz villages were burned and 150,000 Kyrgyz were killed. A third of the Kyrgyz fled to China before the Russians had forced submission to their rule. The area remained part of Russia until well after the Russian Revolution and formation of the Union of Soviet Socialist Republics. In February 1926 the land of the Kyrgyz became an Autonomous Republic in the Russian Federation, and in 1936, a Union Republic of the Soviet Union with its capital at Frunze (now Pishpek). During this period, the Kyrgyz began to abandon their old nomadic ways under pressure from the Russians. Between 1926 and 1939 the urban population increased by 50 percent and the capital city of Frunze (Pishpek) nearly tripled in size.

Independence. By 1989, the rulers of the Kyrgyz republic had begun to press for more independence from the Union. In that year they voted to change the name of the country from the Kyrgyz Soviet Socialist Republic to the Socialist Republic of Kyrgyzstan. This name change was not recognized by the USSR, but laid the groundwork for independence that came in 1991 with the breakup of the USSR. By that time, the lives of the Kyrgyz had been drastically altered, and their economy was closely tied to that of Russia and its neighboring former Soviet republics. As a result, Kyrgyzstan quickly endorsed the idea of a Commonwealth of Independent States.

Culture Today

Soviet denomadization. For many years after coming to the attention of the Soviet Union, the Kyrgyz resisted Soviet rule. Rebellions were frequent but, having never organized their own centralized government, the nomadic people were no match for the Soviets. Still clinging to their old lifestyles of herding goats, cattle, and horses throughout the valleys of the Tien Shan Mountains, the Kyrgyz became subjects of Soviet denomadization programs. From 1929 to 1935 the Soviet Union actively pursued a policy of developing collective farming and herding—locating the Kyrgyz herders on permanent lands. The transition was a difficult one; in time the herds of the Kyrgyz were reduced to about one-fifth of their pre-Russian period. Displaced Kyrgyz began to move to the cities and larger towns to seek jobs in mining and industry. The black felt tents were abandoned for permanent houses and the Kyrgyz turned to industry. Coal, petroleum, and natural gas found in the mountains provided energy and jobs. Cities and towns arose in which steel, steel products, motors, and cement were manufactured. Still, few Kyrgyz participated in this industrial growth, preferring to continue raising cattle and sheep, but on more permanent grazing land. The Kyrgyz still prided themselves on the quality of their horses, bred for sturdiness and small size and used for travel, labor, and food.

Food and clothing. For centuries the Black Kyrgyz of the Tien Shan Mountains lived on the meat from their animals, as well as on milk and dairy products. They even prepared a fermented drink, *kemmel*, from milk. Such products are still the staple foods of the Kyrgyz, but are now supplemented with fruits and vegetables imported from the steppes north in the northern part of Kyrgyz land.

Long robes of fur once sheltered the Kyrgyz men from the fierce mountain winters, while women dressed in heavy woolen clothing. These fur and woolen clothes are still the style among the ranchers and herders outside the city. They are often augmented by knives

A Kyrgyz woman in traditional costume plays her three-stringed instrument.
From the Library of Congress.

tucked into a belt. With industrialization, these traditional clothes have given way to Western-style work clothing in the towns and cities.

Before becoming part of the Soviet Union, Kyrgyz herders built small villages in the lower regions of the Tien Shan Mountains. Inhabited by extended families, these villages comprised mud-walled houses with flat roofs on which hay for their prized horses was stored. In summer, the houses were closed while the Kyrgyz moved to yurts—round, black felt tents erected on good grazing land higher in the mountains. As they moved to the cities and towns, both mud houses and yurts gave way to the concrete houses and apartments typical of Soviet housing everywhere.

Horses. Both the Kara-Kyrgyz (Black Kyrgyz, or today's Kyrgyz) and the Kazakh-Kyrgyz are known for their excellent horsemanship and for their small but strong horses. At one time, the clans of the Kyrgyz could be identified by the color of their horses, but both the clan structure and the fondness for horses has given way under the industrialization brought on by the Soviet Union. However, such sports as horse racing and polo are still popular among these mountain people.

Religion. The Kyrgyz were introduced to Christianity early in their history, but were later persuaded to join Islam. Today most Kyrgyz are Sunni Muslims, but have mixed this religion with bits of Christianity as well as earlier beliefs, to create patterns of worship that are different from other Sunnis.

Language and literature. The language of the Kyrgyz, Kyrgyzian is a Turkic language. Since the people were long nomadic and not well organized as a nation, little was written using this language until Russian settlers brought the Cyrillic alphabet of the Russian written language. However, the Kyrgyz oral tradition was strong from early times. One of the most popular pieces of oral literature created before the fifteenth century was "Manas," a long-verse lyric about Kyrgyz independence. The Russian script has been adapted to the Kyrgyz oral language and is the current standard for writing. One of the most popular writings today is *The Ascent of Mt. Fuji* by Chingiz Aytmatov. This is a story written about the moral compromises made by the Kyrgyz during their rule by Joseph Stalin.

Arts. Kyrgyz artists have been active—even during the Russian rule. Before and during this period a great many songs were composed. They are played on the *komus*, a three-stringed instrument played in the same manner as a guitar. Under Russian leadership, Kyrgyz arts expanded into motion pictures. The Kyrgyz Motion Picture Studio has been in operation since 1942, and today produces pictures about Kyrgyz history and life.

Education. The Soviet Union also brought public education to the Kyrgyz, and the process of denomadization encouraged the Kyrgyz to take advantage of these schools. The Soviet Union permitted teaching in the Kyrgyz language, an added incentive to attend school. By 1950, there were 1,650 elementary and secondary schools with more

A Kyrgyz family at meal time. *From the Library of Congress.*

than 500,000 students. There were also 24 technical schools to provide training for jobs in the new industries, and six colleges and universities. By 1990 these numbers had grown to nearly 1,800 elementary and secondary schools, 109 technical schools, and 10 colleges and universities.

For More Information

Gregory, James S. *Russian Land, Soviet People.* New York: Pegasus Press, 1968.

Slobin, Mark. *Kirgiz Instrumental Music.* New York: Asian Music Publishers, 1969.

Stewart, John Massey. *Across the Russias.* Chicago: Rand McNally and Company, 1969.

LATVIANS

(lat′ ee ans)

Migrants from the Black Sea area who settled on the Baltic Sea
coast and became traders of amber.

Population: 1,388,760 (1989 census).
Location: Eastern shores of the Baltic Sea.
Languages: Latvian, an ancient Indo-European language akin to
Sanskrit; Russian.

Geographical Setting

Due to their shared geography and history, Latvia, Estonia, and Lithuania are also referred to as the "Baltic States."

The Republic of Latvia, until recently part of the Union of Soviet Socialist Republics (USSR), lies along the shores of the Baltic Sea and the Gulf of Riga, bordered by Estonia to the north, Lithuania to the south, and Russia to the east. Referred to by Peter the Great as the "Window to the West," Latvia is the crossroads between Eastern and Western Europe, with the Baltic Sea connecting it to Germany, Scandinavia and onwards. This strategic location along the well-traveled sea routes of the Baltic Sea has been the cause of political struggle and warfare throughout Latvia's history.

The country itself covers 24,600 square miles of undulating plains with stretches of sandy beach along the coast, a land mass about the size of West Virginia in the United States. About one-third of this land is forested and one-tenth has been developed for agriculture. A major energy source for the people of Latvia is peat. Peat bogs cover 10 percent of the land.

The capital, Riga, the major cultural, political, and trade center of the country, is situated at the mouth of the largest river, the Dau-

Latvians

- Latvians in Latvia
- Latvians in Other Countries

Latvians live across the Gulf of Finland from their Finnish relatives.

gava. Riga was once an important shipping center for trade between Scandinavia and the Byzantine Empire, and grew to be one of the three largest cities on the Baltic Sea. About 600,000 people live in the city.

The climate of Latvia is not severe, although the land lies on the same latitude as northern Canada. Influenced by the warm gulf streams in the North Atlantic, summers are humid and bring in the heaviest rainfalls of the year. Summer temperatures average around 64.2 degrees Fahrenheit. Winters are relatively mild: the average temperature in January, the coldest month, is 23.4 degrees Fahrenheit. The skies of Latvia are usually partly cloudy, with only 30 to 40 days of sunshine throughout the year.

Historical Background

Ancient origins. The origins of present-day Latvians, who form a bare majority (51.8 percent) in their own country, can be traced to the settlers of an ancient tribal group. Known as the Balts, this tribe probably migrated from the Eurasiatic steppes north of the Black Sea and served an important role in the distribution of amber. The first historical records of the Balts were those of the Tacitus, a Roman who wrote of the important amber trade. This trade, through Germanic middlemen, reached a peak in the first two centuries A.D. before it began to decline with the expansion of Slavic peoples over Central and Eastern Europe. By the tenth and eleventh centuries, Latvia was beginning to feel pressures on all fronts. The Varangians or Vikings of Sweden began to push toward the shores of the Courland region from the west and the Russians began to penetrate from the east. The Germanic Saxons ultimately came to dominate the region for centuries.

German rule. In the twelfth century, with the expansionist movement of the Crusades losing ground in the Middle East, the Germans began to turn toward the non-Christian peoples of the East. Arriving at the eastern shores of Latvia, they called the country Livonia (or Livland) after the Livs who occupied the territory. The Germans established Christian missionary posts and a number of bishops took control of the area. Bishop Albert of Buxhoevden founded the Order of Knights of the Sword in 1202 to aid with the Christianization of Latvia. By 1237, when the order merged with the Knights of the Teutonic Order, they had conquered all of what is now Latvia. Under German rule, the Livonian confederation (union of territories that included Latvia) lasted for over three centuries, replacing the local nobles in a feudal organization of the land and peasants. In general the condition of Latvians was that of any nation under conquest. The peasants were forced to pay taxes to the German conquerors while providing their hard labor for a share of the food from the land.

In the fourteenth century the union of the Polish and Lithuanian crowns created the strongest power in the region. This combination waged long wars against the Russian kingdom in the east. Since these battles were often on Latvian soil, the suffering of the people already laboring under the weakening and less-effective Teutonic Order increased. By the sixteenth century, the Latvian people were subject to ruthless exploitation by the declining German knights and lords. The Teutonic rule eventually came to a close with the battles of the Livonian War (1558–1582) initiated by the Russian army led by Ivan IV (Ivan the Terrible).

Polish and Swedish sovereignty and the Russian encroachment.
As the region broke out in war over the Latvian territory, Latvians,
instead of uniting, turned to whichever political source was most
advantageous. Consequently, by 1561 most of Estonia and parts of
Latvia had fallen under the domination of Sweden and Denmark.
The greater part of Latvia came under the Kingdom of Poland-Lithuania.

The rulers of Muscovy (Russia) had failed to reach the shores of
the Baltic Sea in Latvia although several of the tsars (emperors) had
tried to do so. Finally, however, Peter I (the Great) penetrated the
Polish and Swedish stronghold during the Great Northern War and
took the capital, Riga, from the Swedes in 1710. By the end of the
eighth century, all of Latvia had come under Russian rule.

Russian domination. Russian rule was harsh. The Latvian peasants
who were laborers in previous serfdoms fell into near slavery. However, the period of Enlightenment in Europe, which spread a philosophy of equality, began to affect the feudal life of Latvians. Shortly
after the Napoleonic Wars in 1817, the Russian Emperor Alexander
I was persuaded to grant personal freedom to the Latvians of certain
areas of Latvia—40 years before peasant liberation in Russia. Still,
Latvian peasants did not gain the right to own the land that they had
tilled for generations until the 1861 emancipation of peasants
throughout the Russian Empire. A nationalist sentiment began to rise
throughout Latvia as the right to landownership greatly increased the
economic strength and solidarity of the local peasants. Courageous
and strong-willed leaders began to sow the idea of self-rule for the
long-occupied Latvian countryside. During the Russian Revolution
in 1905, the idea of an independent Latvian state was openly proposed. However, it was not until World War I that this dream would
be realized.

Latvian independence. On November 18, 1917, the Latvian People's
Council proclaimed independence. A government was formed by the
leader of the Farmers' Union, Karlis Ulmanis. However, the Soviet
Union took command of the capital at Riga and established a Communist government for Latvia. The Ulmanis government was forced
to move to Liepaja, where it was protected by the British. German
troops again set their eyes upon Latvian territory with plans to develop a base of operations against the Soviets. Through the persistence of the Red Army and Latvian troops, all of the German troops

abandoned Latvia in December of 1919. Soon thereafter a troop of 33,000 Latvian soldiers removed the remnants of the Red Army in the province of Latgale.

A Latvian constituent assembly was elected in April of 1920 in Riga. On August 11, a Latvian-Soviet peace treaty was signed releasing all Russian claims for Latvian territory. The Latvian government was composed of a president with a unicameral parliament or *saeima* composed of 100 officials elected from various parties for three years. The stability of this government was weakened, however, by the extreme number of political parties allowed under a law which permitted seven citizens or more to form a party. The result of this fragmentation was a nearly endless change of governments. In the short period of Latvian independence (1918 to 1934) there were a total of 18 governments. Karl Ulmanis, the first prime minister of Latvia, was elected four times to the presidency and initiated constitutional reforms in 1934.

In spite of the changing government, this period of independence brought major changes for the Latvians. The Agrarian Reform redistributed more than half of the land to landless farmers. Latvia began to export grain in the 1930s after being an importer in the '20s. Education was improved, with expenditures for instruction increasing to nine times more than those in the early 1900s. Illiteracy was reduced and schools, training colleges, and academies were established.

Incorporation into the Soviet Union. Latvian independence was short-lived within the power struggles leading up to World War II. Although the Baltic states of Estonia and Lithuania joined Latvia in a search for peace and security through diplomatic relations, the Soviet Union made a secret agreement with Nazi Germany under the Nazi-Soviet Non-Aggression and Friendship Pact for the acceptance of Soviet occupation of the Baltic states. On June 17, 1939, the Soviet Red Army entered and occupied the entire country. On July 20, a new Saiema (parliament) voted for the incorporation of Latvia in the USSR and on August 20th this was officially accepted by the USSR. A year of terror followed the occupation with an intense drive to exterminate Latvia's leaders and spread Russian language and culture by force. On the night of June 13-14, the Soviets arrested and deported to labor camps more than 15,000 Latvians. During the strife of World War II, one out of five Latvians fled their homeland for Central and

Eastern Europe. With this new migration, a total of 300,000 Latvians lived outside Latvia.

At home, the culture, economy and lifestyle of the Latvian people underwent great change. In 1949, Latvian farms were made collective and state-controlled. During the Soviet domination, from 1940 to 1990, Latvia and the other Baltic States were mostly closed to foreign visitors, so little was known of the conditions there. A Swedish ship was allowed to visit Riga in 1956, and its crew reported a city in squalor and with signs of much cruel treatment of its inhabitants. However, as the Baltic States became industrialized, many Russians moved to Riga to work in the factories and on the shipping docks. Later in Soviet rule, there were reports of much improvement in living conditions in the country as the population of Latvians was supplemented by a Russian managerial and work force that would make up more than a third of the country's population

Although Latvia remained one of the most prosperous and industrialized regions while controlled by the Soviet Union, the memory of independence kept resistance movements alive abroad and among the Latvians at home. With the liberalization of the Soviet Union under Mikhail Gorbachev in the late 1980s, nationalist movements gained momentum in trying to assert more control over Latvian internal affairs. As economic conditions worsened in the Soviet Union, Latvians were among the first to declare themselves an independent nation (see LATVIA).

Culture Today

Latvians today have lived under great change with, first, the liberalization policy of the Soviet Union, and then the rise of independence movements in Latvia and abroad. Throughout Soviet control, long-standing traditions and customs bonded Latvians throughout the world. Latvian associations around the world continue to bring Latvian immigrants together to renew their ties to their culture and homeland.

Language. The Latvian language is spoken by about 1,500,000 people throughout Latvia. The language, which belongs to the Baltic branch of the Indo-European family of languages (including Lithuanian), has been the country's official language since 1918. While the earliest texts of the Latvian language, including the Catholic catechism, date to the sixteenth century, the grammar was not written down until the eighteenth century. However, the literary language of Latvians was well-developed by the nineteenth century. Latvian is spoken in three dialects: East Latvian, West Latvian, and Central Latvian.

Family life. Long-standing cultural customs and traditions celebrate family ties and events in the lives of family members. Many of the Latvian customs are centered around life events such as the naming of a child, marriage, and death. During Latvian weddings, ritual folk songs are sung as the bride's wedding veil is replaced with a women's scarf to mark her transition to married life. These joyous occasions usually extend into second-day fetes joined in by relatives and close friends.

Holidays. Many festivals are celebrated in accordance with the changing seasons. During the winter season, family members visit each other's houses—in colorful masked processions through neighborhoods—during the festival of Martini from November 10 to around Christmastime. Disguised in costumes as Gypsies, bears, horses, and sheaves of grain, the members sing and dance and parade through the neighborhood with homemade noisemakers. The masqueraders represent the good spirits whose songs and dances are intended to bring good luck to the families of the community.

Everywhere in Central Europe, Christmas and New Year's Eve are important holidays. Among the Latvians these holidays are celebrated with lavish feasts of traditional foods such as pig's snout, bacon rolls and boiled brown peas. Easter also brings neighboring families together. One custom has people swinging high from a pole between two trees to bring tall grains in the next fall's harvest.

In June, near the summer solstice, the festival of *Janu* involves singing, dancing, and special preparations. Houses are given a yearly cleaning, and beer is brewed a week ahead. The day before *Janu* is special for collecting herbs, flowers, and greenery to use for making wreaths and garlands that decorate the homes and the festive outfits of women and men. In the evening, bonfires are lit for singing, dancing, eating, and storytelling throughout the night.

Clothing. Latvians are proud of their native dress, which includes long-admired designs and ornamentations. The patterns are unique to the various regions of Latvia and are worn on festive holidays and national events. Along the seacoast and the Estonian border, the people called Tamnieki use colorful combinations of blue, yellow, green and black for decorative borders on wool and linen fabrics sewn into long wraps and shawls for women. In the Alsunga and Kuldiga districts a 1,500-year-old tradition of ornamenting indigo-blue wraps with bronze spiral pendants is followed by women today. During the sixteenth and seventeenth centuries, new techniques for crafting bronze jewelry and belts were introduced. These bronze pieces are inspiring embellishments for Latvian dress. In Letgalu, the bronze accessories are attached to headdresses worn by men and women. The intricate designs of the native dress have been recognized as a highly skilled folk art.

Food and shelter. Increased industrialization in Latvia has demanded a rapid increase in urban housing to meet the flood of new city-dwellers. The capital of Latvia, Riga, has an Old Town which holds some of the older European-style buildings with apartments. Many similar buildings were destroyed during World War I and II. Since the Soviet occupation of Latvia, most of the housing units were nationalized under the former Soviet government. New housing units were also built in large development tracts to meet the increasing population in the urban areas. Due to the density of the population, the majority of these units have been small one- and two-unit apartments in which whole families reside.

Collective farms produce most of the food grown to feed the populations, and several food industries have been developed to export food to other former Soviet republics. While the Latvian government is struggling to reorganize land ownership, almost all of the farms in Latvia are collectively run by the government. Latvians are also struggling to make changes within a government that had set quotas for the amount of crops to be harvested, milk to be produced and eggs to be laid. Animal husbandry is the main branch of agriculture in Latvia while meat and dairy products comprise a large part of the Latvian diet. Given the bountiful seas that border one-fourth of Latvia, fish is also an important part of the diet and of the country's commercial trade. There are favorable conditions in Latvia for grain, potato, sugar beets, and vegetable cultivation to provide a well-balanced diet.

Religion. Long before Christianity came to Latvia, the Latvians had a developed religious life centered around three divine beings: Dievas, Mara and Laimea. The beliefs of ancient Latvian religion are recon-

Sorting and washing vegetables at a canning factory in Latvia. *From the Library of Congress.*

structed from more than a million surviving myths and folklore. Dievas, the sky god, was the most powerful of the council of gods. The feminine counterpart of Dievas, Laimea, the goddess of fate, decided the fate of all newborn Latvians and mediated between Dievas and Mara. The modern version of the ancient religion, called Dievturiba, inspired a revival during Latvia's independence. Today the Dievturi religion has numerous followers in Latvia and abroad.

Most present-day Latvian people are either Catholic or Lutheran, although religious worship was generally discouraged under Soviet rule. Since the invasion by the Soviet Union in 1940, many of the important Latvian churches have been converted to other uses or burned down. For example, St. Peter's Church in Riga was converted to a museum. Such transformation has led to a decrease in the members participating in the Church, and in the availability of pastors to lead congregations. Lutheran church members fell from 1,094,787 in 1935, before the Russian invasion, to 350,000 in 1969. Churches decreased in number from 297 to 182 and pastors from 288 to 102 (Lutheran World Federation figures).

The arts. The arts in Latvia thrive through local, community-based drama groups, choirs, ensembles, orchestras and dance companies. Song festivals that have been held since the 1870s are some of the most popular events in Latvia, as well as in immigrant communities all over the world. In Latvia, every five years, the local districts and towns hold song festivals to choose their best choir, orchestra, and dance company to send to Riga for a national festival. These festivals provide contemporary forums for the vital folk traditions that have been passed down from generation to generation for centuries.

Latvian folk songs, *dainas*, form the richest part of Latvian musical heritage. There are some 400,000 published folk songs in existence, in addition to more than 1,000,000 unpublished and unrecorded songs in existence. Folk songs are sung at weddings, funerals, and other communal occasions and are accompanied by a number of

Dancing in traditional festival costumes at the Fisherman's Festival at Riga, Latvia. *From the Library of Congress.*

traditional instruments. One of the most celebrated folk instruments is the *kokle*, a string instrument found throughout the Baltics. Played since the thirteenth century, the *kokle* thrives in Latvia and immigrant communities. Folk dances are also popular and are performed to the folk songs and music. The Lativan National Opera, renamed the "The Opera and Ballet Theater" under the Soviet Union, began a flourishing ballet tradition in Latvia.

Latvians have a long tradition of excellence in wood crafts. Latvian furniture is often beautifully carved. Latvian women are also well-known for their skill in embroidery. Traditional Latvian costumes reveal this skill in heavily embroidered skirts, blouses, and shawls.

Literature. Literature written in the Latvian language draws from the rich folklore and poetry of its people. Written non-religious literature began in the eighteenth century with Latvian G. F. Stender, who produced tales of country life that incorporated folk songs. During the awakening of the Latvian nationalist movement in the mid-nineteenth century, folklore became an important source of inspiration for the revival of Latvian culture. Juris Alunans's landmark book of verse, *Dziesminas* ("Songs"), written in 1856, is considered to be the birth of the Latvians' national artistic poetry. A cornerstone of Latvian literature appeared in 1879 with the publication of *Mernieku laiki* ("The Time of the Land Surveyors") by the brothers Reinis and Matiss Kaudzites. This novel was the first to provide a realistic, although somewhat romantic, portrayal of Latvian peasantry and has been translated into a number of languages.

At the turn of the century, socialist ideas spread in Latvia and gave rise to a movement known as the New Current, which adopted a more universal outlook. Janis Rainis, a poet, playwright, and lyrical writer is one of the best-known writers of this movement. His works such as *Joseph and His Brothers* have found an audience throughout the world. During the era of Latvian independence, expressionist writers actively contributed to the development of Latvian culture. Janis Veselis (1896–1962) founded his writing on the folklore and legends of the religious beliefs of ancient Latvians. Veselis developed a special type of legend—*teiksma*—as a romantic reconstruction of Latvian history. Alexsandrs Čaks, the greatest of modern poets, is known for his rebellious style and for his collection of patriotic poetry, such as *Mirrors of Imagination* (1938).

After the occupation by the Soviet Union, Latvian expression was suppressed and many Latvian writers exiled. While many writers were forced to write Socialist propaganda, restrictions were loosened after Stalin's death in 1953, resulting in the first work of the period, *The Unfinished Song*, which dealt with the themes of banishment to Siberia. Three poets, Ojārs Vacietis, Vizma Bel, and Imants Ziedonis, have tried, with their revolutionary poetry, to mobilize Latvian consciousness against the oppression of Communist rule. Latvian writers in exile in Western countries have published more than 600 new literary works since 1945 and have founded literary magazines such as the *Jauna Gaita* ("The New Course") as a means to express the struggle of Latvian people for their independence.

For More Information

Rutkis, J. *Latvia: Country and People*. Stockholm: Latvian National Foundation, 1967.

Simanis, Vito Vitauts, ed. *Latvia*. St. Charles: The Book of Latvia, Inc., 1984.

Spekke, Arnolds. *History of Latvia: An Outline*. Stockholm: Goppers, 1957.

LITHUANIANS

(lith′ oo ai′ nee uns)

Early settlers of the Baltic Sea coast.

Population: 2,955,690 in Lithuania (1990 census).
Location: Lithuania and Byelarus.
Language: Lithuanian, an ancient Indo-European language most nearly related to Latvian.

Geographical Setting

Lithuanians

Lithuanians in Lithuania
Lithuanians in Other Countries

The land of the Lithuanians, consisting mostly of the modern state of Lithuania, is part of the great plain that extends from Poland through Russia to the Ural Mountains. It is a land of fertile soil, cold winters, and cool summers. Low and flat, the territory lies on the Baltic Sea and is crossed by three large rivers: the Nemunas River, which begins in Byelarus and flows into the Baltic Sea; its tributary the Neris, along which lies the capital city Vilnius; and the Kaunas. The northern half of the country averages about 300 feet above sea level. In the south the land rises to between 300 and 600 feet. The highest hill in Lithuania is just over 800 feet high. Seventeen percent of the land is forest, providing some wood for building and fuel. Otherwise, until the development of nuclear energy plants, Lithuania had no energy resources of its own, and came to be dependent on other sections of the former Soviet Union for energy to operate its industries.

Historical Background

Origin. About 800 B.C. small groups of people from regions around the Baltic Sea began to settle in the area that is now Lithuania—until 1991 a republic in the Union of Soviet Socialist Republics. On hilltops overlooking plains and rivers, leaders who later took on the status of dukes, built forts with great earthen buttresses and around the forts, villages. The villages were composed of one-room, rectangular huts clustered together in a circle. The grand dukes thus ruled the area of present-day Lithuania, successfully warding off invasion by the Slavs in the fifth century and Swedes about A.D. 650. The fortifications and surrounding homes grew into towns, still ruled individually by dukes until the thirteenth century, although they were often threatened or forced to pay tribute to the neighboring Prussians. In that century, Mindaugas, one of the dukes, unified their feudal states and won recognition as an independent state from the threatening Prussians. Mindaugas, therefore, is credited for establishing the nation of Lithuania. In exchange for independence, Mindaugas made Christianity the official religion of Lithuania. In the two centuries that followed, Lithuania expanded south and west (into the area now Byelarus and western Ukraine) and became a leading empire in feudal Europe.

Lithuania and Poland. The Duchy of Lithuania grew more powerful when, in 1485, Lithuania and Poland were united by marriage of their rulers. The Lithuanian-Polish union grew as a result of mutual ambition to ward off Prussian invasion and to invade Russia. In 1501, Lithuanians demanded that the grand duke of Lithuania be recognized as king of Poland. That accomplished, the union of the two countries was confirmed by the formation of a parliament in 1569. The major division between peoples of the countries was language: one-third of the population spoke a form of Russian, while more than one-fourth spoke Polish.

Russia and Prussia. By the eighteenth century, both Russia and Prussia had begun to dominate eastern Europe. In three annexations between 1772 and 1795, Russia took the Russian-speaking portions of Lithuania while the remainder fell to Prussian rule. Then, in 1839, the Roman Catholic religion was officially replaced by the Russian Orthodox Church, and Russian law replaced Lithuanian state law. Lithuania became the Russian "Territory of the Northwest." To further consolidate their claim in Lithuania, Russian rulers abolished the use of other languages in 1864. Only Russian and a form of the Lithuanian language written with a Russian alphabet were permitted. Lithuanians were uneasy with the restrictions and pressed for freedom of speech, finally winning a measure of freedom in 1905. Restrictions on Lithuanian writers were repealed, and they responded by adding stories, plays, and poems to the Lithuanian folklore that had been collected by Jonas Basanavičius.

World Wars. In World War I, Germany occupied Lithuania and recognized it as independent from Russia. The separation was confirmed in a 1920 treaty with the Soviet Union, which formed Lithuania out of the Russian provinces of Kovno, Vilnus, and parts of Grodno, Suvalki, Courland, and Memel. The great powers of the war accepted this arrangement. Now with a land area only a small fraction of the once expansive and powerful Grand Duchy of Lithuania, the new country struggled to remain free. Lithuania warded off Polish demands on land and Russian attempts to dominate the country. Germany again occupied Lithuania between 1941 and 1944. Then in 1950, despite resistance by Lithuanians, their homeland became part of the Union of Soviet Socialist Republics. In 1990, as the Soviet economy threatened to break down, Lithuania joined Estonia and Latvia in declaring independence from the Soviet Union. Soviet troops were sent into Lithuania to enforce obedience to Moscow. The Lithuanians resisted stubbornly, until in 1991 the Soviet Union recognized Lithuanian independence. The Lithuanian Soviet Socialist Republic promptly changed its name to the Republic of Lithuania. Today most Lithuanians live in their own homeland. A few live in the neighboring country of Byelarus, and more live in the United States and other Western nations, having fled Soviet oppression.

Culture Today

Agriculture and industry. The Lithuanian territory is mostly rich agricultural land, but includes amber among its natural resources (90 percent of the world's amber, which is used in chemical industries and in jewelry, comes from Lithuania). Once a land of small family farms on which the father was the authoritarian leader, Lithuanian land has now been formed into large cooperatives and mechanization has replaced the old family's animal-drawn plow. However, shale oil deposits and new nuclear power plants have enabled Lithuanians to develop an industrial economy which is fed with raw materials from Lithuanian forestland and farms. Cloth, shoes, and processed foods from fish, meat, and dairy products are major commercial products. With the development of nuclear energy plants, metal-processing has become an important part of the Lithuanian economy.

Family life. Life under communism tended to replace local authority with state-wide government. However, the traditional, patriarchal family is still powerful among Lithuanians. Although the father is still the economic and moral authority, more land is now state-owned and he has little to pass on to his sons. Usually a man, his wife, and their children form the family unit. Only in about one-fifth of the households are grandparents included in this home. Another one-fifth of all Lithuanians today live alone.

Under communism, the government assumed some of the roles of the head of the family, while issues of health, welfare, and education became the responsibilities of trade unions.

Food, clothing, and shelter. The home of the typical Lithuanian family varies in style according to the region of the country. Eastern Lithuanian farm families live in small cottages. An enclosed stove in the main room of the cottage serves for cooking and for heating both this room and the adjoining sleeping rooms. Western Lithuanian homes are larger, while in the north, Lithuanian farmers and cattle raisers live in structures that include a barn and a threshing floor.

Before annexation by the Soviet Union, most farm families lived in small hamlets near their farmland. In the 50 years of Soviet domination, these old hamlets and villages were largely abandoned in favor of new village-like establishments on the large collective farms. In addition, Soviet policies led to industrialization and its resulting migration to the cities. Now about 25 percent of the people live on the farm collectives. Others live in the cities in structures that vary from single-family homes to large apartments.

Food production, along with amber collecting and processing shale oil, made Lithuanians among the most prosperous people in the former Soviet alliance. The Lithuanians grow wheat and a large variety of fruits and vegetables, which they eat along with meat products such as ham, bacon, and sausage. Dairy products are also important ingredients in Lithuanian diets. Dairy farming and hog farming are carried on by 40 percent of the agricultural communities. Under Soviet rule, Lithuanians were encouraged to explore the fishing potential in the land's three large rivers and in the Baltic Sea. As a result, fish has taken a place in the diet of many Lithuanians.

Religion. Lithuanians are a religious people. Ninety-five percent of them claim to be Catholics, in spite of religious persecution under Soviet rule in retaliation for the church's resistance to the Soviet takeover of Lithuania in the 1940s. Religious festivals are popular among Lithuanians and are often celebrated with feasts, as are marriages and funerals. As many as a hundred guests might attend a typical wedding, each bringing food or drink. The wedding becomes a party with the guests sometimes enacting a mock war between the bride's family and that of the groom—a tradition thought to be a vestige of a more ancient wedding practice in which the bride was kidnapped by the groom.

Early tradition, before Christianity appeared in Lithuania, called for cremation of the dead, then later for burial in wooden coffins in mounded graves protected by massive rocks. Under Christianity cremation lost favor, only to be revived in the sixth century.

Education. Under Soviet rule, a school system was developed that provided free and compulsory education for twelve years. As in Russian schools, students attend a common school and then are placed in more specialized high schools according to vocational needs, interests, and scholastic abilities.

A class learns to play an old Lithuanian instrument, the Kanklis. *From the Library of Congress.*

Arts and literature. Interest in the arts was exhibited early in Lithuanian history. Burial sites of the second century contain the bodies of women wearing woolen caps from which hung coiled-wire temple ornaments. These burial grounds also revealed headcloths, necklaces, bracelets, woolen cloaks, toe-rings, and other decorative objects. Soon after contact with the Romans, Lithuanians also became interested in glass beads. That the interest continued through the ages was demonstrated by the foundation of the Vilnius Drawing School in 1886. One Lithuanian and internationally known painter in recent history was M. K. Čiurlonis. Under Soviet rule, the creation of art objects was limited by the insistence on productions of social realism. Still,

Lithuanians are noted for their works in ceramics, wood carving, and textiles.

There were few, if any, Lithuanian writers during the most powerful days of the Grand Duchy. Its folk history and songs were chanted by bards called *burtininkas*. But under the sixteenth century power of the clergy, these bards were discontinued and the ancient literature disappeared. The Lithuanian language, as are the languages of their Baltic neighbors, is one of the oldest in Europe. It is most akin to the ancient Sanskrit language but with influences from Greek and Roman. Adopting Roman characters for writing in this language rather than the Cyrillic characters of their neighbors, Lithuanian books first appeared in 1547 with the publication of a Roman Catholic catechism. This was followed in the 1600s by a Lithuanian grammar book and dictionary. In the middle of the eighteenth century, Kristijonas Donelaitis began an interest in writing about the Lithuanian people with *The Four Seasons*. However, during the long rule of the Russian tsars, writing in the Lithuanian language was mostly forbidden. Before World War I, Lithuanians printed books abroad and smuggled them into the country to preserve their language. Many who distributed these books were exiled to Siberia for their crime against the tsarist state.

Under Joseph Stalin, Lithuanians were again forbidden from publishing in their own language. However, two religious leaders, Bishop

Dancers perform the Shopachnaya, a Lithuanian folk dance. *From the Library of Congress.*

M. Valančius and Bishop G. Baranauskas, continued to publish Lithuanian books and rally the people to preserve their language. More recently, Lithuanian writers inside the Soviet Union have confined themselves to social realism topics, while exiled Lithuanians have written strongly about their struggle for freedom in such works as Jueagas Daumantis's *Fighters for Freedom* (1975) and Javis Rejaujis's *Genocide in Lithuania* (1980). Perhaps the greatest writer of the twentieth century is V. Krévé Mickevičius, who has popularized short stories and lyrics.

Music is a popular recreational outlet among the Lithuanians. There are three nationwide music festivals each year, and every fifth year there is an international singing festival in which nearly all Lithuanians participate.

For More Information

Davies, Norman. *Heart of Europe: Poland—Politics and Government.* New York: Oxford University Press, 1984.

Porter, A. *Lithuania.* Annapolis, Maryland: John's Hopkins University Press, 1990.

Senn, Alfred E. *Lithuania Awakening.* Berkeley, California: University of California Press, 1990.

MAGYARS

(mag' yars)

Ancestors of Finnish, Iranian, and early Magyar peoples who lived in Hungary.

Population: 13,700,000 (1990 estimate; 10,375,000 in Hungary).
Location: Hungary, Czechoslovakia, Yugoslavia, Romania.
Language: Hungarian.

Magyars

Magyars (Hungarians) live in Austria, Hungary, Czechoslovakia, Romania, and in the Vojvodina region of Yugoslavia.

Geographical Setting

Magyars make up 95 percent of the population of Hungary, which is located in the lowland center of the middle basin of the Danube River. The country is a landlocked Central European country which, for physical as well as cultural reasons, is divided into three geographical zones: Transdanubia, the Northern Hills, and the Great Plain. Transdanubia, a small plains area with undulating hills that are extensions of the Austrian Alps, is dotted with lakes. Budapest—the capital of Hungary—as well as the cities of Székesfehrvár, Estergom, and Pecs are located in Transdanubia. North of Budapest, the Northern Hills provide much of the mineral wealth of the country. Miskolc, an important mining and industrial center, Eser, and Tokay, famous for its wines, are in this region.

The Great Plain, an extremely flat, sand-dune expanse, is bordered by the Danube and its main watershed, the Tisza. It is the horse-riding, cattle-herding people of this region that many foreigners picture as typical Magyars. Although these animals now roam Hortobágy, now a national park, and some of the wild uncultivated countryside, much of the land has been reclaimed for cultivation by regularly flooding the Tisza River. Additionally, large cities, such as Debrecen and Szeged (known for its paprika), are in this part of Hungary.

Historical Background

About the ninth century A.D. people of Finnish-Ugric descent left their homes in the area between the upper Volga River and the Ural Mountains in present-day Russia and began moving west across the great plains between the Ural and Carpathian mountain ranges. In 896 a tribe led by Arpád, and known as Magyars, moved across the Carpathians into a western flatland in present-day Hungary.

Early raiding society. From that base, the Magyars earned a reputation as warriors, preferring frequent raiding of small German kingdoms to farming. However, Germans resisted the raids and, by 955, Otto the Great had gathered a German army that was able to defeat the Magyars. This stopped the westward aggression of the Magyars and they settled along the Danube and Tisza rivers. Gradually, they expanded their territory east, north, and south until their country, Magyarorszag, reached its greatest expanse, in the eleventh century.

On Christmas Day in the year 1001, Stephen was crowned king of Hungary with recognition by the Pope, Sylvester II. (Stephen was cannonized in 1083, and is the patron saint of Hungarians.) Following St. Stephen's death in 1038, a decade of discord arose over who should succeed to the throne, during which time there was a revival of the old religions. Eventually Ladislaw I (the saint) reunited the country under Christianity. During his reign (1077–1095) Hungary laid its first claim to part of Croatia. The reign of the Arpad family continued for 300 years, until 1301.

Austria and Turkey. In 1222, nobles of Hungary persuaded King Andrew II to accept the Golden Bull, a pact that defined civil rights for noblemen. However, in 1521 the Turks seized Belgrade in preparation for war, and in 1526 the king of the Magyars was killed. The Magyar nobles were divided as to a successor. Most of the nation fell under Austrian rule as Ferdinand of Austria was elected king by the nobles, while the center of the country came under Turkish rule. When the Ottoman Empire began to decline about the end of the seventeenth century, Hungary fell to the Austrians. In the Thirty Years War, Hungarian princes were a powerful force for Protestantism against the religious fervor of the Austrian emperor and the Jesuits. In 1683, the then-powerful Magyars joined in the defense of Vienna that turned the tide of Turkish advances. Hungary remained part of an empire with Austria from 1687 until the end of World War I. An Austro-Hungarian monarchy was established in 1867 that gave the Magyars a measure of self-rule, but the monarchy collapsed in 1918 with Austria-Hungary's defeat in World War I.

World War I settlements. For Hungary, the settlements that followed the war were tainted by secret agreements made in 1915 and 1916 as to the setting of new boundaries in Central Europe. Hungary was seldom invited to state its position in the peace conferences that continued through 1920. The result was the setting of boundaries that reduced Hungarian land by more than 70 percent and left large Magyar minorities in the newly shaped states of Czechoslovakia, Romania, and Russia. Finding little interest in their cause among France, Great Britain, and the United States, Hungarians turned to the once-feared Russians for support and the government of Béla Kun leaned toward communism. This situation did not encourage friendship with the West, and the government decided to settle its own border dispute with Romania. Defeated in that move, Kun resigned in 1919 and the government was revived the next year by Nicholas Horthy as a kingdom without a crowned monarch. This condition prevailed until 1947. Meanwhile, the peace conference at the Trianon Palace in Paris established the boundaries of a drastically reduced Hungary. Two-thirds of the old Hungary had been given to its neighbors, including much land heavily populated by Magyars.

Hungary between the wars. From 1918 to 1945, Hungary concerned itself with appeals to every party involved in adjusting the Hungarian boundaries, so that large Magyar areas would be reunited. Among the major powers, only the United States expressed interest in such adjustments, but Hungary was not sufficiently important to this nation to encourage action. It was left to the Central European nations to resolve their differences, a situation that resulted in the formation of a "Little Entente" of Yugoslavia, Romania, and Czechoslovakia, which pressed its case at Hungarian expense. No changes were made in the boundaries established by the Trianon Treaty.

World War II. Beginning in 1938, Germany began to exert influence on its neighbors. For Hungary, this meant pressure to allow the passage of German troops whose destination would eventually be Romania. In 1940, the Hungarian government sought to resolve one of its greatest land disputes by allowing German troops passage through Hungary in exchange for a promise of the restoration to Hungary of Romanian-held Transylvania. By 1944, Germany had violated that pact by invading Hungary, and again the Magyar people were drawn into conflict. Settlements following the second World War did little to change the boundaries established by the Trianon Treaty.

Communism. In 1945, Hungary began a land reform movement that broke large landholdings into small peasant-owned farms. This reform was followed by adoption of a Soviet-style communist government. A Hungarian Catholic leader who represented 60 percent of the people, Cardinal Jósef Mindszenti, protested the new government and was imprisoned for many years by the government led by Mátyás Rákosi. Rákosi had organized a communist movement in 1925, been exiled to Russia, and returned to lead the Communist party in Hungary until he again fled to Russia in 1956.

Under Hungarian-style communism, peasants owned the land but were encouraged to form "cooperatives." By 1953, 25 percent of the farmland had been formed into 5,315 cooperatives. However, private owners of farms were still managed through government-prescribed obligations to deliver their produce on a quota basis. This and other government interventions caused many farmers to lose their farms, and resulted in a continued general decline in the economy. The decline was reversed in 1956 and 1957 when the government raised wages by 20 percent and abolished the farm quotas.

Meanwhile, Mátyás Rákosi had consolidated his power in the style of Joseph Stalin, by purging those with differing opinions. In 1953, his actions were disputed and a moderate leader, Imre Nagy, was installed only to be ousted in 1955. A revolt against the advance of Russian communism in 1956 was suppressed with the help of

Increased freedom brought changes in street names in Budapest, Hungary.
Courtesy of Leah M. Cadavona.

Russian troops. A new Russian-supported government was installed, led by János Kádár. A new economic plan raised wages and moved Hungary toward industrialization. Twelve years later continued unrest ultimately resulted in a "new economic mechanism" under which the rights of peasants to own land were confirmed. However, the always independent Magyars were not satisfied with progress under communism. By the end of this century there was some easing of communist controls of factories and farms.

By the early 1980s, under Kádár, Magyars were able to carry on private enterprises as long as this activity was in addition to their required work in state-run businesses. In 1982, the government began to decentralize some industries. At that time, Hungary was considered one of the most open and liberal of the Communist-bloc nations. The economy reflected both the changes and the successes. Between 1949 and 1980 farm workers dropped from 56 percent of the work force to 13 percent. Most urban households boasted washing machines and electric refrigerators by 1980, and one of three homes owned automobiles.

In 1989, a series of changes inside and outside government recognized that the demonstrations of 1956 reflected the desires of the people. Statues of the hero of the 1956 uprising, Nagy, were given ceremonial burials. A constitutional court was appointed. National elections were called for. The Young Communists Union gave way to a new Hungarian Democratic Youth Federation. The presidential council was replaced by a president of the republic. The Hungarian government began to relax its long abstinence from dealings with the West. In the fall of 1989, Hungary opened its borders to East Germans wishing to pass through en route to West Germany. This initiated a series of events that resulted in the union of the two Germanies and the destruction of the Berlin Wall.

In March and April 1990, Hungary held its first multiparty elections since 1945, with 28 parties and groups represented. Today Hungary is governed by a freely elected unicameral National Assembly, which appoints the president and council of ministers.

Culture Today

The mixture. The Magyars of Hungary were originally a Finnish people. As they moved into Europe, they were invaded by Austrians and Turks, and in turn, overran some German groups. The combinations of these various groups resulted in the Magyars of today. As with most peoples of Central and Eastern Europe, the Magyars resulted from the mixing of people moving about and seeking land in the region.

Language. The Magyars did not develop a written language until A.D 1200; however, they had begun to build a rich folklore in tales and songs early in their history. These folktales and songs tell stories of the Magyars' adventures as mobile warriors before they settled in the Danube Valley. Hungarian is written using Roman characters but without a "W." A system of accents indicates the 15 vowel sounds and 26 consonant sounds that complete the language. This language has been used in preference to Latin as the formal language of the Magyars since 1844.

Religion. Religion was one of the forces that unified the Magyars. About 1000 the Magyar king known as Stephen I was converted to Christianity and tried to convert all the people. Since that time, the Magyars have been divided among Protestants and Roman Catholics. Today about two-thirds of the Magyars are Roman Catholics and one-fourth are Protestants.

Changes in the 1980s included a greater tolerance of religious differences. Churches and synagogues reflect with modern, Gothic, Byzantine, Roman, and Renaissance designs.

Economy. Originally, the Magyars disdained farming as a way of earning a living. The first Magyar invaders of Europe were warriors who preferred raiding other people or hiring themselves as soldiers to warring countries. However, after their defeat by Otto the Great, the Magyars settled into the Danube Valley, where they became farmers and herders. Farming is still a major occupation on the plain east of the Danube, and sheep and goat herding, in the hills. Land reform under the Communists in 1945 protected the small farmer and redistributed the larger landholdings. Peasant families were allowed to stay on their farms but were encouraged to form cooperative units. Today most of the land is owned by the peasants but has been organized into cooperative farm units for more efficient use of modern farm equipment.

As with other European countries, Hungary under communism has pushed for industrialization. Coal mining and iron mining, the development of forestry products, and the production of cotton fabrics and rolled steel has resulted in an evolution of farmhands to

**Pushcarts have been popular for
transporting goods in the villages of
Hungary.** *Courtesy of the Judah L.
Magnes Museum, Berkeley, California.*

factory workers. A 1968 ruling and additional legal changes in 1982
transformed Hungarian industry from a system of complete government ownership to a combination-style in which some small-scale
industry is owned and operated as private enterprise.

Ninety-four percent of all land is owned by the state or owned
cooperatively by the peasants. The land is organized into private and
collective farms on which wheat, maize, sugar beets, potatoes, and
grapes are grown. Poultry and pigs are the main livestock. Crops and
livestock are used to make traditional dishes such as gulyas, a stew
of meat and vegetables. Meat, fruit, and vegetables are also used for

A husband and wife work together to cut firewood on a Hungarian farm. *Courtesy of the Judah L. Magnes Museum, Berkeley, California.*

foreign trade. Fifty percent of all Hungarian products are developed for export.

Family life. As with most peoples, increased mobility in the twentieth century has taken away much of the family structure's significance and security. Since World War II, industrialization has forced peasants out of the countryside and into city factories and taken women out of the homes to work elsewhere. As a result, children spend a large proportion of their time in school and, in the largest Hungarian city, Budapest, in youth group activities.

Hungarian girls in holiday dress wait to greet returning troops. *From the Library of Congress.*

Scarcity of housing is one force holding families together. Particularly in large cities, entire families are sometimes confined to one or two rooms in an apartment building. Young people frequently live with and care for elders so that they can acquire the apartment when the elders die. Tall apartment buildings are becoming the standard of housing. Complexes of multistory buildings have sprung up in even the smaller cities.

Rural families and some city families live in their own single-family dwellings, which are one- or two-story structures with tiled roofs and stucco facades. Overall, about half the Magyar population live in private, single-family homes.

Clothing. Along with industrialization and international trade there has been a change in Hungarian dress to a more Western style. Traditional dress is now only seen in festivals or among the sheepherders in the hills. The traditional woman's attire consists of an embroidered long dress bound at the waist with a sash and topped with a ruffled collar. An ankle-length train trailing from the waist often decorates the costume. Older women are still often seen wearing scarfs over their hair. Traditional men's attire includes plain skirts with embroidered vests. Shepherds still wear their traditional boots, baggy trousers, and loose shirts with a blanket thrown across one shoulder. Flat, wide-brimmed hats complete the outfit.

Food. Most foreigners are more familiar with Hungarian food than with any other aspects of Magyar culture. Though goulash, a soup of beef, onions, potatoes, and spices, may be the best-known dish elsewhere, it is primarily associated with the Great Plain region in Hungary. Magyar food is distinguished by its emphasis on the spice paprika, a mild, sweet, red pepper that gives flavor and color to Hungarian dishes. *Csirke paprikas* (paprika chicken) is a sauteed and stewed chicken in a sauce of onion, green peppers, and paprika. Both peppers and cabbages are often stuffed with ground meat and served with tomato sauce. Meals include salads of sliced cucumbers, or grated cabbage with a vinegar-based dressing.

The primary meal of the day is eaten at midday. Breakfast usually consists of bread or buns with butter and jam, while supper (eaten late) is often deli-style with open-faced sandwiches of cheese, salami, or cold cuts. Today, in the industrial cities, lighter lunches and heavier dinners are the rule.

Hungarian cooks are also known for pastries. *Palacsinta*, a thin crepe-like pancake, may be filled with jams or savory fillings such as smoked ham and sour cream. Sweet dumplings are stuffed with plums and pastas are cooked with ground walnuts and poppyseeds.

Politics. Magyars have always had a reputation for being free-spirited. This freedom has led to both disaster and cultural growth. The rebellion of 1956 cost the lives of 10,000 young people, but paved the way for a new style of politics. About nine-tenths of all Hungarians are non-Communists but they have formed an alliance with party members for a share in political activity. Efforts are directed toward involving the people in decisions about major issues by encouraging media discussion and the participation of local councils in decision-making stages.

Literature and arts. Magyar accomplishments in art, literature, and science are many. Today, no less than seven Magyar Nobel laureates live and work in the United States, including the famous scientist turned anti-nuclear advocate Edward Teller, and John von Neumann, a pioneer of computers.

A rich folklore reminds Magyars of their days of roaming and warring. Once they had settled onto rich farmland, the Magyars turned to art and architecture as an expression of their independence. Three cities were established on either side of the Danube River—Buda, Obuda, and Pest—and grew together to become Budapest, one of the most colorful cities of Europe. The parliament building in this capital city is one of the most ornate of European buildings.

Another building in Budapest reflects Hungarian interest in music. A great opera house has stood in the city for decades. The best-known musical artists are composers Franz Liszt, Bela Bartok, and Zoltan Kodaly. Liszt is perhaps best known for his symphony *Faust* and his *Twenty Hungarian Rhapsodies*. Bartok worked in the United States and was a pioneer of modern music.

Hungarians regard their poets and other authors highly, even though few Magyar authors are well-known outside their own country. Sandór Petöfi, Endre Ady, and Attila József are popular poets. Gyula Illyés, a poet, and playwright István Örkény wrote in the 1970s and 1980s about life in Hungary, in an age when poetry was being replaced by realistic writings of worker life. The novelist Mór Jójai wrote during the 1800s and Ferenc Molnár authored many plays, novels, and short stories in the 1900s. Magyar writing frequently reflects the pride of the people in their country. Mihály Vörösmarty wrote "Szozat" in 1837 out of concern for his homeland and it has become a national anthem. The poem begins (Reményi 1964, p. 77.):

O Magyar, keep immovably
    Thy native country's trust,
For it has borne thee, and at death
    Will consecrate thy dust!

Two writers gained international fame during the Russian domination. Gyula Illyés was sentenced to prison for his anti-government activities in 1934, yet continued to write novels and poetry prolifically and to win many international awards. István Örkény's wartime experiences as a forced laborer and prisoner of war in Russia provided his subject matter.

The internationally known Magyar painters include Victor Vasarely, who originated Op Art, and Laszlo Moholy-Nagy, who was head of the New Bauhaus (or Institute for Design) in Chicago. A noted experimenter in art, Moholy-Nagy created with plexiglass and other unusual materials.

Recreation. At the right time of the year, Magyars take to the hills in search of mushrooms. This tradition is so popular that during the peak summer period, professional botanists establish stations in the cities where findings can be brought for identification.

In parks, Magyars can be seen playing chess at nearly any hour. Huge playing boards made of painted cement or tiles that accommodate life-size pieces can even be seen. Hungarians are credited with creating the first "thinking machine," a computer designed for playing chess.

Magyars often socialize in cafes or bars. Dark strong espresso coffee is common, although beer and wine are popular drinks as well. Some Hungarian wines are quite famous, particularly Tokay, and many Magyars own their own small vineyards, where they produce wine for themselves and their families.

For More Information

Balassa, Iván, and Gyula Ortutay. *Hungarian Ethnography and Folk-lore.* Budapest: Corvina, 1984.

Illés, Lajos, editor. *Nothing's Lost: Twenty-five Hungarian Short Stories.* Budapest: Corvina, 1988.

Sugar, Peter F., editor. *A History of Hungary.* Bloomington, Indiana: Indiana University Press, 1990.

MONTENEGRINS
(mon teh neh′ grinz)

People living along the Adriatic Sea in Yugoslavia.

Population: 600,000 (1990).
Location: Southern Yugoslavia.
Language: Serbo-Croatian.

Geographical Setting

Montenegrins are one of the peoples of the disintegrating state of Yugoslavia.

The smallest of the former Yugoslavia's six republics, Montenegro is slightly larger than Connecticut. It lies just north of Albania along the coast of the southern Adriatic Sea. The name means "Black Mountain" in Venetian-Italian, as does the Serbo-Croatian, *Crna Gora*. Montenegro is made up almost wholly of the dark and rocky limestone mountains—the southern Dinaric Alps—for which it is named. The mountains extend south into Albania and north into coastal Yugoslavia. Rather than eroding, limestone slowly dissolves in water, so that the mountains are pitted with hollows and caves. Rivers do not flow gently downhill, but rush through steep gorges or follow the hidden underground courses to emerge miles from their origins. Little soil is carried by the rivers and deposited in the lower regions, making farming extremely difficult. Villages grew up in the isolated pockets of arable land, which are called *polja*.

Montenegro's capital, Titograd, lies in its only plain, the plain of Zeta, on the Morača River in the south. South of Titograd, Montenegro shares with Albania the Balkans' largest body of water, Lake Scutari. North of Titograd runs the Piva River, part of which is now a lake formed by the Mratinje Dam and power station. East of the northern Piva rises lofty Durmitor, at 8,274 feet, Montenegro's highest mountain. Along the Adriatic coast lie a number of resort areas. They enjoy the Mediterranean climate of coastal Yugoslavia, without the cold winters of the inland mountains.

Historical Background

Buffer state. Montenegrins are descended from Serbs, and thus are closely related to Yugoslavia's largest ethnic group (see SERBS, YUGOSLAVS). Serbs entered the area in the early A.D. 600s, perhaps at the request of the Byzantine emperor Heraclius, who wished them to act as a barrier against attacks on the Greek Empire from the north. It was a role the people would play repeatedly, as various powerful states—Byzantium, Bulgaria, Serbia itself, Turkey, Venice and Austria—struggled to control the lands around Montenegro. The rugged terrain made the territory easy to defend. In the late 800s, Byzantine monks converted the Serbs to Orthodox Christianity.

Flowering of Serbia. By the 1100s, Serbian tribal leaders had created two strong states independent of Serbia's powerful neighbors, the Byzantines and the Bulgars. One, in Serbia proper, was called Raska; the other, in present-day Montenegro and nearby parts of Herzegovina, was called Zeta. The two states united about 1170, and over the next 200 years the Serbian nation became the most powerful in the Balkans.

Arrival of the Turks. In 1389, however, invading Ottomans defeated the Serbs, and over the next century conquered nearly all Serbian territory (see SERBS). Only in the most rugged and inaccessible parts of Zeta were the Serbs able to successfully resist the Turks. For the next 400 years, as the Ottoman Empire ruled the Balkans, they fiercely guarded their independence and their Serbian culture.

Refugees and warriors. Montenegro—as the independent remnant of Zeta became known—turned into a refuge for Serbs fleeing Turkish rule. The Turks continued to attack the mountainous domain, but could not conquer it. Neighboring Albanians, who had converted to Islam under the Ottomans, also carried out continuous raids into Montenegro. Under such conditions, the people gained a reputation for being courageous and warlike. A new culture began to emerge based on that of medieval Serbia; the culture developed separately from the majority of Serbs, who remained under the Turks.

***Vladika* leadership.** Political and religious organization centered around military leaders. Local headman led the village or tribal units. Overall leadership fell to the *vladika,* or Orthodox bishop, who was elected by the tribesmen (rather than being appointed by the church). The vladika's official power was only spiritual, but in fact he became the central military and political authority as well, rallying the tribes for defense against the constant invasions by Turks and Albanians.

The Njegoš dynasty. In 1697, the office of vladika became hereditary and restricted to the Njegoš family. The dynasty ruled for over 200 years. Often leading Montenegrins in battle personally, the Njegoš vladikas doubled Montenegro's territory at the expense of the Turks. In 1851, Daniel Petrović Njegoš formalized his political authority by taking the title *Knez,* or Prince. His successor, Nicholas I, ruled until 1918, when Montenegro became part of the Kingdom of Serbs, Croats, and Slovenes. In 1929, the kingdom's name was changed to Yugoslavia. In 1945, having expelled German and Italian occupiers, Communist leaders came to power in Yugoslavia (see YUGO-SLAVS).

The death of the dictator Josip Broz (Tito) in 1980 brought about considerable unrest as the various people of Yugoslavia contended for position in the new government. Riots and uprisings were common throughout the 1980s. By 1991, this bickering had resulted in declarations of independence by Slovenia, Croatia, Boznia-Herzegovina, and Macedonia, and consideration of independence by Montenegro. As this is written, the outcome of this civil war has broken up the nation of Yugoslavia.

Industry, mobility, and, above all, education have changed Montenegrin society. Yet the old ways, born of isolation and warfare, remain close to the surface.

Culture Today

Warrior tradition. Centuries of constant fighting shaped Montenegrin culture. Older Montenegrins remember battles in which they took part, such as the July 1941 uprising against Italian occupation in World War II. The very oldest Montenegrins recall boyhoods spent battling Turks, Albanians, or Bulgarians in the Balkan Wars of 1912–13, or Austrians in World War I. No less important to them are battles of the remote past, however. Poems and legends celebrate the exploits of ancestors, and show a strong sense of family pride and honor. Montenegrin clans (groups of families all related by blood) competed to collect the heads of Turkish enemies. They would display the heads in villages and cities as symbols of their courage. In the old capital, Cetinje, tourists may still see rows of Turkish skulls lined up behind the town's monastery. The Montenegrins have continued their military tradition in modern times. While they make up only about 4 percent of the overall population, Montenegrins comprised almost 20 percent of the generals in the Yugoslav army in the 1970s.

Family life. Already important in Serbian culture, the family became the Montenegrins' chief support in their poverty, isolation, and hostile environment. Its basic unit was the *kuća*, or household. In the past, this included not only a couple and their unmarried children, but also their surviving parents or even grandparents, various aunts and uncles, and often married children and their spouses. To the women fell the work of maintaining the kuća: cleaning, cooking, simple repair, and, above all, agricultural labor. Males over the age of 16 were armed at all times. Their main job was to defend the kuća against raids. The men supplemented the kuća's income with spoils brought back from raids of their own. Today, the extended kuća has been replaced mostly by smaller households. Improved agricultural techniques and the men's availability for work allow smaller units to feed themselves. Also, more and more young people seek education and careers in the cities. They go to Titograd, or to other cities in Yugoslavia, such as Belgrade.

Brastvo. A number of kućas, related by blood, make up the *brastvo,* or clan. People in the brastvo most often share the same last name and live in the same village or region. Similar to the Serbian *vamilija,* the brastvo has been larger and played a more important social role. In the past, it was the basic military and political unit in Montenegrin society. A collection of brastvos constituted the tribe, through which the people conducted warfare. The brastvo, however, claimed a Montenegrin's fundamental allegiance. If a member's honor was injured, or if a member was killed, it was his brastvo that took revenge on that of the offender. While such "blood feuds" are no longer common, the ties of the brastvo remain strong in social life.

Food, clothing, and shelter. Despite industrial investment in recent decades, Montenegro remains one of Yugoslavia's poorest regions. Especially in isolated rural areas, the diet is simple. The women bake bread in cast-iron pots before a fire. Sheep and cattle are kept both for their meat and their milk, which is made into a rich, cheeselike spread called *kajmak* and eaten with the bread. Many households also have several beehives, which are tended by the women and which supply honey. The people grow vegetables such as potatoes, onions, turnips, and cucumbers in the sparse soil. Meat is grilled or prepared in traditional Serbian ways, like the spicy sausage called *čevapići.* Chicken is roasted or made into soup. Montenegrin wine is popular throughout Yugoslavia.

Like their food, Montenegrins' everyday clothing is simple and sturdy. Workclothes consist of heavy fabrics like cotton or wool, most often in black or other dark colors. Traditional costumes are more colorful, with flowing silken dresses for women and silk shirts for men. These are topped by wool vests or jackets in red, black, and gold. The men wear the traditional *kapa*, a round cap with a black border that commemorates the defeat of the Serbs at Kosovo in 1389.

Wood is rare in the rocky countryside, so most houses are made of stone. The spartan two- or three-room dwellings rarely have gas or electricity, so cooking is done with a wood fire. Floors are often packed-earth. In cities and larger towns, drab apartment buildings have been constructed to deal with the inflow of people.

Religion. Along with the Serbs, Montenegrins were converted by the Byzantines and thus adopted the Greek Orthodox form of Christianity. Unlike those converted to Roman Catholicism (such as the Croats), Orthodox converts were allowed to form their own independent churches and hold services in their own languages (Catholic services, until recently, had to be held in Latin). Thus, Montenegrins worship in the Serbian Orthodox Church. However, the military role played by Montenegrin religious leaders created an independent spirit that persists to this day. Their religion has been an important marker of the people's identity in the years of struggle against neighboring Muslims. In the past, Montenegrins who converted to Islam have been executed by the larger Orthodox community. Today, religion continues to play an important role in Montenegro's alliance with Serbia in the current civil war (see YUGOSLAVS).

Because of their isolation, Montenegrins, more than many other European cultures, have retained folk beliefs in their practice of Christianity. Many of the rural people, for example, have only a vague outline of Christian dogma. Yet they maintain detailed traditions concerning supernatural beings such as witches, ghosts, vampires and magic spirits.

Literature. Like the Serbs, Montenegrins use the Cyrillic alphabet given to Orthodox Slavs by the Byzantine monks who converted them. Like other Slavs, the Montenegrins had no alphabet before their adoption of Christianity. Their strong tradition of oral folklore (poetry and legends about the exploits of ancestors and other heroes) means that Montenegrins are born-poets as well as soldiers. Montenegro's most famous poet, Rade Njegoš, for example, ruled as vladika from 1830 to 1851. Known simply as Njegoš, he is regarded by Montenegrins much as Shakespeare is by the English. His best known poem, "The Mountain Wreath," treats the tragic events of Christmas 1702, when his ancestor Vladika Kanilo ordered the execution of Montenegrins converted to Islam.

Montenegro's most respected modern writer, Milovan Djilas, was also a political leader. For years the right-hand man of the Yugoslavian Communist leader Marshall Tito, Djilas was forced from the Communist party in 1954. For the next 30 years, Djilas wrote books and articles that often challenged the Communist leadership. For asserting his independent views, he was jailed for five years in the 1960s. Among his many works is a biography of the poet Njegoš.

The arts. Like other Slavs, Montenegrins take a lively interest in the arts. Many paint or sculpt, either as a profession or simply for relaxation. In the Middle Ages, Montenegrin painters were trained in Venice and produced the icons (religious paintings) that decorate the region's monasteries. Much of Montenegro's art—past and present— harks back to military or religious themes from history. Musicians still sing the *pesme*, Serbian songs accompanied by the *gusle*, a one-stringed fiddle, or by the *tambura*. Part of the Serbian oral tradition, these are epic poems set to music, commemorating battles and heroic deeds of the past.

For More Information

Boehm, Christopher. *Montenegrin Social Organization and Values.* New York: AMS Press, 1983.

Hodgson, Bryan. "Montenegro: Yugoslavia's 'Black Mountain.'" *National Geographic,* November 1977.

Nyrop, Richard F., editor. *Yugoslavia: A Country Study.* Washington, DC: Department of the Army, 1981.

Singleton, Fred. *A Short History of the Yugoslav Peoples.* Cambridge, England: Cambridge University Press, 1985.

POLES
(poles)

A Slavic people of northern Europe whose land has frequently been ruled by Germans and Russians.

Population: 39,000,000 (1990 estimate).
Location: Poland, a Central European country bordered by Czechoslovakia, Germany, Lithuania, and the Baltic Sea.
Language: Polish, a Slavic language.

Geographical Setting

Poland is a large, bowl-shaped plain carved and flattened by the Vistula River as it flows northward from the mountains to the Baltic Sea. Long winters and wet springs produce much marshland, but most of the northern two-thirds of the country is fertile farmland. Southern Poland, separated from Czechoslovakia by the Carpathian Mountains, is rich in coal and other minerals.

Historical Background

Origin. According to Polish folklore, Poland originated when a peasant boy named Piast encountered two tall strangers who predicted that he would be chosen as the ruling prince. The building of a Polish people and nation does, in reality, trace its origin to a Prince Mieszko in A.D. 965—the first ruler of the Piast house. This prince married a Czech princess and began a family that was to govern the Slavic people of Poland until 1138. His son Bolesław became the first king of the kingdom and extended its influence from Prague to Kiev. But the kingdom was to grow to a federation of nobles with large landholdings worked by serfs. When in 1138 Bolesław divided his king-

Poles

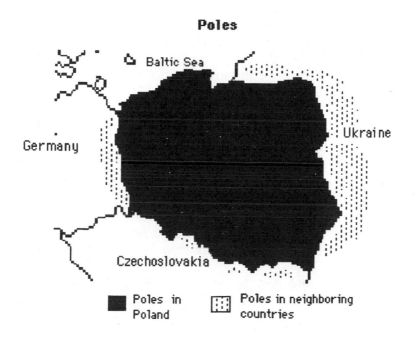

Poles in Poland
Poles in neighboring countries

Polish land once extended far beyond the present boundaries. As a result, large populations of Poles live in neighboring countries.

dom among his sons, the old kingdom of Poland fell into a period of fragmentation during which the chief driving force was competition among the nobles for Kraków and its rank as the seat of the senior prince. Not until 1320, under Władysław I, was the kingdom reunited. Under his successor, Casimir the Great (1333–1370), the kingdom was firmly established with a code of Polish law and the second European university (after Prague), the Jagiellonian University. The Jagiellonians were rulers of Poland's eastern neighbor, Lithuania. In 1386 Poland and Lithuania were united when the Polish queen married the ruler of the house of Jagiellon, the Grand Duchy of Lithuania. Poland and Lithuania then began 187 years of joint rule and expansion. In an eastern corner between them lay the nation of Prussia. In 1226 a prince of part of Poland, Conrad of Mazonia, had invited Teutonic knights to help against the Prussian forces. These knights came to control the Baltic coast and were a constant threat to Polish-Lithuanian unity. In 1410 the Poles and Lithuanians defeated the Teutonic knights at the Battle of Grunwald. During the next century the Kingdom of Poland and Grand Duchy of Lithuania was to expand its territory eastward and south to become the dominant power of the region. When the last of the kings of the house of Jagiellon fell in 1572, the kingdom reverted to rule by noblemen. For the next 223 years Poland would be ruled by a succession of indifferent kings elected by the nobles. In this time only four kings were of Polish descent.

Russians and Turks had long been antagonistic to continued Polish growth, and the Polish acceptance of the Catholic religion, beginning with the first Piast king, had not eased this situation. In 1683 Poland was attacked by Turks who set siege to Vienna. Jan Sobieski, who broke this siege, is a national hero of the Polish people. Russia and Poland fought one another for centuries, with the boundaries of Polish territory expanding until 1772, then gradually retreating. In 1772, 1793, and 1795, Prussia, Russia, and Austria claimed parts of Poland and the old kingdom disappeared.

World War I to World War II. A reestablished Poland of 1918 was much smaller in territory than it had been at the time of the country's division in the 1700s. At first organized as a republic, it fell under military rule between 1926 and 1939. Then in 1939 Poland was divided between the invading countries, Germany and Russia. In the five years that followed, 20 percent of the Poles were killed in German camps or Russian "corrective labor" programs.

After World War II, some Polish territory taken by the Germans and the Soviet Union was restored, but Poland fell under the influence of the USSR. A "Polish Committee of National Liberation," formed under Russian sponsorship, became the provisional government after Russia drove out the Germans. Life under Soviet influence was uneasy. The Soviet Union became the chief user of Polish goods and labor. For example, Polish shipyards supplied 75 percent of Russia's merchant vessels. In 1956 and again in 1970 laborers struck for more human rights—for "bread and freedom." In 1968 university students had joined the protests and formed a Committee for Student Solidarity. This organization spearheaded revolts in the next years. A workers' strike in 1970 was brutally suppressed, but was the beginning of a stronger worker rebellion. The movement was strengthened with the support of the Roman Catholic Church and was greatly stimulated by the election of the Polish Archbishop of Kraków, Karl Cardinal Wojtyla, as Pope of the Roman Catholic Church. (Cardinal Wojtyla became Pope John Paul II.) By 1980, many workers had formed a single trade union, Solidarity. Led by Lech Wałęsa, this union successfully struck at the large Gdansk shipyards, and succeeded in forcing the Communist leadership to accept trade unions that were not under Communist party leadership, and to modify censorship of the press. The union was outlawed in 1980 by a government led by Piotr Jaroszewicz, but continued its actions while the suspension was contested in the courts. In 1981 the rebellions had grown so that the government felt a need to abolish the Trade Union Council, but labor leaders continued their resistance, as they do today. The Communist party continued to dominate Poland through the Sejm, a 460-member council of deputies. This group elected a 17-person Council of State that governed Poland through a series of plans to collectivize farms and improve industry.

By 1987, unrest in Poland had forced the government to change its policies drastically and to announce a plan to remodel the government. Partially free elections were held in 1989 and, after constitutional changes in 1990, completely free elections were held. The Sejm was converted to a lower house of a bicameral legislature. A 100-member senate completed the National Assembly. Finally, the Communist party was overthrown and a democratically elected government installed in 1990. At the same time, the chairman of the Council of Ministers, General Wojciech Jaruzelski, agreed to resign as leader of the country.

Culture Today

Traditions. Poland is a land with little ethnic diversity. The World War II solution restored some land occupied by Polish people in the west, while leaving eastern land largely inhabited by Lithuanians and Byelarussians in the hands of the Soviet Union. The result is that most of the residents of Poland are Poles of Slavic descent, and most are Roman Catholics. The Polish people dress in Western clothing and work in industry and agriculture much like other Europeans. Once Poland was a country of feudal estates and peasant farmers— a pattern characteristic of most of the countries of Central Europe. In 1931, 52 percent of the people were peasant farmers living on small farms of 5 to 50 hectares. Their homes were wood or plaster houses with thatched roofs. There the father was ruler, while the wife's work was in the field and kitchen. In this environment, a family's closest friends were other relatives. School was optional for the farm workers.

Under communism. At first under the guise of land reform that promised to redistribute all landholdings over 125 hectares (312.5 acres), the Communist rulers slowly began to encourage collective farming. The idea of cooperative farms was abandoned in 1956. By the time they were overthrown, about a third of the Polish farmers had been organized into state-owned farms. The remainder of the farmland is still privately owned. Polish farmers' primary crops are rye, wheat, oats, sugar beets, and potatoes. Little of the livestock raised is exported except to Russia. At the same time, encouraged to produce for the Soviets, industry has grown to employ 40 percent of the Polish workers. These workers process foods for shipping, mine coal, and produce steel, textiles, and chemical products. So the number of Poles still active in agriculture has been reduced to 25 percent of the work force.

Food, clothing, and shelter. The many experiences with rule by others has influenced Polish life. The cities vary from the ancient capital of Kraków, with its Austro-Hungarian-style marketplace where textiles are sold in the great Cloth Hall, to modern cities such as Nowa Huta, recently erected as a suburb of Warsaw to house the new city workers.

In the countryside, Polish homes are stone, brick, or wood one- or two-room houses with thatched roofs. In the cities, people live in

The marketplace in Kolomna, Poland. *Courtesy of the Simon Wiesenthal Center for Holocaust Studies.*

brick or stone houses, or in cement-block apartments erected under Communist rule. Because the population is growing and because many Poles are moving to the industrialized cities in search of work, housing is in great demand in Poland.

Dress also varies, from the European styles of the cities to the drab denim and heavy boots of the farmland, and from province to province in the traditional clothing still often seen on holidays or Sundays. The traditional costumes include loose-fitting trousers tucked into boots and long vests or short jackets decorated with embroidery. Women wear full skirts covered with white lace aprons and a highly decorated vest over a white blouse. Women sew together cloths of different colors—red, orange, green, blue—to make a popular coat of many colors.

Education. Poles have long respected education, although it was not always affordable. The delight with a good student is even seen in Polish literature. Konstantyn Galczynski's "Monument of a Student" begins

A street in Makow, Poland. *Courtesy of the Simon Wiesenthal Center for Holocaust Studies.*

In a certain Polish city—the truth must now be told,
A statue of a student stands, admired by young and old.
. . . In honor of her dearest children, those forgotten students . . .
(Gillon and Krzyzanowski 1964, p. 465)

Before the present form of government took charge, Poland had begun to encourage an educational system free to everyone. Today primary education is required for children seven to 14. After age 14, students may go on for three or four years of secondary education, either in a college preparatory program or in a vocational program. Poles have had great universities since 1364 when the University of Kraków became the second university established in Central Europe.

Religion. Ninety percent of the Poles are Roman Catholic and new churches are being built in Poland in spite of socialist attempts to discourage religious beliefs. The persistence of organized religion is a reflection of the independent spirit of Polish people. The bond between the Polish people and the Roman Catholic Church was bolstered by the 1978 election of a Polish religious leader to become Pope, the first Polish person to be so honored.

Literature and arts. Poles have been characterized as highly individualistic and stubbornly resistant to leadership that demands absolute obedience. These qualities characterize Polish art of the past, but recent governments have supported art that favors the Communist philosophy. Some Poles have strayed from this path in the twentieth century, however. Poets such as Julian Przybos and Julian Tuwim have celebrated Polish uprisings and written verse opposing the Communist regime. Other recent poets (Jozef Putrament and Tadeusz Borowski, for example) have written works revealing their faith in the new form of government. Earlier writers won fame throughout the world. Henryk Sienkiewicz was awarded the Nobel Prize for Literature in 1905 for his novel *Quo Vadis?* Again, in 1924, the Nobel Prize was awarded to a Pole, Władysław S. Reymont, for his work *The Peasants.*

In music, such famous musicians as Frédéric Chopin and Ignace Paderewski composed and conducted music in Poland. Much of the work of Chopin was inspired by Polish folk songs. Arthur Rubinstein is a Jewish Polish composer who escaped Russian domination to create popular works in other countries. Music and dance have long been favorite pastimes of the Polish peasants. The mazurka and the polka are Polish dances that resemble American square dances.

Recreation. While dancing, as everywhere, is one of the most popular recreational activities, Polish people also enjoy sports—particularly basketball, boxing, cycling, running, soccer, and swimming. Under Soviet domination, sports participation was encouraged by the establishing of national teams in nearly every sport, including table tennis. Poles also enjoy hunting. Once great forests covered much of the land and wild animals were abundant. Today, the forests are disappearing, but hunters still search for wild boars.

St. John's Eve is one of the most popular holidays. Originally a pagan celebration designed to drive out devils, it is now celebrated with great bonfires around which the young people dance and over which boys try to leap, carrying buckets of water to douse on the girls.

Values. Polish people have reputations for hard work and closeness to the soil. Their most coveted desires reflect their solid working-class background, and are not unlike other Western nations. A survey of school students rated these goals as most important: equal opportunity, a good standard of living, freedom of speech, citizen participation in government, economic self-sufficiency, obedience to authority, a mechanized industry, independence, strong central government, and freedom of political expression, initiative, and action within limits.

With independence from the disintegrating Soviet Union, the Polish people have achieved the freedoms they desired. There has been some progress toward mechanization of industry, but this industry was created largely to supply Soviet needs and will need to find new markets. Nevertheless, Poles are far from self-sufficient. Now with the freedom to act, some predict a long struggle of 15 or 25 years to regain economic balance with European neighbors.

Achievements. Often the subject of ethnic jokes, the Polish people have suffered through four partitions of their land, one so complete that, for a time, Poland ceased to exist. And in the 1860s, during which much of Poland was under Russian rule, Poles were discouraged from reading and writing in their own language. Still, the history of Poland is one of great accomplishments. The great astronomer, Nicholas Copernicus, made observations that helped to describe the universe. Marie Curie was born and educated in Poland, though she lived in France while experimenting with radium. Highly reputed authors, such as Joseph Conrad, were also born in Poland. Recently,

Polish engineers and scientists have loaned their abilities to the United States space program, devising such space aids as the vehicle used to traverse the moon. Zbigniew Brzezinski, a Polish emigrant, became a security adviser to the United States president Richard Nixon.

For More Information

Dziwanowski, M. K. *Poland in the Twentieth Century*. New York: Columbia University Press, 1977.

Kolankiewicz, G. *Poland: Politics, Economy and Society*. New York: Columbia University Press, 1987.

ROMANIANS

(roh may' knee uns)

Slavic people who live in the area of the Carpathian and Transylvanian mountains and who have adopted the language and habits of their early Roman overlords.

Population: 23,180,000 (1990 estimate).
Location: Romania, Moldova, Yugoslavia.
Language: Romanian, a Romance language.

Geographical Setting

The Carpathian Mountains run roughly north and a little west to south through Romania, and the Transylvanian Alps cross the land east to west. These two ranges form an arc of 8,000-foot mountains that divide the country into three parts. The mountains drop to a wide plain on the south, and cut into river valleys that run southward to the Danube River, which forms Romania's border with Bulgaria. This is the ancient land of the Vlachs. East of the mountains, rolling hills give way to a higher plain or plateau that extends into Ukraine, the Moldavian Plateau. This plain is also traversed by many rivers flowing into the Danube River. Northwest of the Alps in a sort of pocket formed with the Carpathian Mountains is a section long disputed between Romania and Hungary, the Transylvania Plateau. Thus the mountains form a "U" in the western part of the country. In the far west the mountains give way to another fertile area, the Tisa Plain. Early Romans managed to cross the Alps from what is now Yugoslavia and conquer the southern and eastern plains of Walachia and Moldavia. This fertile region was united under the Romans with the province southwest of the Carpathians called Dacia.

In winter, cold winds from the Arctic blow across the Moldavian and Walachian plains from the Russian steppes. Temperatures fall

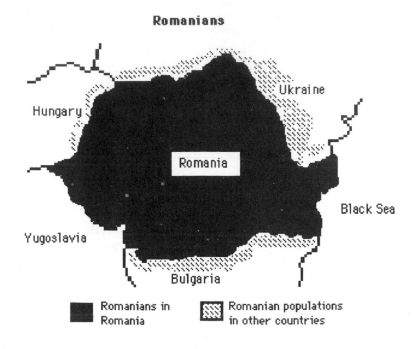

Romanians

Romanians live in Romania and in its neighboring countries.

so that the Danube River is frozen for up to three months of the year. In the summer, winds from the south bring warm Mediterranean temperatures tempered by Romania's distance from the sea.

Historical Background

Early history. When the Romans expanded into the country now known as Romania, they found people who farmed and herded cattle. These people lived in a well-organized kingdom in which two classes, nobles and peasants, were distinguishable by their headwear. Peasants, merchants, and soldiers wore long, uncut, and uncovered hair while the aristocrats only were permitted to wear felt hats. The Romans called the people Daci. By the second century B.C. these people had established a kingdom under the monarch Orolas. Between 85 and 89 A.D. the Dacians and Romans engaged in two wars. At first beaten, the Romans eventually began to gain the upper hand. The Dacian king delivered his crown to the Romans acknowledging his subservience, and peace was arranged when the Romans agreed to pay tribute to avoid future raids by the Daci.

Goths and others. The Romans eventually dominated this region on the north bank of the Danube and divided the old kingdom into two parts and then into three. Then, in A.D. 256, an army of Goths led by General Gallienus crossed the Carpathian Mountains and drove the Romans from Dacia. From this time through the twelfth century the land of the Romanians was overrun by Slavs, Avars, Bulgars, and Magyars. This mingling of peoples created the Romanians. The strong influence of the Romans is still evident in the Romanian language. So strong was this influence that it has been suggested that the Romanians of today really originated from a settlement of Romans established by Emperor Trajan (A.D. 53–117). This claim is widely held by Romanians and as widely disputed by Hungarians. It is supported by the Romanian language, a Romance language similar to Latin. The language witnessed a great influence by the Romans in the comparatively short time that they controlled the region.

Vlachs. In the thirteenth century Vlach people (see VLACHS) in the south invaded the land from Greece. They united with those already living in the area to become the ancestors of today's Romanians. In 1310, part of present-day Romania became the kingdom of Walachia under Radul Negru, a vassal of the ruler of Hungary. The Vlachs eventually formed two kingdoms, Walachia and Moldavia, and added to the mix that formed today's Romanians. The land disputes between Romanians and Magyars have continued through the ages.

Turks. In 1601 Michael the Brave united the people of Romania for a brief time, but after his death the country again divided into two kingdoms. From 1717 to 1739, part of Walachia known as Little Walachia fell to Austrian domination. The remains of the two kingdoms were both taken under Turkish domination in 1774. Freed from the Turks in the mid-1800s, they were united into the country of Romania by the Paris Peace Conference of 1858.

Romania. In 1864, under Prince Couza, Romania established a senate and adopted a constitution. However, the despotic prince chose not to uphold the constitution and was soon forced to abdicate the throne. Prince Charles, of the royal Austrian Hohenzollern family, was persuaded to take his place. Charles was recognized as hereditary ruler of Romania in 1866, but his attempt to give Romania a solid government was thwarted by the Franco-German War of 1870. That war turned the Romanian people against their German ruler.

Russians. By 1877 Romania was threatened by Russians who had begun a war with the Turks in which Romania sided with the Russians. After a Russian victory in which Romanians provided important support, Romanians expected to gain land. This was accomplished by acquiring Dobruja in the southeast, but the Romanians were forced to give up Bessarabia, an area along the Black Sea. For a time it seemed that Romania was to gain in regional strength and territory. However, the Congress of Berlin, held in 1878, again divided the land. Walachia and Moldavia remained Romanian, but Transylvania was taken into Hungary. Hungarians, Bulgarians, and Romanians found themselves divided among the three countries.

World wars. During World War I, the Romania government sided with the Germans. Following the war, the Treaty of Neuilly returned the province of Dobruja from Bulgaria to Romania. In 1940 Germany and Italy took it upon themselves to arbitrate the land disputes of the Magyars and Romanians. Transylvania was then split, with half of it restored to Hungary. In the same year, a fascist group called the Iron Guard began in Romania. Early in World War II, King Carol abdicated his throne and the country sided with the Germans under Iron Guard leader Ion Antonescu. This pro-German government was overthrown in 1944 when King Carol's son Michael returned to the throne. The same year Russian troops entered the country. King Michael agreed to a Communist coalition government. General Antonescu was executed as a war criminal in 1946 when Soviet troops were stationed in Romania and strengthened the country's already-developed Communist organization. Again the region was divided. The Soviet Union claimed outright the provinces of Bessarabia and Bukovina.

A 1946 election saw 89 percent of the votes for a coalition dominated by Communists. By 1947, the king had been forced to abdicate and a Romanian People's Republic was declared. The leader of the Romanian Communist party was Gheorghe Gheorghiu-Dej, who became chairman of the council of ministers by 1952 and president of the state council in 1961. Upon his death in 1965, Nicholae Ceauşescu became leader of Romania. By the late 1980s, corruption had become evident in many parts of the government, leading to a great deal of discontent. This was fueled by actions of Ceauşescu such as his proposal to destroy eight thousand villages in Transylvania (mostly inhabited by Magyars) and to resettle the people in multistoried housing complexes. Both Hungarians and exiled Romanians protested this proposal. The Romanian government came under fire from international human rights groups. Finally, a revolt upset Ceauşescu, who was tried and executed in 1989. Political parties began to form in Romania and the country held multiparty elections to elect a bicameral legislature and president. But the wary Romanians moved away slowly from communism. Communists won 1990 free elections. However, new regulations call for a popularly elected president who is, when elected, not allowed to be a member of any political party.

Independence and democracy. When Romania broke with the Communists in 1989, the economy was in shambles, and the democratic government sought to enforce stringent controls to revive it. But without capital for improvements, progress was slower than mine workers and others would tolerate. The government came under con-

In 1990, citizens of Romania protested in Bucharest for 55 days. They were opposing a new Communist government. *Courtesy of Emanuel Tanjala.*

stant harassment, and, in September 1991, the prime minister, Petre Roman, was forced to resign.

Culture Today

Economy. In the 1960s, after Russian troops had left, the people of Romania embarked on an effort to industrialize their country. Oil resources provided the financing to develop mining and textile industries. The plan was so effective that today Romania has had the highest rate of industrial growth in Europe in the last decade, 11 percent a year. Once the country was so closely tied to the Soviet Union that the Romanians were kept in relative poverty as their government "sold wheat to Russia and gave them oil." Industrialization, however, had threatened Romania's role as "breadbasket" for Europe. With the recent change in governments, Romanians are faced with the need to rebuild an almost completely collapsed economy.

Food, clothing, and shelter. Fifty-one percent of Romanians live as farmers, raising wheat, barley, maize, and grapes, along with cattle and sheep. Once the average farmer tilled a portion of land owned

Already hard-pressed, the citizens of Bucharest, Romania, found themselves lining up for food after the governmental upsets of 1991. *Courtesy of Emanuel Tanjala.*

by wealthy landowners and paid the landowner for relative freedom. During the reign of Prince Couza, the wealthy landholders were forced to give portions of the land to the farmers who worked it. These were small plots, and Romanian farmers remained poor. Under communism, the farms were collectivized, with farmers joining others to plow and plant by decree of the government.

Old stone and wood houses, often with thatched roofs, provide shelter for the farmers and for people who gather in small villages in the hills. There are few large towns or cities in Romania. The typical Romanian outside the large industrial cities lives in a two- or three-room wooden house. In the mountain areas the homes are loosely scattered and villages are spread over more land, while on the rich farm land of the plains, villages are more compact.

While Western-style clothing is beginning to find a way into the countryside, Romanian peasants can still be seen in homespun clothes of plain colors. Western-style clothes had already become the style in the larger towns and cities, during domination by the Soviet Union.

Many Romanian foods include grilled meats. One popular dish, *mititei*, is made of cylinder-shaped meatballs. Bread is part of nearly every meal; *mamalîga*, a breadlike cornmeal is popular, since corn is a major product of Romanian farms.

Spinning wool has been practiced in much the same way for 2,000 years in the village of Sapinta, Romania. *Courtesy of Emanuel Tanjala.*

Family life. The family remains the most important social unit in Romania. Fathers are autocratic family leaders. Land is passed from the father most often to the oldest son. Other sons are paid for their inheritance, while daughters depend on their dowry, a gift-giving that goes with the bride at each wedding. There once were many small family industries in Romania. These included wood carving, carpet weaving, pottery making, and glass painting. Romanian family industries became famous for their decorations of eggs. These small industries were organized into communal actions by the Communist leaders.

Two important legacies of the Soviet era can be seen in education and medicine. In the early 1900s, Romania had one of the highest rates of illiteracy in Europe, despite the fact that the Communist management made education free and compulsory. Medical care was also directed by the government and made available free of cost to everyone.

Religion. The isolation of the Romanians is reflected in religion as well as other aspects of Romanian life. While they originated in the land of the Eastern Orthodox Church and espouse Orthodox beliefs, the Romanians of the last century developed their own Romanian Orthodox Church. There are large minorities of Roman Catholics

A summer kitchen in Vrancea, Romania.
Courtesy of Emanuel Tanjala.

and Unitarians. Under communism, religion has become less influential, but many Romanians still claim to be religious.

Language and arts. Throughout history, the fate of the Romanians has been bound with the many river valleys of the plains. Living in the valleys made it possible for Romanians to resist endless incursions by foreign forces and to preserve their own way of life. Not until the return of the Vlachs were the people themselves united. The language of the Vlach people, who were believed to have been driven from southern Romania in the tenth century by the Goths and then to return in the thirteenth century, is still part of the language of Romania. Many words in this language are of Slavic origin. However, Romanian is primarily derived from Roman sources.

World-famous Romanian authors such as Mihail Sudoveanu write about the good times and bad times in Romania in such books as *Tales of War* and *Evening Tales*. In 1960, George Calinescu wrote *The Black Chest*, describing four generations of Romanian life as viewed around the family of an exiled Polish military officer. Perhaps the most noteworthy author at the turn of the century was George Cosbuc, a poet whose themes were nature and nationalism. Many fine Romanian authors wrote in French, and Romania turned to France for its dramatic productions.

However, during Communist rule, writers were encouraged to work on government-recommended subjects. The government controlled plays that were written and acted, sponsoring their production in village clubs, houses of culture, and trade union clubs. During this period, some of the best writers and musicians left Romania to produce works in more open environments. One musical composer, Eugene Ionesco, whose most famous work is "Romanian Rhapsodies," moved to France to continue his musical creations.

The shifting of nationalities and boundaries in Central Europe is demonstrated in the press. Of about 1,700 newspapers in Romania, 74 are printed in languages of people with whom Romanians have been mixed—Magyars, Germans, Serbians, Ukrainians, and Armenians.

Song and dance mark Romanian festivals, religious or secular. On holidays, parades and folk dance festivals are held in many Romanian towns. Folk dancing is in the circle-dance style also seen in Greece. The dance is accompanied on violins and by Romanian instruments such as the *coliza*, a kind of lute, and the *tambel*, related to the dulcimer. Folk melodies and folk literature remain popular as well. A government policy of making the arts accessible to the people has resulted in the opening of more than 8,000 cultural houses, theaters, museums, and libraries.

Romanian artists created many painted folk-art pieces, and used their artistic talents to paint and decorate buildings. The folk art of Romania features geometric designs and stylized plants and animals. Much of the inspiration for Romanian folk art reflects the people's closeness with nature. This closeness is seen in their favorite recreations: trips to the forests or to the seacoast. A line from a verse in an ancient poem is the theme for much literature, "The forest—the faithful brother of Romanians."

Romanian children sell carpets in Hungary. *Courtesy of Aleksandar Albijanic.*

Romanians have won international acclaim as filmmakers. In 1990, the popular actor Sergiu Nicolaescu turned to history to make an award-winning film, *Mircea*, about the prince who rallied the Romanian people to defeat the invading Turks.

Sports. Romanians are avid sports enthusiasts and support athletic achievements in track and field, soccer, and other Olympic sports through national athletic federations. In 1991, the president of the Athletic Federation, Iolana Balas, symbolized Romania's enthusiasm and achievement. She is remembered throughout Romania for her achievements in the high jump, an event she won in the 1956 Olympic

The posers in this photograph are modeling the old style Romanian costumes. *From the Library of Congress.*

Games. At age 15 she was the champion of Romania and from then until her retirement in 1967, Balas won 146 consecutive high jump events. Her career included setting world records on 13 different occasions.

Change. Although certain Romanian traditions have been maintained, efforts to improve their standard of living have forced Romanians to accept changes. In the 1960s the people struggled with religious taboos, finally legalizing abortion and relaxing marriage laws to make divorce easier. However, Romanians have had a problem that is shared by few other groups—under-population in a growing industrial economy. There are not enough working people for the growing industries. As a result, after ten years of liberalism, the Romanian leaders declared abortion illegal, placed a tax burden on childless families, and reinstalled more difficult divorce laws.

For More Information

Iliescu, R. "Return to Romania." *New Choices for the Best Years,* vol. 30, December 1990, pages 18–22.

Hockenos, P. "The Winter of Our Discontent." *Nation*, vol. 252, January 7–14, 1991, pp. 14–16.

RUSSIANS
(rush' uns)

The largest society within the 15 republics that
made up the former Union of Soviet Socialist Republics.

Population: 145,000,000 (1991 estimate).
Location: Russia and other former Soviet republics.
Language: Russian.

More than 85 percent of the people of the Republic of Russia are
Russians and speak the Russian language.

Geographical Setting

The Russian homeland lies between the Ural Mountains in the east and Byelarussia and Ukraine in the west. The low-lying and often swampy region extends north-south from the frozen tundra along the White and Barents seas to the rolling steppe, or grassy plain, north of the Black and Caspian seas. In between grows a band of dense forest which includes the ancient city of Moscow. From this area originate Russia's greatest two rivers, the Volga, flowing south to the Caspian Sea, and the Don, flowing south to the Black Sea.

Russia's climate is characterized by extremes: warm, humid summers contrast with the severe cold of the Russian winter. Rainfall is moderate to light, with much of the precipitation coming as snow during the long winter months.

Historical Background

Rus. Russians are descended from the Eastern Slavs, a Slavic group that broke into three branches around A.D. 1200. The other two branches are treated in separate entries (see BYELARUSSIANS and UKRAINIANS).

Origin. About the fifth century A.D., Slavs from the region of the Baltic Sea and near the Elbe and Danube rivers began to migrate along the rivers of the great plain of Russia. On rivers such as the Dnieper, the settlers built a large number of tribal towns at strategic points on trading routes. At the southern tip of one network of trading routes was the town of Kiev. Far to the north, situated on a river and a lake, was the community of Novgorod. Over the centuries, Kiev attracted increasing concentrations of people and power, which, along with the entire trading network, became burdensome to manage. About the middle of the ninth century, some influential people of Novgorod invited the Scandinavian kingdoms to send a ruler to govern them. One Scandinavian leader, Rurik, responded, accompanied by a band of warriors, and established unity among the peoples in the neighboring areas of Novgorod. His coming in 862 marked the beginning of the empire of Russia. Scarcely a quarter-century thereafter, the regent of the ruler at Novgorod, Oleg, changed the seat of government to Kiev. From that time to 1200, the Eastern Slavs formed a loose confederation of states known as Kievan Rus centered in its foremost city. Oleg, the regent who made Kiev the capital, was standing in for the real king, Igor, who took the rule when he was of age. His wife, Olga, was converted to Christianity in 955, setting the religious tone for the country.

By the eleventh century Kievan Rus had become a major power, but this power was short-lived as Kiev was plagued by outside invasions. In the 1100s, the Slavs in the south began to be plagued with waves of invaders from the the east. To escape them, many residents of the southern and western steppes fled eastward toward Kievan Rus. However, the eastern invaders continued to pester them.

The Tatars. Most devastating was the conquest of Kievan Rus by the Mongol people, who captured the capital in 1240 and remained in control for nearly 250 years. During this invasion, the Slavs fled northeast to distant Moscow where Prince Dimitry met and defeated the Mongols in 1380. The Mongols retaliated and continued to control Russia from the steppes, allowing Russian princes to keep their positions in exchange for money and absolute obedience.

Rise of Moscow. During the Mongol, or Tatar, domination, the town of Moscow rose to preeminence, and by the late 1300s its rulers claimed to be princes of "all Rus." The Muscovites thus took the name of the former Kievan state, from which the term "Russia" comes. Two factors contributed to Moscow's success: its strategic location near the heads of the Don and Volga rivers, enabling it to control vital trade routes, and the Tatars' recognition of Moscow's rulers as collectors of tribute (the money paid to the Tatars).

Tsars. Tatar recognition made it possible for a series of strong central rulers to take power. This tendency was reinforced both by the example of the powerful Tatar Khan and by the ultimate need for unity in order to overthrow the Tatars. Ivan the Great (ruled 1462–1505) added to Moscow's territory and finally shook off Tatar rule. He was the first prince of Moscow to call himself "tsar," meaning "Caesar." He also began the practice of using European architects and craftsmen to beautify Moscow, which the tsars began to see as an imperial capital, "the third Rome." Ivan's grandson, also called Ivan (ruled 1533–1584), went on the offensive against the Tatars, winning victories that opened the vast eastern land of Siberia to Russian colonization. Less successful were his attempts to gain a foothold on the Baltic coast. For his Tatar victories, and for his ruthless domination of the Russian nobles (many of whom he tortured and killed) he is called Ivan Groznyi (Ivan the Terrible).

Imperial Russia. Later tsars continued to enlarge Russian territory and to maintain their grip on absolute power. Peter the Great (ruled 1689–1725), by defeating the Swedes, finally broke through to the Baltic, where he built the new capital of St. Petersburg—Russia's "window to the West." St. Petersburg represented Peter's attempt to end the long isolation of Russia from Western Europe, an isolation dating from the time of the Tatars. Still, only the Russian nobility became westernized; the serfs (peasants who had become legally bound to the land under the autocratic tsars) remained poor and backward.

Social unrest. The gulf between the peasants' harsh existence and the glittering life of the nobles created stagnation and social tension in the 1800s. While Western Europe undertook the industrial revolution, Russian peasants, who made up 90 percent of the population, continued to live much as they had in the Middle Ages. Few tsars

Catherine the Great built a school for aristocratic women in St. Petersburg. It became the Smolny Institute. During the Revolution, Lenin used this church on the school campus for his headquarters. *Courtesy of Portia Chambliss.*

The Church of the Resurrection in St. Petersburg, also known as the "Church of the Spilled Blood," was the site of the assassination of Czar Alexander II (1818–1881), during whose reign Russians were granted a constitution. *Courtesy of Portia Chambliss.*

were concerned with the peasantry. A notable exception was Alexander I, who attempted to abolish serfdom in the Baltic provinces. Only by the end of the century had Russians developed a small, urban, industrial population of 3,000,000 workers out of the empire's 128,000,000 people. During the 1800s, writers, including Leo Tolstoy, Alexander Pushkin, and others, and socialist thinkers, such as Alexander Herzen, helped spread ideas of reform. By the end of the century, peasants, workers, and intellectuals were all dissatisfied with Russia's old social structure.

Revolution (1917). In 1905, following the defeat of her navy by Japan, Russia underwent a year of strikes, riots, and popular demonstrations. Tsar Nicholas II agreed to the election of a parliament, or *duma*. In the next years, this parliament was periodically disbanded and reestablished. Nine years later Russia entered World War I. The strain of the war—about 2,000,000 Russians died in three years—added to the misery of poverty and famine in the land. Civil uprisings in St. Petersburg and elsewhere forced the tsar to abdicate in 1917.

Communism. After three years of bloody civil war, the Communist party under Vladimir Ilyich Ulyanov (Lenin) emerged in power. Surviving nobles and many wealthier Russians fled to establish expatriate communities in Europe or America. For about the next 70 years, communist ideas provided the context in which Russians lived, worked, and thought. In 1924, the Union of Soviet Socialist Republics was formed, with the Russian Socialist Federative Soviet Republic being the largest.

Dictatorship. With Lenin's death in 1924, the nature of Soviet communism took a new direction. Joseph Stalin seized personal control of the Communist party and thus of the USSR. Under the new dictatorship, all dissenting opinion was ruthlessly suppressed. Russians and other Soviet citizens lived in an atmosphere of suspicion and fear, in which all faced the threat of arrest by secret police. Recently revealed information indicates that, in the 1930s, about 20,000,000 Soviets were executed or sent to lingering death in Siberian prison camps. Hand-in-hand with these political "purges" went Stalin's economic policies. A series of "Five Year Plans" industrialized the country, and the entire agricultural system was "collectivized." Widespread resistance led to the deaths of two to three million peasants before the process was complete.

War. Adolf Hitler's German army invaded Russia in June 1941, quickly advancing through Russian territory and soon besieging Leningrad, Moscow, and Stalingrad. The eventual Russian victory at Stalingrad (1942) allowed the Soviet Army to repulse the German attack. In the spring of 1945 the victorious Soviet Army advanced into a defeated Germany, where they met the Western Allies. The fighting, however, had caused immense suffering and devastation throughout the land. More than 20,000,000—soldiers and civilians alike—and millions of others were maimed or wounded. World War II affected the Russians in a way unparalleled in the West. To Russians, the war is called the "Great Patriotic War."

Cold War and recovery. The USSR's role in the war and Joseph Stalin's negotiations after it left him in a strong position in Eastern Europe. Puppet Communist governments were installed throughout the region, all under the influence or the direct control of Moscow. Although the dominant country in the Communist world, the USSR was soon in confrontation with the West. This atmosphere of international distrust, called the "Cold War," persisted into the 1980s.

A slow but steady economic recovery began during the rule of Stalin, even though his tactics were often repressive. On his death in 1953, Nikita Krushchev became party leader and attempted to undo Stalin's more repressive policies. Krushchev was overthrown in 1964, and replaced by the more authoritarian Leonid Brezhnev. Like Stalin, Brezhnev balanced political repression with economic progress. Still, the gulf between the USSR and the Western world, especially in high technology and consumer goods, remained wide.

The Gorbachev era. In 1985, a new Soviet leader came to power. Mikhail Gorbachev, younger than his predecessors, initiated a program of bold political reforms. Two of his ideas have been especially well-publicized: *perestroika* (restructuring) and *glasnost* (openness). At first, Gorbachev attempted to retain the central ideas of communism, but with the addition of greater democracy. Even though he was a skilled politician, Gorbachev at times had to struggle to keep pace with the processes he began, a struggle in which he was not always successful. In October 1991, Russians undertook a revolution less violent but just as profound as that of 1917. It brought about the government's admission that the communist experiment had failed, followed by a reorganization of the union, with each republic much more independent than in the past.

Uncertain future. In 1991 Russians faced a daunting array of problems. While the old communist system was harsh, repressive, and inefficient, it at least provided the necessities of life for most of the people. This old system was disrupted so suddenly that nothing was developed to take its place. Market shelves, in 1991, were nearly bare in major Russian cities. The crumbling of the economy led to great disillusionment with Gorbachev's policies. The mood in Russia in 1991 was one of growing uncertainty and fear, even as Russians enjoy freedoms that they never before had.

Politics. For most of his time in power, Gorbachev survived by taking a moderate course between two extremes. Old-style conservatives, or Stalinists, wish to return to the days of authoritarian rule and a state-run economy. The radical reformists, led by Boris Yeltsin, the president of the Russian Soviet Republic, wish to adopt a capitalist market economy like those in the West. As great democratic reforms were initiated—including an openly elected parliament—the conservatives grew more dissatisfied. Many were the military and government leaders of the old system whose power had declined with reform. In August 1991, a group of high-ranking conservatives placed Gorbachev under arrest and attempted to take control of the government. Their failure was due in part to strong and decisive action by Yeltsin, who mobilized popular and political resistance to the coup leaders, forcing them to abandon their plans.

Yeltsin's actions seemed to break the power of the conservatives. The results were immediate and dramatic. On reassuming Soviet leadership, Gorbachev suspended the once all-ruling Communist party, thus abandoning communist doctrines. This left a major task of redistributing the wealth of property and institutions formerly owned by the government. Before the coup attempt, Gorbachev had resisted efforts of the republics to become independent. After it, he abandoned that policy and most of the 15 Soviet republics declared their independence. That left a question of how the independent republics would share power with the central government. The issues became cloudier as lesser "autonomous" regions sought their own freedom from the republics that had managed them. A new factor on the political scene was the stance of mayors of major cities such as Moscow and St. Petersburg (formerly Leningrad), who tended to be forces for radical change.

Culture Today

Food. Russian staples are potatoes, cabbage, fish, and bread. Meat, normally rare and expensive, has become even more so in recent years. Distribution of food is spotty, and most vegetables grown locally come only seasonally and disappear quickly. As foods are less and less available to the public, Russians eat away from home more frequently. Many jobs offer cafeteria service of some sort, where the main meal of the day may be eaten. Demand for restaurant tables is high. Long lines form, especially in the evenings, and most dishes may be gone by the time a customer is seated.

Despite such conditions, meals are generally lively and social, whether taken with friends or family, in public or private. They are times to share the conversations that seem to offer Russians as much nourishment as food. Philosophy, literature, science, and politics—the talk ranges widely as courses are served, toasts are offered, and small glasses of vodka are downed.

This old windmill is maintained in a cultural park near St. Petersburg.
Courtesy of Portia Chambliss.

In the long, cold winter months, Russians prepare a variety of rich and tasty soups. These are almost always served with a dollop of sour cream, or *smetana.* Most famous is *borshch,* or borscht, made from beets, cabbage, and meat. In the summer, borscht is served cold. *Shchi,* also made from cabbage, includes as well turnip, carrot, onion or leek, and beef. Fish soups, such as *solianka,* that include onion, tomato, cucumber, lemon, butter, and sometimes beef, are popular. Many soups also include potatoes or dumplings. Two well-known meat dishes are chicken Kiev, prepared with butter and herbs, and beef Stroganov, in which mushrooms, onions, and smetana are simmered with strips of beef. The traditional dark Russian bread is made

This Russian woman is wearing a typical peasant costume. *Courtesy of the National Anthropological Archive of the Smithsonian Institution.*

from rye, though wheat is used increasingly. In past times, wheat was used mostly for *kasha*, a thick gruel eaten with butter or smetana. Caviar is available easily and inexpensively in Russia, and is eaten as an appetizer, or with a variety of accompaniments such as *bliny*, Russian pancakes served with smetana.

The most popular drinks are tea—always with lemon and often with a sugar cube placed in the mouth before drinking—and mineral water. From wheeled tanks, street vendors serve *kvas*, a cooling drink made from fermented dark bread. Though beer and wine are drunk, the king of Russian liquors is vodka ("little water"), which is distilled from potatoes.

Clothing and shelter. Russians' clothing, like that of other Soviet citizens, is mass-produced and often of poor quality. Utility rather than fashion is generally foremost, and shortages are common. As with other consumer goods, an item such as winter galoshes might arrive suddenly. Long lines form immediately. People buy more pairs than they need, hoarding against the future or thinking of friends and relatives. Men usually wear inexpensive suits, women simple, cotton-print dresses with perhaps a cardigan sweater. In the 1980s and 1990s, however, Western-style casual clothing has become increasingly popular, especially among the young. Blue jeans and athletic shoes, for example, may be easily purchased on the black market. Russians dress

Wood was an abundant building material for the farmers of Russia.
Courtesy of Portia Chambliss.

well against winter cold, wearing fur-lined hats, coats, and boots. Western winter clothing—nylon parkas, good quality wool sweaters, for example—can also be found on the black market.

Before communism and its rapid industrialization, most Russian peasants lived in simple wooden houses without plumbing and with only crude furnishings. In small villages, the houses lined streets that were dry and dusty in summer, turning to deep mud in fall and spring. The Soviet regime, in industrializing, drew many former peasants to cities and planned factory communities. Housing shortages have been a constant problem, despite massive building efforts. Many Russian families still live in small one- or two-room apartments, or share a single room in an apartment with other families. High Communist party officials, by contrast, enjoyed privileges in housing as well as in other areas. They had luxurious flats or houses in the city, as well as comfortable summer houses, or *dachas*, in resort regions like the Crimea.

Family life. It has been in the realm of the family that Communist party ideas have most conflicted with Russian tradition. In a communist society, the individual family is supposed to wither away, to be replaced by the "family" of society. Early party officials attempted to undermine the bond between family and child. Children were encouraged to betray parents who resisted communism. Yet family ties remained strong, and party dogma was ultimately forced to accept them.

An emotionally warm people, Russians lavish attention on their children. Progress in school is followed in detail, day by day, and parents are in close touch with teachers. Physical contact is regular and open, both among children and adults. In the past, most families were large, with grandparents and other in-laws living with a couple and their children. As the society has become more urban, this extended family has been largely replaced by the single married couple with children. Urbanization has also led to a higher divorce rate, however, of about one in three marriages.

Women. Communism accepts unconditional equality for men and women. Since 1917, women have received pay equal to that of men, and they rapidly came to make up over half the labor force. With casualties high among men in World War II, women undertook economic and social responsibilities that they have since kept. Most Russian doctors are women, for example, and women account for about 85 percent of all health-care workers. They occupy senior positions in government and administration, making up 60 percent of those with university or technical educations. In the family, however, a woman is still expected to perform domestic tasks such as cooking and cleaning. She might have help from her mother or mother-in-law, who may also do much of the day's shopping. This invariably involves several hours of standing in line. It is common to see a line of older women, many of them war widows, waiting patiently to buy whatever has become available.

Religion. Although communism rejects religion, the Russian Orthodox Church has remained a potent social force. Most churches, while maintained as museums or other cultural institutions, were closed in the years after the revolution, and all religions were forbidden from seeking converts. The church had been closely associated with the hated tsars. Museums, however, proudly display religious art, especially icons—small paintings on wood panels—for which Russia is famous.

Under the Soviet system, the people were taught from childhood that religion is simply empty superstition. Russians are well-educated in science, and scientific ideas were presented in such a way as to pour scorn on religious beliefs. Many accept such ideas but still turn to Christianity as a link with Russia's deeper, pre-Soviet past. Others, especially the old, worship as committed Christians. Open worship, which once would have threatened one's career advancement, has become more common in the age of Gorbachev. A growing number of Russians have become Baptists.

Language. Russian is a rich and complex language whose tone can vary from the purity of the eighteenth-century poets to the breezy slang of youths in Moscow or St. Petersburg. Illiteracy, widespread before the revolution of 1917, has since then virtually disappeared. Today, Russians are deeply attached to their language, and education is such that most can quote long passages of literature they learned in school.

Literature and the arts. Russians possess one of the world's great literary traditions. The 1800s saw its flowering, as novelists such as Leo Tolstoy and Fyodor Dostoyevsky examined both society at large and the inner lives of individuals. The poetry of Alexander Pushkin and others celebrated the natural beauty of Russia in resonant and dramatic verse. The classic Russian authors, only a few of whom are mentioned here, continue to sell to an avid reading public. Today's Russians also enjoy adventure, detective, and science fiction stories, along with novels, such as those of Valentin Rasputin, that describe life in the countryside and explore changing values in the society.

In the last days of the tsars and early days of the Soviet reorganization after 1917, Russian authors such as Anton Chekhov and Vladimir Korolenko could write works of protest or stories, such as Korolenko's "Makars Dream," about peasant life. But in 1934 the Communist party established the Russian Association of Proletarian Writers. For the next 30 years this organization forced writers into production of propaganda for communism. After the death of Joseph Stalin, this heavy censorship began to waver, and by 1954 Ilya Ehrenburg was again able to write critically of the Russian situation. His book *Ottepel* ("The Thaw") was critical of the reign of Stalin. In 1991 the days of heavy and automatic censorship seemed over, and writers enjoyed a new freedom. Many of them, once imprisoned by the system they criticized, helped bring about its downfall.

Many arts, however, such as ballet and classical music, flourished under the Soviet system. Children are trained in such performing arts from an early age, and great dancers or musicians are revered in society. Among the many ballet companies, the world-famous Bolshoi Ballet is the most prestigious.

Sidewalk artists are popular attractions in some streets of Russian cities. *Courtesy of Portia Chambliss.*

Russia has a rich tradition in art. Before 1863, Russian artists had formed an Academy of Fine Arts. From this sprang the Artists Guild, which persists today. In 1870, a group of artists formed the Society for Traveling Art to carry their works to the Russian people. The *predvizhniki*, or wandering artist shows, exhibited throughout Russia and were approved by Lenin, who called the artists traveling brothers. Great artists such as Vasili Kandinsky, the inventor of Russian abstract art, and Kazimir Makevich exhibited their works before the 1930s. Like the writers, however, artists who sought to express themselves in paintings or other works were persecuted by the Communist party. Under the Soviet system, art was encouraged only if it complied with the party doctrines, and those doctrines were subject to varying interpretations depending on the local authorities enforcing them. Social realism, really artistic propaganda for the Communist party, became the accepted art form. It is represented by the stainless steel sculpture eulogizing a truck driver and a woman farmworker that was produced by Vera Muchina in 1937. The result of this coercion was a general fear within the community of artists that was reflected in underground production of works protesting the suppression of the regime or, in the cases of some artists, destruction of their own works lest the authorities find something offensive in them. Artists who dared to work outside the party lines were not allowed to show their works nor were they supported by the government. Artists like Pavel Filonov survived largely on bread while attempting to portray the dismal life of the average Russian in the period between the two world wars. Still, artists are respected and admired in Russia. Unlike the art world of the Western nations in which art works are produced and then offered for sale, much Russian art is commissioned—paid for in advance of its production.

Economy. The central feature of the Soviet economy was central control from Moscow, which embraced all aspects of production and distribution. Underneath this economy has existed a busy "black market," in which individuals buy and sell goods without central control. Though illegal, the black market has permeated all levels of society. It is estimated that the black market accounts for perhaps 30 percent of the overall economy. Often goods can be found only in this market.

A major problem with the decentralization of the union will be the transfer of agriculture and industry to private hands. The *kolkhozy* (collective farms) and *sovkhozy* (state farms), huge agricultural

Recreation time at a Soviet collective farm. *Courtesy of the National Anthropological Archive of the Smithsonian Institution.*

communities controlled by the state, have resulted in many farmers being familiar with only a small part of the farming process. Such institutions have also robbed the people of incentive to produce, because all profits are claimed by the state.

While Russian leaders like Boris Yeltsin promote the idea of a free market, the society has no real understanding of or experience in what such a market entails. The people have a deep suspicion of those who attempt to make a profit in a business transaction, for example. Profound social change must occur before a new Russian economy can emerge.

Diversity. Of the 145,000,000 people who live in Russia about 66,000,000 live east of the Ural Mountains and the broad sweep of the Volga River. Railroads, highways, and active resettlement has resulted in Slavic Russians from the west becoming the dominant group throughout the region but particularly in the steppes, where agriculture under the Communist regime was developed rapidly, along with industry. Most of the more than 100 ethnic groups that have mingled with the western Russians in the land east of the Volga have merged or are merging with the dominant culture successfully—sometimes by force and sometimes by the power of industrialization and mechanized agriculture. Only a few of these societies are mentioned here to illustrate the variety of cultural backgrounds of the people of Russia.

Tatars. The history of the people known as Tatars begins in Bulgaria with various Turkic tribes forming an eastern Bulgarian khanate about the ninth century A.D. In 1236, the grandson of Genghis Khan, the Mongol leader, overran the Khanate, and Mongols merged with the local tribes under Mongol rule for the next 200 years. That rule came to an end in 1552 when the armies of Peter the Great took control. Even though the Tatars rebelled against Russian rule several times (1553, 1574, 1582, 1606, 1667), they remained firmly under the control of the tsars. People called Tatars (the term has been used in many definitions) settled along the middle and lower Volga River and were spread throughout the southern part of Russia into China. At the time of World War II, Tatars made up 23 percent of the people of Crimea.

Peter the Great set the pattern of Russianization that continued through the early days of Communism. Although Peter established a Tatar province on the Volga River, he set out to integrate the people under his rule. By 1744 these efforts had focused on religious differences and Tatars, who were Sunni Muslims, were forced to pledge loyalty to the Russian Orthodox Church. For a short period under Catherine the Great, religious freedom was expanded, but her successor revoked this attitude.

Tatar groups supported the Russian Revolution in the early 1900s, fighting the aristocracy in the region of Gorky, and in 1917, a Volga-Ural Tatar State was formed. Five years later, this had become an Autonomous Soviet Socialist Republic like an adjacent area with a large Tatar population, the Bakshir A.S.S.R. Even so, efforts continued to separate the Tatar population from its past. In 1926 the government decreed that the Arabic alphabet be replaced with the Latin alphabet, and in 1939 this was replaced with the Cyrillic letters.

Highways were constructed, railroads linked the Tatar capital of Kazan to Moscow, 350 miles west, and irrigation systems improved the agricultural output of the Tatar farmers. Oil was discovered in Tatar territory and the farmers were affected by industrial development. The Tatar A.S.S.R. became an important contributor to Russian economy. Nevertheless, when World War II threatened the area with German invasion, the Tatars who had remained in the Crimea were accused of collaborating with the enemy. This seemed to be a false charge, but the Tatars, who were nearly one-fourth of the Crimean population, were packed into boxcars, without food or water, and transported from their homes to new locations in Uzbekistan.

With the collapse of the Soviet Union, the Volga Tatars became concerned that their products would be used to support all of Russia at their expense. By now, so thoroughly Russianized as to be indistinguishable from other Russians, these Tatars in 1992 threatened to establish their own country—speaking against total independence but demanding more voice in their own economy.

In 1992 there are about five million people called Tatars in the Soviet Union who are themselves divided into various smaller ethnic groups. Seven hundred fifty thousand Volga Tatars are divided among those of Kazan, Mishors, Kasimov, and Astrakan. A group of Siberian Tatars lives along the Irtysh River, and the Crimean Tatars form part of the population of Uzbekistan.

Yakuts. About 300,000 people known as Yakuts migrated north from the region of Lake Baikal and were spread across the vast basin of the Lena River when Cossacks invaded the land in the 1600s. The Cossacks built forts along the river to control the population and exploit trade, for which they settled the town of Yakutsk—now a city of nearly 200,000 and the capital of what was the Yakutsian Autonomous Soviet Socialist Republic.

That these people migrated from the south and west is attested to by their language, one of the oldest dialects of the many Turkic languages throughout eastern and southern Russia. The Yakuts worked their way through the southern forests to steppe land and on north through tundra to the north coast of Asia. Small groups, hardly more than extended families, spread through an area that is two-fifths as large as the total continent of Europe. But the Yakuts were perhaps farther along the way to the new civilization than some of their neighbors. They built substantial homes, furnished them with wooden benches for sleeping and other household tools and remained in them for most of the year. They became herders of reindeer and cattle, migrating from permanent log houses with ice or skin windows to live in the summer in birch bark tents as they sought grazing land for their animals. In time, some Yakuts became farmers, clearing small plots of land in and near the forests to grow grains. By the time of Vitus Bering's expeditions of the early 1700s, the Yakut agricultural and hunting industry was able to supply this band of explorers with needed rations.

In the far north, some Yakuts became traders, encouraged by the Russian interest in furs. Adaptable people, the Yakuts early espoused Christianity, and then merged it with their older shamanistic religion. They took quickly to education and took an important part in the growing trade of the region.

Gold and silver were discovered in the region. Russian adventurers multiplied—some pursuing the fur trade and others seeking a fortune in mining. Yakutsk became an important supply and trading center linked to Moscow by the trans-Siberian railway.

Today, the capital of Yakutsk is a modern city with growing importance in trade, industry, and mining, and the Yakuts are adapting to a new lifestyle. For a time, Yakutsk was a checkerboard of Russian wooden houses side–by–side with Yakut birchbark tents. But in the 1990s, the Yakuts have abandoned their yurts for the more substantial wooden structures. Now, the Yakuts have taken up warm factory-spun fabric clothing to replace or supplement their earlier fur dress. So adept were they at processing furs and hides, that the Yakuts had never taken to weaving or felt production.

Nentsy. Far north in the tundra region at the mouth of the Ob River about 25,000 reindeer-dependent people still live in portable housing that allows them to follow their herds of reindeer and to add to them new stock from the wild reindeer that roam across the tundra to the north coast. The men hunt wild reindeer and other animals for food and furs while the women tend the temporary villages, setting up the double-layered teepee-shaped dwellings to form the community, then tearing them down and packing all their equipment onto sleds, again drawn by reindeer, to follow the men. Some Nentsy have settled along the Ob River to become fishers. An important property of each Nentsy family is the hunting dogs, bred and trained to help with the herding. Although exposed to Christianity and to Islam, the Nentsy are still inclined to call in a shaman in times of need.

For a more complete example of life in northern Siberia, see TUNGUS.

For More Information

Maclean, Fitzroy. *Portrait of the Soviet Union.* London: Weidenfeld and Nicholson, 1988.

Parker, W. H. *The Russians: How They Live and Work.* New York: Praeger Publishers, 1973.

Smith, Hedrick. *The New Russians.* New York: Avon Books, 1991.

Tweddell, Colin E. and Linda Amy Kimball, *Introduction to the Peoples and Cultures of Asia.* Englewood Cliffs, New Jersey: Prentice-Hall, 1985.

SERBS
(serbs)

One of the Slavic peoples, living mostly in the territory that was, since World War II, Yugoslavia.

Population: 10,000,000 (1990).
Location: Yugoslavia.
Language: Serbo-Croatian.

Geographical Setting

Most Serbs live in the Republic of Serbia, the largest of the six republics which made up Yugoslavia until 1992. Serbia occupies the greater part of eastern Yugoslavia, and includes the "autonomous provinces" of Kosovo and Vojvodina (see YUGOSLAVS). Few Serbs live in Kosovo, to the south, but Serbs make up the majority in the northern province of Vojvodina. Serbs also constitute substantial minorities in central and western Yugoslavia, in the republics of Croatia and Bosnia-Herzegovina.

In the north, around the capital city of Belgrade, and in Vojvodina, spreads a vast and fertile plain where much of Yugoslavia's wheat is grown. Through the plain flow two historic rivers, the Danube and the Sava. At Belgrade, the Sava joins the Danube, which continues west to the Black Sea. In places, the Danube is nearly two miles wide. South of Belgrade rise wooded mountains and valleys with rolling meadows. An extension of the Transylvanian Alps (a part of the Carpathian Mountain complex) forms an eastern border with Romania; mountains in the southwest also separate Serbia from rocky Montenegro (see MONTENEGRINS). In the northern plains, winters are severe with light snow and summers hot and humid. In more mountainous southern Serbia, winters are snowy and cold; higher areas have short, cool summers.

Serbs

Greater Serb population
Lesser Serb population

Serbs hold the central and south of the land that was Yugoslavia. About 600,000 Serbs live in the northern land of the Croats.

Historical Background

Arrival and conversion. Serbs arrived in the Balkans probably during the 600s, part of the mass Slavic migration out of southern Ukraine and Poland. They settled south and east of the Croats (see CROATS), probably at first in the areas now called Kosovo, Montenegro, and Bosnia. Serbian tribes and clans (groups of interrelated families) fought among each other for dominance; they also faced raids by neighboring Bulgars and by the powerful Greek empire of Byzantium. In the late 800s, Byzantine monks converted the Serbs to Orthodox Christianity and established Byzantine culture among the Serbs. For most of the next two centuries, the Byzantines ruled the Serbs, though weakly.

Independent state. By the 1100s, two Serbian principalities had emerged, Zeta, in present-day Montenegro, and Raska, in southern Serbia. The Grand Župan of Raska, Stephen Nemanja, overthrew

Byzantine rule and united the two principalities in the late 1100s. Nemanja allied his state closely with the church. He abdicated in 1196 to become a monk, having founded a dynasty that would last some 200 years. His son became the first archbishop of the newly independent Serbian Orthodox Church.

Flowering of medieval Serbia. The Serbian Empire reached its high point under Nemanja's descendant Stephen Dushan in the mid-1300s. Dushan conquered territory that included most of modern Yugoslavia and Albania. Encouraging trade and the arts, Dushan also gave Serbia a legal code that combined Byzantine law with Serbian customs. Dušan even aspired to win the throne of Byzantium. To help defeat the Serbs, the Byzantines invited the Ottomans—who had taken Turkey from them—into Europe. Though Dushan held back the Turks, his successors lacked his abilities. The Serbian Empire began to disintegrate soon after Dushan's death in 1355.

Turkish conquest. By the 1300s, much Serbian territory had been conquered by the Turks. In 1389, the Serbs lost the famous battle of Kosovo, in which the Serbian leader, Prince Lazar, died. Serbians still commemorate the battle's anniversary. Though the Turks were unable at first to follow up their victory, in 1459 they wiped out the last resistance, and the Serbian state ended. For over 300 years, the Islamic Turks held Serbia under military occupation as part of the huge Ottoman Empire. Only in the small, mountainous coastal area of Montenegro were they unable to take over.

Turkish rule. Many Serbs fled north into Hungarian-ruled Vojvodina or Croatia before the Turkish advance, particularly the nobles and other town- and city-dwellers. The Serbs who remained were mostly the peasants who lived in small villages. At first, the Turks occupied the towns and mostly left the villages alone. Elected leaders ran the villages and collected taxes to give to the Turks; Serbian church officials led the Serbian community as a whole.

Revolt. By the late 1700s, however, Ottoman rule had become more oppressive, as corrupt Turkish officials plundered the powerless Serbian peasants. In 1804, with a weakened Turkey at war with Russia, France and Austria, Serbs seized the opportunity to revolt. They were led by a man called Karadjordje or "Black George." For almost ten years, Karadjordje ran an independent Serbian government in Belgrade, and, even though he was unable to read or write, organized the Serbs for independence. In 1813, the Turks defeated Karadjordje; a successful second revolt in 1815, led by Miloš Obrenović, resulted in the Turks' declaring in 1829 that Serbia could govern itself. However, not until 1867 did the last Turkish troops leave Serbian territory. In 1889, the Congress of Berlin recognized Serbia's complete independence.

Serbia and the Yugoslav idea. Until 1903, the Serbian kingship passed between Karadjordje's and Obrenović's descendants. In 1903, the last Obrenović ruler was assassinated, and Petar Karadjordjević became king. A movement had arisen during the 1800s that aimed to unify the Serbs and their Slavic neighbors. This Yugoslav ("south Slav") idea, as it was known, came to fruition in 1918, when the south Slavs declared Alexander king of a new state: the Kingdom of the Serbs, Croats and Slovenes, which in 1929 became known as the Kingdom of Yugoslavia. In 1934, Alexander was assassinated by Croats seeking independence. During this period (1921–1937) a Communist party had arisen, been declared illegal, and continued to operate. In 1937 Josip Tito became general secretary of this party. In 1941 German troops occupied Yugoslavia, inciting a deep rift between pro-German and anti-German factions that led to a civil war. In 1945, having defeated the occupying Germans and Italians, Communists came to power in Yugoslavia.

In both the kingdom and the Communist state that followed, Serbs dominated the government and the army. The forceful personality of Josip Tito, Communist leader of Yugoslavia for 35 years, was able to hold the people together. In 1990, ten years after Tito's death, Croatian and Slovenian resentment of Serb dominance led to attempts to secede from Yugoslavia's federal system. In June 1991, the Serbian-led federal army attacked Croatia, and a bitter civil war followed. Some of the complex issues involved are discussed below. In mid-1992, as this is written, Croatia is in the process of forming a separate nation. The Yugoslavian army, largely Serbs, has now turned its attention to Bosnia-Herzegovina.

Culture Today

The Serbs face two main problems in achieving peace with their neighbors. Both obstacles arise from the region's complicated and violent history, yet hold a vital interest for Serbs today.

Croatian Serbs. First, about 600,000 Serbs live in Croatia, the republic controlled by the Serbs' historic rival, the Croats (see CROATS). Some are descendants of families that fled the Turks; these people live mostly in the interior of Dalmatian Croatia. More, however, are from families who moved into a military buffer zone between Turkish territory and the Croatian lands controlled by Christian rulers of Austria and Hungary. The Austro-Hungarian Habsburg emperors offered incentives in order to populate the areas now on the Croatian border with Bosnia. Most of those who moved there were mostly Serbs.

Thousands of Croatian Serbs were killed by right-wing Croatian leaders (the *ustaše*) during World War II. Today, the Serbian leaders fear that if Croatia becomes independent, Serbs in Croatia will lose their civil rights. In 1990, the Croatian Serbs voted in favor of self-rule, and during the 1991 civil war they set up their own government.

Kosovo. The second obstacle to peace concerns the Serbian province of Kosovo. As one of the earliest areas of Serbian settlement, Kosovo has strong historic overtones for Serbs. A number of monasteries, built by the Serbs in the 1200s and 1300s, grace the region—including the monastery at Peč, the ancient center of the Serbian church. Kosovo is also the site of the battle (in 1389; see above) that Serbs consider central to their historical identity.

Yet in the 1600s, Serbs began migrating north from Kosovo and have continued to do so up to the present. Ethnic Albanians who also lived there (and who also fought the Turks at Kosovo) remained. Today, Albanians outnumber Serbs in Kosovo by nine to one. The Serbs have refused to allow the Albanians to govern themselves, insisting that Kosovo remain a province of Serbia. They don't want to lose a region so crucial to their heritage, and they fear that the Albanian Kosovars would want to unite with Albania, which borders Kosovo on the southeast.

Religion. Much of the Serbs' trouble with the Croats and Albanians stems from religious differences. The Slavic Croats, once closely related to the Serbs, were converted by the Roman Catholic West, while the Serbs took the eastern Greek Orthodox form of Christianity. Christianity itself had split along cultural lines—Greek east versus Latin west—and the split between Serbs and Croats reflects the boundary between the two cultures. The Albanians, formerly Christian, converted to Islam after the Turkish conquest.

For the Serbs, as for the Croats, religion has played a central role in defining cultural identity. Under Islamic rule, Jewish and Christian populations each made up a separate *millet* or administrative division. The millets were self-supervising, with the highest religious official acting as administrative head. Thus, during the years of Turkish occupation, the Serbian Orthodox Church became very important in Serbian society. During the decline of the Ottoman Empire, the church became identified with Serbian nationalism. Religious leaders led early revolts against the Turks in the 1700s. The church continues to be a major force promoting the Serbian cause, though its influence weakened under Croatian persecution in World War II and during the years of Communist rule.

Language. Serbs and Croats speak the same language, called Serbo-Croatian. Like other Orthodox Slavs, the Serbs use a modified version of the Greek alphabet, called Cyrillic. The Cyrillic alphabet was devised by the Byzantine monks who converted the Slavs, and is named for the most famous of them, St. Cyril. Croats use the Latin alphabet (also used in English). Like religion, the Serbs' alphabet has become an important symbol of their culture.

Food, clothing, and shelter. Favorite Serbian dishes include a spicy sausage (*čevapići*), grilled meats, and chicken soup. Like all Yugoslavs, Serbs enjoy coffee, wine, and *sjvovia*, the plum brandy that is the national drink. Serbian folk costumes generally comprise a white shirt for both men and women, topped by embroidered cotton or wool overgarments. Men often wear dark, somber browns or grays: their vests, short jackets, and leggings all of the same hue. Women's costumes tend to be more colorful, with different colored patterns gracing a vest, skirt, and apron. The costumes are worn on holidays and special occasions. Homes are generally built of wood, though modern cities such as Belgrade (capital of Serbia as well as of Yugoslavia) feature concrete apartment buildings in the utilitarian style of European Communist regimes.

Family life. Like their Slavic neighbors, Serbs share in the *zadruga*, or large extended family. The zadruga developed as a way of pooling labor and ensuring security for the group. A rural phenomenon, it was a source of strength for the Serbs during the years of Turkish rule, when most Serbs lived in small, agricultural villages. A distinctively Serbian family relationship is the unusually strong bond between brothers and sisters. For men, strong friendships arose within the family rather than outside it; those that might arise outside were thought of in family terms. Thus, "blood brotherhood" (*pobratimstvo*) and "godfatherhood" (*kumstvo*) meant a serious commitment to supply help in times of need.

Serbian religious customs are often conducted within the context of the family. They sometimes represent old customs that predate Christianity but survived its arrival by mixing with Christian ritual. For example, the Slava, a major religious festival, celebrates a family's patron saint. The tradition reflects the old custom of worshiping a family protector. Today, on a family's Slava day they open their home to friends and relatives and serve special dishes such as Slava Cake and Slava žita, a wheat dish made with sugar, spices, and walnuts.

Folk poetry and literature. The Serb's tradition of oral folk poetry represents one of the strongest and most distinctive elements of their culture. The *pesme*, or songs, are accompanied by the *gusle*, a violin with one string. The most famous pesme commemorate the battle of Kosovo (see above); others celebrate the exploits of popular heroes like the *uskoks* and *hajduks*. These were pirate and outlaw bands who fought the Turks during the Ottoman occupation. Like Robin Hood, the hajduks of legend robbed the rich Turks and gave to the poor Serbian peasants. This rich tradition influenced European writers like Jacob Grimm (the fairytale author), who compared them favorably with the Greek epics of Homer.

The pesme also continue to influence modern Serbian literature. The best-known Serb author of this century, Ivo Andrić, viewed the pesme as cutting across the cultural boundaries between the Orthodox, Catholic, and Muslim communities of his native Bosnia. His most famous novel, *The Bridge on the Drina,* helped him win the Nobel Prize for Literature in 1961. In it, a bridge on the Drina River serves as the setting for a number of dramatic events that reveal the passions of the novel's multiethnic characters.

For More Information

Andrić, Ivo. *The Bridge on the Drina.* Chicago: University of Chicago Press, 1977.

Danforth, Kenneth C. "Yugoslavia: A House Much Divided." *National Geographic*, August 1990, pp. 92–123.

Doder, Dusko. *The Yugoslavs*. New York: Random House, 1978.

Jordan, Robert. "Yugoslavia: Six Republics in One." *National Geographic*, May 1970, pp. 589–633.

Pavlovich, Paul. *The Serbians: The Story of a People*. Toronto: Serbian Heritage Books, 1983.

Viorst, Milton. "A Reporter at Large: The Yugoslav Idea." *The New Yorker*, March 18, 1991, pp. 58–79.

SLOVAKS
(slo′ vaks)

Slavic people who settled near the Bohemian forest in northwestern and central present-day Czechoslovakia.

Population: 5,288,000 (1990 estimate).
Location: Czechoslovakia, particularly Slovakia.
Language: Slovakian.

Geographical Setting

The Slovak people live in all parts of Czechoslovakia but are most concentrated in the eastern section of the country. Czechoslovakia is a country divided into three parts by mountains. The heavily populated western region is a plateau ringed by mountains and separated from central Moravia by the Bohemian Mountains. Central Moravia, in turn, is separated from Slovakia in the east by the Little Carpathian Mountains. While Slovak people live in all three regions and in Poland and Hungary, they are most concentrated in the Slovakia region. The Carpathian Mountains swing in a broad arc separating Slovakia from Poland in the north and east. The land of the Slovaks slopes down from this high mountain range into fertile river valleys cut by several tributaries that drain into the Danube River. The Danube forms part of the southern boundary of the land. Slovakia is fertile farmland. Winters are severe and summers warm in this middle-European region.

Historical Background

Beginnings. Before the fourth century A.D. small bands of Slavic people had established themselves in northeastern Europe. In this

Slovaks

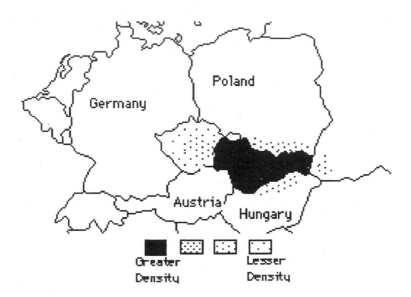

While Slovaks live in most parts of Czechoslovakia, as well as in Poland and Hungary, the majority live in southeastern Czechoslovakia.

area they were dominated first by the Goths, then by the Huns. More slowly than their rulers, the Slavs moved toward Central Europe, migrating west before the seventh century to the area that is now Czechoslovakia and establishing a county called Moravia. The eastern region of this country was overrun by the Magyars of Hungary about 905 and the Slavs fell under Magyar rule. In the west, Czech people who were part of the Slavs founded a nation called Bohemia on land shared with the Germans. Thus, the Slavs in what is now Czechoslovakia became divided. Those in the west were influenced by Europeans, those in the east related most closely with the eastern nations. With the rise of the Austrian Habsburgs, Bohemia fell under their rule in 1526 and remained part of the Austrian Empire until the people rebelled over religious matters in the 1600s. Meanwhile, eastern Slavs were governed by Hungary and Poland. These Polish- and Hungarian-influenced Slavs of the eastern region developed their own language and became known as the Slovaks.

Troubles in the west erupted into the Thirty Years' War, in which Bohemians, Danes, Swedes, and French were involved in actions against the Austrian states. In this turmoil the Czechs, who had had a measure of self-government under the Habsburgs, lost their political independence.

World War I. Before the 1840s, the Slovaks had begun to develop a sense of national identity. In 1843 L'undovit Štur, a Slovak writer, pressed for a Slovak literature ("Let us write in Slovak"). It was not until 1848 that the Slovaks began to demand their own nation. Later, in 1907, Andréy Hlinka began to discuss a unified Slavic state which he called Czechoslovakia. Still, little came of the Slovak claims until after World War I when Czechs (the western Slavs) and Slovaks joined in rebelling against Germany. In 1918, Czechs and Slovaks, two groups of Slavs who had come to the area at the same time but had grown apart as they were influenced by successions of rulers from east and west, joined to form the country of Czechoslovakia. Now differences became more apparent. In the west, Czechs inhabited the area that had once been Bohemia, a highly industrialized part of the old Austro-Hungarian Empire. In the east Slovaks inhabited a more mountainous area north of Hungary and farmed the mountain valleys. The two peoples formed a democratic government under the presidency of Tomáš Garrigue Masaryk and the country began to build economic prosperity and political freedom. Then, in the 1930s, Germany claimed a right to the part of Bohemia in which 3,000,000 Germans were living. They were supported within Czechoslovakia by a fascist Populist movement and by some Germans in the country. With the consent of other countries, Sudetenland, the far western section of the country that was heavily inhabited by Germans was occupied by Germany. Supported by Germany, radical parties in Czechoslovakia demanded that the country be divided so as to form a federated state with eastern and western Slavs governing themselves. Reflecting little experience in industrialization or self-government, a vote over federation indicated that only 40 percent of the Slovaks were in favor. Most felt that they benefitted by union with the Czechs. However, a radical minority prevailed with German assistance and in 1939 Slovakia became a separate protectorate of Germany. The government of Slovakia was restructured to be pro-German. Small parts of the country were given to Austria and Hungary, but Slovakia remained a German supporter. Finally, in 1939 the

Germans took command of all of Czechoslovakia and held it through World War II. After the war the country was reunited, Germans were evicted, and Czechs moved into the Sudetenland once occupied by them. A 1946 election gave power to a coalition of which the Communist party was the strongest group but with Czech President Edvard Beneš retaining control of the government. A 1948 coup confirmed Russian domination and Czechoslovakia became the Czechoslovakia Socialist Republic, with two groups, Czechs and Slovaks, proportionally represented.

The struggles for independence. The Slavic people have always sought independence. Finding personal liberty inhibited under Russian influence, Czechs and Slovaks resisted, declaring a more open society. In 1968, this movement was suppressed by invading Warsaw Pact countries (the alliance of Communist states). Still, political leaders resisted. A 1977 manifesto protesting the lack of civil rights resulted in the arrest and imprisonment of many Slavic leaders.

Slavic leaders. Protests over this action took place in 1979 and 1983. Then in 1989, a "velvet revolution" featuring mass protests and dissention within the government resulted in a reform of the government. In 1990, the land of the Czechs and Slovaks held its first free election since 1946. Twenty-seven parties and groups competed for seats in two regional governments as well as in the federal government. The country was divided into two states, Czech and Slovak, with their own governments operated under the direction of a federal assembly. Slovaks were guaranteed the right to use their own language. However, Slovaks were outnumbered by Czechs in the new country nearly three to one and were soon challenging Czech's authority, and some Czechs, meanwhile, were demanding independence.

Culture Today

The union of Slavs. The early Slavs migrated west through the Carpathian Mountains. These people of a racial stock called "Alpine" were dark haired, stocky people. While some of them pushed west into land held by Germanic tribes, one group of Slavs lingered in the high plateaus of the Carpathians. This group, the Slovaks, came to be influenced and sometimes dominated by the Hungarians while the advance groups were influenced by the Germans. The result has been that the original group of Slavs has grown apart. Only the fear by Czechs, Slovaks and their dividing group, the Moravians, that they might find themselves minorities in their own land has forced them to unite under one government.

Division. Before Communist management, the Slovaks living in the rugged Carpathian lands survived by farming and tending sheep in the time-honored traditions of animal-powered plows and human muscle. In the west, the Czechs of Bohemia were joining with their German neighbors to establish trade and industry and to build the great city of Prague. The Slovaks' major city, Bratislava, was established, not with trade routes to Prague, but along the routes to Vienna and Budapest, where there was a market for the farm goods.

Czechs looked down upon the Slovaks as backward and unkempt. To the extent that most Slovaks felt a need to be under Czech guidance, the Slovaks agreed. At first, Slovaks were little-educated and unprepared for self-government, and they were not encouraged to industrialize even though their mountainous land held many mineral resources. It was not until the Slovaks gained relative equality under communism that industrialization began, and not until 1980 that the first major highway was completed between the Czech capital of Prague and the Slovak capital of Bratislava. Czech and Slovak societies were merging once again into one uneasy Slavic unit.

Farm life. Until the country fell under Communist control, the Slovak families farmed individually owned small farms. While some private ownership remained, the Communists encouraged organization of village collectives. Over time, more than 95 percent of the farmland became operated by a few agro-collectives. Sugar beets, wheat, potatoes, and barley are the main products of the farm collectives, along with poultry and hogs, which outnumber cattle.

Changing economy. The Communists, however, also encouraged the people of Slovakia to develop the land's industrial potential. As a result, nearly 40 percent of Slovaks are employed in mining and other industries. The modern collective farming techniques have reduced farm laborers to only 12 percent of the laborers. Coal, iron, and copper account for most of the mine employment. Under communism, industrialization grew so that Slovakia has joined Bohemia and Moravia in becoming one of the most industrialized sections of the world.

Food, clothing, and shelter. City and town people in Slovakia wear clothing that cannot be distinguished from the apparel of Western Europeans. However, peasants in the hill country still wear traditional dress, including dark woolen suits and knitted hats. Women dress in plain-colored full skirts, aprons, blouses, and scarfs.

As elsewhere in the countries guided by the Soviet Union, rapid industrialization and the resulting movement of the population to cities and towns and from farm to factory resulted in a shortage of housing. Today, the city worker in Czechoslovakia most often lives in a small flat or apartment with one or two rooms housing two to five people. Country houses are small stone, brick, or frame houses— sometimes with thatched roofs. These homes are often immaculately kept, and decorated with brightly colored decals on white plaster walls. The walls are often decorated by wall hangings such as hand-painted plates.

Movement to the cities, however, has had less effect on Slovak preferences in food. Slovaks count bread, potatoes, and meat as staple foods. They, like their Hungarian neighbors, also enjoy a wide variety of pastries, and are fond of the wines they produce. Their Czech countrymen prefer beer.

Recreation. The cold climate of the Czechoslovakian mountains encourages winter sports. Ice hockey is the national sport. Some schools take students on special holidays to ski and skate in the mountains. The Slovaks join their Russian neighbors in preferring cross-country skiing to slalom and other ski activities.

Religion. Most Slovaks profess to be Christians and most belong to the Roman Catholic Church. Their great celebrations are centered around religious events. Slovaks are tightly affiliated with their church community, and have often preferred to take instruction from the local church leaders rather than from the Communist government.

In religion, too, Slovaks differ from their Czech countrymen. Slovak Catholicism is likely to be more traditional than the more liberal Czech version.

Literature. Czechs and Slavs speak, read, and write variations of an older Slavic language to which Latin, German, and Greek words and phrases have been added. In language debates that took place in the early 1800s, the Slovaks elected to adopt the western dialect of their language that was most nearly like the language of the Czechs. In their own version of the language, Slovak, there is a rich heritage of literature.

Slovak interest in reading has done much to separate their country from Soviet domination. While opting for communism and aligning themselves with the Soviets, the Czechs and Slovaks very early began to use their books and newspapers to establish their own self-government. In the 1950s and 1960s, while the Soviet Union was pressing for closer alliances with Czechoslovakia, writers were busy reminding the people of their independence. A congress of the Slovak Writers Union in 1954 was the forum for decrying the tightening bonds between Moscow and the Czechoslovakian leader, Antonin Novotný. Through this forum, writers spoke of Stalinism as "monstrous and horrible" and declared that it wiped out trust, confidence, and understanding. Shortly after this conference, Ladislav Mňačko gained fame with his book *Delayed Reports*, which lamented Czechoslovakia's passive acceptance of Stalinism. At the same time, Ladislav Bublik was writing about the terrible life in Czechoslovak prisons under communism, and Ludvik Vaculik was preparing to publish *A Busy House*, which was an attack on Stalinist practices in his country.

One outcome of the velvet revolution was the elimination of the country's laws of censorship. As a result, publications of all major political organizations have blossomed, including the magazine *Rudé Lidové*, the voice of the Czechoslovak Communist party, and Fórum, the magazine of the Czech Civic Forum, the umbrella political organization that dominates federal government. The Slovaks continue to be influenced by the past. Of the nine newspapers circulated in the Slovak capital of Bratislava, one is published in Magyar, while 20 major magazines are published in Slovak.

For More Information

Czechoslovakia: A Country Study. Washington, D.C.: American University Press, 1980.

Szulc, Tad. *Czechoslovakia since World War II*. New York: Viking Press, 1971.

SLOVENES

(sloh veens')

Slavic people of a former northwest republic of Yugoslavia.

Population: 2,000,000 (1991 estimate).
Location: Slovenia, the northwest portion of the former state of Yugoslavia.
Language: Slovenian.

Geographical Setting

Slovenia, now independent, but once the northernmost of Yugoslavia's six republics, shares its mostly Alpine geography with neighboring parts of Austria and Italy. The high, craggy Julian Alps, near the meeting point of the Austrian, Italian, and Slovenian borders, dominate the mountainous region. Lower Alpine ranges rise to the east, generally running in an east-west direction, between the Sava River valley and the Austrian border. The Sava itself, one of Yugoslavia's most important rivers, rises in the Alps near the Slovenian capital of Ljubljana. From Austria, parallel to the Sava and to the north, flows the Drava River. Both rivers run through Slovenia, flowing southeast to join the mighty Danube at or near Belgrade, the Yugoslav capital. On the headwaters of the Sava, north of Ljubljana, lies Lake Bled, one of Europe's most famous mountain resorts.

Southeast of the Julian Alps lies a region of limestone plateaus called karst (or *kras* in Slovenian). Extending inland to the area of the Kupa River, the karst features elaborate cave systems and underground rivers. The vast and spectacular caves at Postojno attract around 250,000 tourists a year. Another tourist attraction of the karst are the intermittent lakes that dry up completely in the summer, only to reappear in the winter and spring. Some of the karst is barren; in other areas, the topsoil allows farming.

Slovenes

Slovenes are mostly concentrated in the north of the dividing nation of Yugoslavia.

Slovenian winters can be cold and snowy, especially in the higher Alps, where skiing and other winter sports are popular. Summers are generally warm and dry, though cooler in the mountains.

Historical Background

German influence. Slovenes arrived in their present homeland during the 600s, about the same time as the two other main branches of the Yugoslavs or "south Slavs" (see SERBS, CROATS, and YUGOSLAVS). Along with the Croats, the Slovenes came under Frankish domination by the 700s. Soon after, German missionaries converted them to Roman Catholicism, the Western European form of Christianity. The missionaries also introduced German culture to the Slovenes, whose lands lay on the southern edge of German territory.

Habsburg rule. During the 1000s and 1100s, the Slovenes became serfs (peasants legally bound to work the land) under the German feudal nobility. In the late 1200s and early 1300s, Slovene lands were absorbed by the growing empire of the Habsburgs, rulers of Germanic Austria. Except for a brief period of French rule, the Habsburgs would control Slovenia until Austria's defeat in World War I (1918). Under the Habsburgs, German culture became stronger among the Slovenes, as German nobles and church leaders came to control more of the land.

Reformation. In the early 1500s, the Protestant Reformation (in which the Protestant Church split from the Roman Catholic Church) enjoyed support among the Slovenes. Protestant schools and churches sprang up in Ljubljana and other towns. Though the Habsburgs successfully crushed Protestantism in Slovenia, new ideas spread by the Reformation had a lasting impact on Slovene culture. Slovene translations of the New Testament, as well as other early efforts of Slovene writers, appeared in this period. The Austrian rulers, in stamping out the Protestant movement, reinforced their control over the peasants. Yet while German became the official language in government and education, the peasants clung to their Slovenian language and folkways.

Napoleon. In 1809, the Treaty of Vienna transferred Slovene lands to the control of Napoleon's France. Though French rule lasted only four years, it brought to the increasingly prosperous Slovenes opportunities for better living conditions and education. In particular, the Slovenian language began to be used in schools.

Economic growth. During the late 1700s and throughout the 1800s, the Slovene economy grew increasingly vigorous. A major trade route led from Austria through Slovenia to the Adriatic port of Trieste. Slovenes exported timber, mercury, wool, cattle, and farm produce, and imported silk, spices and coffee. A middle class arose, made up of prosperous merchants who sent their children to the best European universities. The Slovenian industrialist Baron Ziga Zois pioneered new farming and mining techniques in the late 1700s. Zois also played an important role in encouraging Slovenian literature.

Yugoslav state. While Slovenes asserted themselves culturally in the 1800s, their prosperity encouraged most of them to be content with Austrian rule. With the collapse of Austrian power following World War I, however, Slovenes joined with their Slavic neighbors to the south in forming the Kingdom of Serbs, Croats and Slovenes (1918), which became the Kingdom of Yugoslavia in 1929. In 1945, Communists came to power in Yugoslavia. Still, Slovenes' prosperity continued to be greater than that of the other Yugoslavs. As the Communist system dissolved in the late 1980s, the more Westernized and better-educated Slovenes pressed for greater self-rule. In June 1991, the Slovene and Croat governments declared independence from the Yugoslav state (see YUGOSLAVS).

Culture Today

Independence. After six months of civil war, in which the Serbian-led federal army attacked territory in Croatia, Yugoslavians have agreed to dissolve their nation. As this is written, Slovenia and Croatia have been recognized as independent nations, and Boznia-Herzegovina and Macedonia have declared their intention to break from Serb-dominated Yugoslavia. However, many complex issues remain to be worked out among the various republics before new and peaceful relations can be established. If the Slovenes maintain independence, it will be for the first time in their long history.

Looking west. Like their Roman Catholic neighbors, the Croats, the Slovenes consider themselves an integral part of Western Europe. They have resented the more numerous Serbs, who have dominated Yugoslavia's army and government. Although Slovenes made up only about eight percent of the Yugoslavia population, Slovenes provided over 25 percent of the federal budget. The Slovenes refer to "floating money down the Sava" to the Yugoslav capital, Belgrade (Danforth 1990, p. 121). Aside from their economic prosperity, Slovenes have Yugoslavia's highest literacy rate, as well as the highest rate of enrollment in vocational education. Slovenes feel that they could do better on their own; an independent Slovenia, many believe, will be more quickly accepted into the European Economic Community than a federal Yugoslavia.

Language. Slovenes speak a Slavic language similar to, but distinct from, Serbo-Croatian. Serbo-Croatian is spoken by both Serbs and Croats, and thus is the most widely spoken language in the Yugoslavian area. Like the Croats, Slovenes use the Latin script, which came with the Roman Catholic Church. Speakers of the two languages can understand each other, and many Slovenes also speak Serbo-

Croatian. Until the late 1980s, Slovenes allowed Serbo-Croatian to be taught in their schools and used it to converse with other Yugoslavs. With the growing separatist movement of 1980 through 1991, however, the question of language assumed greater importance for the Slovenes. They have traditionally mistrusted the Serb-dominated federal army; one complaint of the late 1980s was the wish for Slovene soldiers in the federal army to serve in Slovenia under Slovene officers speaking Slovenian. Many older Slovenians also speak German, which was widely taught under Austrian rule.

Religion. Slovenes have remained strongly Roman Catholic into the 1980s. Polls taken over recent decades have consistently indicated that they have the smallest percentage of atheists among Yugoslav national groups. In the 1800s, the mostly Slovenian Roman Catholic clergy played a crucial role in promoting Slovenian ethnic identity and in preserving the Slovenian language. Today, surveys of the people show that, more than any other national group, they approve of a stronger role for the church in society.

Literature and the arts. The earliest Slovenian literature was the New Testament translation mentioned above, carried out in 1555 by Primoz Trubar. In the mid-1700s, a monk named Marko Pohlin wrote the first non-religious poetry. The industrialist Baron Zois encouraged a Slovenian literary movement in the late 1700s; writers also flourished during the French occupation of 1809–1813. One poet, Valentin Vodnik (1759–1819), praised the French emperor Napoleon in his poems. Like other poets of the Romantic movement in literature, Vodnik drew heavily on the oral folk traditions of the peasants for his material and inspiration.

Peasant traditions also inspire the folk festivals that Slovenes hold each summer. Folk dances and music are performed at the popular tourist resort of Lake Bled, as well in the cities of Ljubljana and Maribor. European classical music also draws crowds at summer recitals, as do opera and jazz.

Food, clothing, and shelter. Slovene eating habits show Austrian influences: Slovenes drink beer more widely than other Yugoslavs, and enjoy more baked goods and pastries. Pork and ham are also more popular than elsewhere in Yugoslavia; pork roast is often served with applesauce (made from local apples). Alpine lakes and streams provide tasty fish such as trout and pike. The people also enjoy meals that are more typically Yugoslav, however. Grilled meats are common, particularly lamb and spicy sausage. Slovenian wine is among Europe's best.

Slovenian folk costumes also reflect nearby Austrian dress. The men wear short jackets with leather shorts, as well as Tyrolean brimmed hats that often include colorful feathers in the bands. Women wear full skirts, brightly embroidered vests and caps, and belts with ribbons hung from them. As elsewhere, such costumes are now mostly seen on holidays or special occasions such as weddings and public festivals.

Slovenia's mountain chalets are wood-shingled or built of stone, like those throughout the Alpine regions of Europe. Farmers' houses are crafted of wood—large and solid structures whose workmanship reflects the people's Germanic thoroughness and attention to detail. Architecture in Ljubljana resembles that of the Austrian capital, Vienna. Buildings in the old section of the city feature baroque churches dating from the 1600s and 1700s. Ljubljana also has a number of buildings from the early 1900s that reflect Viennese interpretations of art nouveau style, with cupolas, spires, arches, and extravagant curlicues.

Family life. While the *zadruga*, or extended families, remained common to other Yugoslavs until recent years, among Slovenes it was less widespread. Greater social mobility and better educational and commercial opportunities made it easier for young people to start their own families. The general prosperity allowed farming to be possible without the large family units of other areas. Even so, the size of families has decreased in recent years, as traditional agricultural ways of life are abandoned for the better wages available in towns and cities. Still, traditional ways reassert themselves on festive occasions when the family gathers.

Recreation. Slovenes have long been enthusiastic about outdoor sports. Hiking, mountaineering, fishing, and hunting are popular pastimes among Slovenes as well as major tourist attractions. More recently, extensive biking paths have been constructed. Skiing is the national sport, however. Aside from the Scandinavians, the Slovenes are the only people to have their own word—*smucka*—for the activity.

For More Information

Cuddon, J. A. *The Companion Guide to Jugoslavia.* Englewood Cliffs, New Jersey: Prentice-Hall, 1984.

Danforth, Kenneth C. "Yugoslavia: A House Much Divided," *National Geographic*, August 1990, pp. 92–123.

Nyrop, Richard F. *Yugoslavia: A Country Study*. Washington DC: Department of the Army, 1982.

Singleton, Fred. *A Short History of the Yugoslav Peoples*. Cambridge, England: Cambridge University Press, 1985.

Viorst, Milton. "A Reporter at Large: The Yugoslav Idea." *New Yorker*, March 18, 1991, pp. 58–79.

TAJIKS
(ta jeeks′)

People of the Hindu Kush Mountains of the Soviet Union and Afghanistan.

Population: 2,850,000 (in Tajikistan: 1990 estimate). Fifty-five and eight tenths percent of the people of Tajikistan are Tajiks, while the rest are of Uzbek, Russian, and other descent. There is no accurate estimate of the number of Tajiks in other countries.
Location: Tajikistan, Afghanistan, Pakistan, China.
Language: Tajik (a Persian dialect).

Geographical Setting

Sweeping across northern Afghanistan and into China, the great Hindu Kush Mountains branch into the small area that was the Tajik Soviet Socialist Republic. Mountain peaks, as high as 24,000 feet, are separated by river valleys that make about 5 percent of the land suitable for agriculture. The altitudes make winters severe in this region except in the low valleys. Here the temperature is among the most moderate in Asia. It is through these valleys that the Tajik migrated from Iran across the northern side of the mountain range into what is now a Tajik member of the Commonwealth Independent of States (made up of former USSR republics). This article deals mostly with the Tajiks in Tajikistan.

Historical Background

Afghanistan. More than 50 percent of Tajiks today live in Afghanistan, a country made up of peoples of various origins. Positioned between the Middle East, Europe, and India, Afghanistan has been

Tajiks

Caspian Sea
Kazakhstan
Uzbekistan
Turkmenistan
Kyrgyzstan
Tajikistan
Afghanistan

Tajiks in Tajikistan

Tajiks in Afghanistan and Kyrgyzstan

Tajiks are Muslim people of the high mountain valleys of Tajikistan and Afghanistan.

a crossroads for people throughout history. Tajiks, who may have been the land's original inhabitants, trace their ancestry to Persia, and to a time as long ago as 3000 B.C. Today, Tajiks represent the largest ethnic group in Afghanistan, yet they are not as influential as the less-numerous Pathans.

Tajikistan. Outside of Afghanistan, most of the remaining Tajik population is distributed througout the south of the former Soviet Union. In the 1960s, Tajiks made up about half the population of Soviet Tajikistan. Uzbeks, a people who once governed the Tajiks, made up the next greatest population. At one time the Tajiks were the majority population in the area, and very early in their history began to develop the irrigation systems that are now used for irrigating cotton crops. Today the Uzbeks greatly outnumber the Tajiks in this region, and recent events have caused some dispersal of the Tajiks into other areas of Asia.

Arabs, Mongols, and Pushtun. Throughout their history the Tajik have been subject to invasions and conquest by neighboring peoples—

the Arabs in the seventh century, the Mongols in the thirteenth century, and the Russians in the nineteenth century. The 3,100,000 Tajiks who now live in the republics of the former Soviet Union gained their own Tajik Soviet Socialist Republic and became part of the Soviet Union in 1929.

Meanwhile in Afghanistan, about 3,500,000 Tajiks were ruled by kings of the Pushtun people until 1973. In 1973 King Zahir Shah was deposed, the Republic of Afghanistan was created, and minority peoples such as the Tajik had hopes for participation in government. Instead a dictatorship was established under the leadership of Lieutenant General Muhammad Daud. This led to a coup d'etat in 1978 when the Democratic Republic of Afghanistan was created. Participants of the coup were members of Khalzi (Masses) Party, which was greatly concerned with the needs of the Pushtun people but had little regard for the Tajiks. Therefore, the Tajiks joined anti-government forces when a civil war erupted. With a friendly government threatened, the Soviets invaded Afghanistan and the Tajik resisted with some success. Four major Soviet offenses were directed toward gaining control of the Tajik in the Penshwar Valley, beginning in 1983. Even though the Soviet-backed government used bombing, shelling, and direct attack, their efforts were unsuccessful. Against these forces, the rebel tactics were to destroy communications and government installations. Recently, some Tajik and other minorities have united with other ethnic groups in their resistance to government forces. Many others have fled to Pakistan.

About two and a half million Tajiks form the majority of people in Tajikistan, where they were encouraged, as citizens of one the former Union of Soviet Socialist Republics, to become settled farmers and ranchers and to develop an industrial base.

Culture

Under Communism, the Tajik economy improved greatly, and the traditional lifestyles were changed. At one time, Tajiks were farmers, herders, and traders on the rivers of western Asia. Many were migrants, driving their cattle north in winter and south in summer to take advantage of mountain- and steppe-grazing. But Soviet management encouraged more sedentary occupations. The Tajiks became settled farmers and cattlemen, while many of them moved to the growing cities to find work in such industries as silk production. One of the world's largest silk mills is in the city of Khodzhent (Lenin-abad).

Economy. In addition to cotton and grapes grown for domestic and trade uses, Tajikistan under the Soviet Union developed its natural resources to build a manufacturing industry. Coal, petroleum, and natural gas were discovered and developed. With these energy sources, textile industries, and plants for the manufacture of a wide range of products including refrigerators, copper wire, and technical lighting equipment were developed. Still, the major occupation of Tajiks is raising sheep, goats, cattle, hogs, cotton, potatoes, and grapes.

A Tajik woman dressed in an old costume. *From the Library of Congress.*

Food, clothing, and shelter. The Tajik of Afghanistan live in mountainous country where they herd and farm on land owned by individuals or jointly held by extended families. The Tajik of the former USSR work on collective farms. One of the principal farm products is cotton, which the farmers call "white gold" because of the price it brings. Their main food crops are wheat, barley, corn, and potatoes. Other vegetables and fruits that contribute to the daily diet are melons, mulberries, grapes, and peas. Bread is baked from any crop that can be ground into flour, including peas and mulberries. Rice dishes are commonly served with *kotrma* (stew) and *kebab* (cubed or ground meat roasted on skewers over an open fire). Dairy foods include milk, yogurt, cheese, and *grut* (curd balls). Fish and wild fowl add protein to the diet, as do walnuts and almonds.

The herders raise sheep, goats, and camels; young men move with the herds in pursuit of the best grazing meadows, living in felt-covered tents (the *yurt* or *chapari*) during seasons of migration. Horses are their methods of transport and donkeys are their beasts of burden.

Permanent Tajik settlements are often clustered communities on rocky land. Tajik homes are low, rectangular dwellings commonly made of unbaked mudbricks and pressed mud on a stone foundation. Roofs are flat and constructed with earth and twigs laid upon mat-covered beams. Other Tajik homes are domed, beehive-shaped structures, while some built at the highest elevations are multi-storied structures made entirely of stone.

Traditional dress includes long-tailed cotton shirts that button at the right shoulder and wide-waisted pantaloons. Old automobile tires are used to make sandals; embroidered shoes or boots are also worn. Those in the country wear cylinder-shaped caps on their heads, covered by the *chader*, a head shawl they place between the teeth to partly cover their faces if strangers approach. Women in Afghan cities often wear the traditional *chadry*, a sacklike veil that reaches from head to toe and has an open-face mask for limited vision. The Soviets urged women to "throw off the veil." The first women to do so were murdered by their relatives because of the shame an unveiled woman brought upon the family, but today few veils are seen among the Tajiks of the former Soviet Union.

Family life. The agricultural Tajik in Tajikistan are a settled people who migrated to highlands to reap wheat and cotton, and raise sheep, goats, and cattle. Some move to towns after the agricultural season to seek work associated with recently developed resources such as zinc, gold, mercury, oil, and gas. These new forms of employment are changing the traditional family unit as men take wives away from the villages into towns. Money made from the employment produces other changes in Tajik life as well. The people now purchase commodities such as bicycles, radios, trucks, and Western-style clothing.

Women and education. The domain of Tajik women continues to be restricted. Although rural women work in the fields, both they and Tajik women in the city are largely absent from public life. In Afghanistan authorities have had little success in bringing Tajik woman into schools, which adds to a general illiteracy among the Tajik of Afghanistan. There, the ability to read and write is limited to about ten percent of the population; however, these skills have been acquired by almost all of the Tajik in Tajikistan. With a total population of less than 6,000,000 (less than half Tajik, and less than half of the total number of Tajiks in the world), Tajikistan has about 1,200,000 students in secondary schools. This emphasis on education is reflected in the reading habits of the Tajiks. More than 1,200,000 newspapers are read daily and more than 9,000,000 magazines are circulated each year.

Religion. Religious training occurs in mosques that are found in most communities. The Tajik are Muslims and some claim to have descend from the founder of the religion, Muhammad. They also worship at shrines dedicated to saints, although this is forbidden by the Muslim religion. Some continue to believe in witchcraft despite the Communist government discouraging this and all other forms of religious worship.

Literature. The Tajiks have a great tradition of folklore. Their first literature, written in the Sogodian language, was produced when they were governed by the Uzbeks. Later, Arabs took control of the Tajiks and the literature disappeared. When the Arabs were driven out, a new literature began in the Middle Ages and an encyclopedia was produced by Abu Ali Ibn Sina. Under Soviet influence, Tajik literature was confined to writings about social realism as viewed by the government in Moscow. The interest in writing and reading is satisfied largely by the publication of sixty-six newspapers in the Tajik language, and in the great quantities of periodicals printed in Tajikistan.

Government. The traditional political group among the Tajik is the *majlis,* or village council. The oldest males of the important families in the community are members of a council that makes decisions for the entire community. In modern-day Afghanistan, workers' unions and political parties have developed and now compete with the majlis organization for final authority in the making of such decisions. In the Tajik Soviet Socialist Republic, politics were dominated by the Tajik Communist party. Recognizing their common interests with other Muslim states and with Russia, the people of Tajikistan formed their own republic after the breakup of the Soviet Union but soon joined the economic union of the Commonwealth of Independent States.

For More Information

Gregory, James S. *Russian Land, Soviet People.* New York: Pegasus Press, 1968.

Salinsky, Audrey. *Central Asia Émigrés to Afghanistan.* 1979.

Stewart, John Massey. *Across the Russias.* Chicago: Rand McNally and Company, 1969.

TUNGUS

(tung' us)

Farmers and reindeer herders of the Siberian plains.

Population: Variously estimated from 30,000 to 135,000 (1991).
Location: Russia, China, Mongolian People's Republic.
Languages: Russian, Tungusic.

Small groups of Tungus people hunt and herd animals in the vast
region from the Ural Mountains to the Pacific Ocean.

Geographical Setting

The Tungus have formed various groups spread throughout Siberia from the Yenisey River to the Pacific Ocean and as far south and east as Korea. This is a highly varied land, ranging from desert edge (the Gobi Desert in the southwest), to coniferous forest, to steppe, and in the far north, tundra. In the southeast there are mountain ranges—the Great Khingan, and farther west, Yablonovyi Khrebet. North of the Gobi Desert, the Mongolian plateau rises then drops into Lake Baikal. Winter temperatures are very severe in the northern region of the Tungus, reaching below -20 degrees Fahrenheit in winter, then rising to the 60-degree range in the warmest months. The few people who live in this area range over a huge expanse of mostly uninviting land. Throughout their known history, the people have survived by hunting fur animals of the north.

Historical Background

There are a number of small ethnic groups spread through the wide expanse of northern Asia. Most of them subsist through hunting land mammals and reindeer herding, or by searching for the large sea mammals that live along the coasts. Between the Ob and Irtysh basins about 25,000 members of the Khanty and Mansi peoples settled in log cabins. Between the Ob and Yenisey rivers there are people known as Sel'kups and Kets. The more than 1,000 Kets speak a language that is unrelated to any nearby languages. Many tribal groups live in Siberia—Negidals, Nanays, Ul'chis, Udeghes, Oraches, Oroks, and Nivkhs (another group with its own unique language). Far north, Nenets, Nganasans, Dolgans, and Yakuts have adapted to the harsh cold and permanent ice conditions, and have become skilled hunters. Spread from the Yenisey River to the Pacific Ocean in the steppe and forest of the lower part of northern Asia are the Evenki and Even. Together these two peoples make up the Tungus and are among the largest numbers of "reindeer people."

These once nomadic peoples who herded their reindeer from one grazing place to another, hunted the forests, and fished the rivers of northern Asia are represented in this book by the Tungus.

Origin. Although little is known about the origin of this nomadic people living in the extreme north of Russia and China, the Tungus appear to have originated in the Amur River basin in eastern Siberia near the border with China. Many still consider this river as their own. Of Mongolian descent, these nomadic people first roamed what is now eastern Siberia. There the Chinese called them *Tung-hu* (which some researchers speculate derives from the Turkic word for hog herders) and the Samoyedes who shared the land referred to them as "younger brothers." Driven by Mongols on one side and Russians on the other, they spread north across Siberia to live by hunting and fur trading. On the Pacific coast, they are known as Lamuts; in Korea as the Tazi. The most well-known group in Siberia are the Evenki, famous reindeer herders.

The "reindeer people." Early visitors to the north country described the people there as cheerful, persevering, open-hearted, trustworthy, and self-reliant. They also seem to have been very adaptable to new situations. Russian explorers classified them according to the animals they used (reindeer, horses, cattle, or dogs), and according to the place they lived (steppe or forest). One group made famous by popular writing has been the Evenki (today, this group numbers about half of all Tungus), including hunters and fur-traders who used reindeer as pack animals and for riding. Other groups herded reindeer for food.

Leaving no written records, the Tungus continued their reindeer-herding life even after Russian Cossacks (cavalrymen) overran their Siberian homeland in the 1600s. The Cossacks demanded payment of tributes; the Tungus resisted and some of them migrated to Manchuria, where they established small, separated settlements.

Missionaries. Between 1600 and 1700, Christian missionaries found the Tungus to be a people with no central government and with religious beliefs entrenched in animism and shamanism. The efforts of the missionaries did little to change the Tungus way of life; the Tungus continued to be herding and fur-trading nomads.

The Soviet Union. Early Russian visitors to the region of the Tungus used the people as fur hunters, sometimes treating them cruelly. It was not until 1917 that Russia organized the Tungus under Soviet rule and began to disrupt old clan establishments by introducing fur farming. Under the Soviet Union's policy of "denomadization" in the 1970s, the Tungus were encouraged to build wood-frame homes, form villages, and establish fur farms. The result was a more stationary lifestyle since Tungus herds were confined to collective farms.

Life for the people of vast northeastern Russia was further complicated when the Soviet Union built rail lines across the southern levels of its land to reach ports on the Pacific. Russians from the west settled along these lines and established industrial cities in the far east. Oil was discovered and developed along the middle of the Ob River, and hydroelectric plants were established to supply energy for the growing industry. All these actions cut into the land of the earlier inhabitants and interfered with their nomadic way of life. Some Evenki were displaced from their land and a few abandoned their old way of life to work in the oil fields. Other small groups were likewise in danger of being absorbed into the growing Russian society, with a resulting loss of their lifestyles and their own languages.

Culture Today

Family life. Before twentieth-century Russian influence, the Tungus did not read or write. They lived in scattered camps of bark-covered houses or tents during summer migrations and in log cabins during the winter. The strongest governmental unit was the family and the clan. Tungus standards of personal conduct and the vast land in which they roamed made the Tungus life peaceful, except for clan and tribal wars over such issues as kidnapped women or stolen reindeer. The women made clothes from animal skins, which they embroidered with beads. Other responsibilities for women included packing and unpacking on the travels, looking after children, curing furs, and cooking. Men and boys hunted, fished, fought when necessary, and built boats of bark and sledges. Men, too, dressed warmly in animal-skin trousers and parkas.

Food, clothing, and shelter. Until Russian settlers began to share their land, the Tungus were dependent on the taiga (the subarctic forests) for all their needs. They hunted animals for fur and food, fished the rivers with nets and with hooks made from wood or metal, and gathered berries for food wherever it was possible. The Russians introduced bread to the Tungus early in their encounters, but it did not become a staple food until these people were persuaded to settle permanently on one living site.

A favorite food was bear meat, and Tungus legends show that bears were held in special esteem. One legend tells of a bear and a boy as children of the same mother. The two grew to contend with one another and the boy won the struggles. The legend illustrates the

A Tungus bark canoe. *Courtesy of the National Anthropological Archive of the Smithsonian Institution.*

respect that bears have among the Tungus. Special rituals were once related to killing a bear, preparing its meat for eating, and disposing of the bear's head. Bear and other meats are prepared by boiling them or by roasting.

The furs of bear, reindeer, and other large mammals were fashioned into clothing; seal and otter skins were used by the Tungus who lived near the ocean. Their clothing included long robes for the women, and for men, trousers and boots. Sometimes the boots were short and were topped by leggings (leather leg wrappings that reached to the knee).

The forest also provided materials for houses. Bark was collected from the trees and steamed so that it could be shaped into panels for tent homes. By the nineteenth century, some Tungus who were in contact with sheep and goat herders near Lake Baikal had begun to substitute cloth tents. Logs were used for home-building in the more settled villages.

Social organization. The social and political organization was the clan, which decided marriages, settled disputes, and enforced regulations. Each clan was associated with a particular river and land area; the nomadism of the Tungus was patterned to conform to this clan territory. A clan was governed by the heads of households, men or women, and had no other government than this common decision-making body, except for the influence of the shaman. When threatened by another clan or planning war themselves, the people of a clan elected a leader for the incident on the basis of strength.

Social patterns were closely governed by the clan. Individual behavior guided by clan principles was correct and reserved toward visitors. The clan members were taught to dislike flattery, oppose

Tungus families near the village of Ola, deep in eastern Russia.
Courtesy of the National Anthropological Archive of the Smithsonian Institution.

lying, and love beauty. They were also taught personal pride and pride in their clan. Women who married into a clan were not accepted as members of the clan; rather they were supposed to remain loyal to their birth clan. Women were taught to pride themselves in good housekeeping, fine handiwork, and good children.

Forest animals. As with other northern tribes, the Tungus felt a strong kinship with the land and with the animals of the north. As Russians, Chinese, and others discovered the wealth of fur to be had in this region, the Tungus were persuaded—sometimes forced—to serve as more diligent hunters. But this was in opposition to long-held beliefs. The north people generally believed in hunting and fishing only when necessary for food. Sometimes they stopped the hunt when enough food had been secured, often when the food supply was adequate only for a single day. The exception to this rule of protection for their animal neighbors was the wolf. The Tungus consider the wolf a symbol of evil, and destroy wolves wherever they are seen.

Religion. The religion of the Tungus is shamanistic. The chief god, Boa, created many other gods to watch over the natural objects and events important to Tungus life. Both feared and revered, the shaman was a dominant force who was thought to be able to call on gods and spirits for assistance in times of need. Tungus clothing included necklaces of animal teeth and claws worn as amulets and thought to have special powers.

The religion of the Tungus holds the dead in high esteem. Burials are important events among some Tungus, with tree-burial reserved for the most deserving. In this form of burial, the dead is placed on a platform built in a tree. A frequent custom in some places in Asia, among the Tungus this practice is reserved for only those people of importance who have died in the prime of life.

Christian missionaries, accompanied by soldiers and traders, encouraged the Tungus to adopt Christianity, and the accommodating Tungus did so. However, their adjustment to Christianity was to incorporate Christian gods and religious figures into their own shamanistic beliefs. An image of a saint, for example, might be added to the ornamentation of the tools of the shaman.

Recreation. Drinking wine was once a recreation among the Tungus. Children were allowed occasional drinks of the liquid, but freedom to buy or trade for drinks was, among some Tungus, reserved for people over 30, and these people did not drink wine while working or hunting. Tungus enjoy card playing, wrestling in various forms, stone-tossing games, and ring dancing. But the most universal recreation is gathering in the evening for conversation or storytelling.

Reindeer people. The most-publicized of the Tungus groups is the Evenki. Evenki people lived by the reindeer, herding these animals like cattle, using the hides to make tents and clothing, and gathering the milk and meat for food. Reindeer were trained as pack animals to aid in the perpetual movement of the nomadic people. When on the move or hunting, the Tungus ride reindeer as others ride horses.

Among the Evenki, a distinction based on wealth was imposed upon the clan structure. Wealthy owners of large reindeer herds ruled over the poorer village residents. When reindeer were needed for travel or warfare, poor neighbors applied to the richer ones to borrow or purchase the needed reindeer. The debts were paid after the need had subsided, but seldom did the poor succeed in completely paying off a debt. Poor Evenki were, therefore, often indebted and subservient to the rich reindeer breeders.

Change in the Soviet Union. In the 1920s, Russia began a literary program designed to enable the Tungus to read and listen to Russian philosophy. The Tungus responded by adapting well to Russian governmental policy and to fur farming as an alternative to trapping. They traded their bark houses or reindeer-skin tents for square, Russian-style wooden houses and outwardly abandoned shamanism when the USSR outlawed the practice. Today, as radio, electricity, motorized boats, and rail transport have increased their communication with other peoples, the Tungus have become successful fur and leather suppliers. Tungus children now attend schools, and Tungus villages are governed as other towns and villages in the former Soviet Union. In the center of Russia, the Evenkski Oblast (self-governing district) houses settled Tungus and provides them with 30 schools and a hospital.

For More Information

Friend, Morton. *The Vanishing Tungus: The Story of a Remarkable Reindeer People.* New York: Dial Press, 1973.

Maclean, Fitzroy. *Portrait of the Soviet Union.* London: Weidenfeld and Nicholson, 1988.

Shirokogoroff, S. M. *Social Organization of the Northern Tungus.* Shanghai: Commercial Press Company, 1980.

TURKMEN
(turk′ men)

Turkic people of Turkmenistan.

Population: 2,477,000 (1990 estimate).
Location: Turkmenistan, the former Turkmen Soviet Socialist Republic.
Languages: Turkmenian, Russian.

Geographical Setting

Bounded by Kazakhstan, Uzbekistan, Iran, and Afghanistan, the land of the Turkmen is mostly a vast desert, the Kara-Kum. This arid region covers four-fifths of the country. Along its eastern border, the Amu Darya separates Turkmenistan from Uzbekistan and to the south an extension of the Elbruz Mountains, the Kopet-Dag, separate the country from Iran and Afghanistan. The Murgab River runs from the southern mountains a short distance toward the desert in south-central Turkmenistan. The farmers of the country depend on irrigation systems from this river and the Amu Darya, and from several oases around the edge of the desert. Salt flats dot the coast of the Caspian Sea which, on the edge of Turkmenistan, is 86 feet below the level of the oceans. Cold winters and very hot summers prevail in the land of the Turkmen.

Historical Background

In the dynasty of the Seljuk Turks, some Turkic people appeared about the eleventh century as nomads wandering the desert and establishing temporary quarters near the rivers or at oases around the Kara-Kum. These people herded sheep, goats, and camels and de-

Turkmen

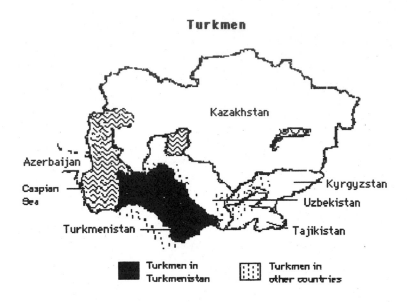

Turkmen are nomadic people who live in Turkmenistan, Uzbekistan, Kyrgyzstan, and Tajikistan.

pended on their animals for food and transportation. Living in small tribes, they were never organized into a political unit of their own, and in this inhospitable land, they were given little attention by others. At various times, the Turkmen found their land claimed by the governments of Persia, Khiva, and Bakhara, but there was no real government of the region until Russia began to take an interest in the country in 1877.

Russia. In that year, Russians began a long process of assimilating the Turkmen by capturing the oasis village of Kyzyl Arvat, inland from the Caspian Sea, in the south of the country. Advancing into Turkmen territory, the Russians next tried to capture the ancient fortress of Geok Tepe. At first (in 1879) rebuffed, the Russians finally took the fortress in 1881, a victory in which 8,000 Turkmen were killed. In that same year, Russia captured the oasis town of Ashkhabad, and by 1884 had moved down the Murgab River to occupy the town of Merv (Mary). That village was again the subject of invasion

Once Turkmenistan was part of the grand empire of Tamer. This richly ornamented building, now abandoned, still symbolizes the architectural ability of the past. *From the Library of Congress.*

in 1918 when Turkey invaded Afghanistan and moved north to take Merv in order to thwart a possible German thrust into Turkmenistan. With the Turks withdrawn, the land reverted to Russian dominance.

The Soviet Union. Turkmen leaders were active in a 1919 movement to unite the Uzbeks, Tajiks, Kazakhs, and Kyrgyz into a semblance of the old empire of Timur (Tamerlaine), and to establish it as a single Muslim state within the budding Soviet Union. Joseph Stalin, fearing that this state would eventually want to become independent of the Union, stalled the decision while carefully building separate economies and encouraging separate cultures. By 1924, he was able to establish five separate republics among the Muslim peoples of the south part of the Soviet Union.

Large irrigation projects were undertaken in what is now Turkmenistan, and the people were encouraged to become sedentary. In addition, deposits of petroleum, natural gas, sulphur, and mineral salts allowed for the establishment of industries in the river valleys and at the oases.

Independence. Long a reluctant member of the Soviet Union, Turkmenistan took an early advantage of the economic problems developing in the Union. In August, 1990, the Turkmen Supreme Soviet declared their state to be a sovereign entity and a zone free of nuclear, chemical, and bacteriological tools of war. In October of that year, the leaders declared their intention to change the government by establishing the position of president. In 1991, with the breakup of the Soviet Union, Turkmenistan became an independent country. However, its economic growth had been, since the 1920s, firmly tied to the other Union republics. To keep their economic ties, Turkmenistan was an early advocate of forming a Commonwealth of Independent States.

Culture Today

World War I was a watershed in the lives of the Turkmen. Before that time, they had wandered from oasis to oasis and up and down the river valleys seeking pasture for their sheep, goats, cattle, camels, and horses. They lived mostly in tents that could be moved easily from one place to another, and they had no government beyond the clan or tribe with which they traveled. The manipulation of the Turkmen following World War I is reflected in their language.

Language. The period following World War I was one of tension between Russia and Turkey. The people of Turkey wrote using the Arabic alphabet, and the Russians used the Cyrillic alphabet. From 1915 to 1928, Joseph Stalin, in order to isolate the Turkmen from Turkish influence or from their preference to unite with other Muslims in a single Soviet state, encouraged the Turkmen to change from an Arabic alphabet to a Latin one. Since 99 percent of the Turkmen were illiterate at the time, this was not a difficult change. But in 1928, Ataturk (father of modern-day Turkey) turned toward the West and, in doing so, changed the Turkish written language to the use of the Latin alphabet. As tensions continued between Turkey and Russia, Stalin began to reconsider his previous decision. With the Muslim peoples of the south firmly separated into five political units, his main concern became Turkmen isolation from Turkey. From 1938 to 1940 schools were established for the now settling Turkmen in which Russian was the official language, and in which Turkmenian was taught using the Cyrillic alphabet of Russia.

Education and literature. Under the Soviet Union, more than 1,900 schools were constructed in Turkmenistan, as well as 9 institutions of higher learning. By 1985, more that 800,000 students were taking advantage of these schools.

There is little written literature directly attributed to the nomadic Turkmen of the past. Those few who could read and write, probably wrote in Arabic—the official language of the Muslim religion. However, Turkmen rapidly learned reading and writing in the Soviet-built schools. Today, the country has a publication dedicated to literature and art, and more than 50 newspapers and 14 journals and magazines are printed in the Turkmenian language. Three Turkmenistan publishing houses print books about science, politics, and fiction.

Housing. The Soviet Union encouraged the nomadic Turkmen to settle in villages and towns, and to confine their herds to lands near these villages. They undertook irrigation systems to encourage this settling and to develop the agricultural potential of the land. Russian farmers and industrialists (now about one-eighth of the population) were brought in to establish farms and to build industries around the newly developed petroleum and mineral resources. Concrete housing units were erected in the towns of the river valleys and in the inhabited oases such as Ashkhabad. In 1992, most Turkmen are now settled on irrigated farms or in towns and villages.

Health. The nomadic Turkmen had few medical facilities before joining the Soviet Union. The Soviets erected hospitals and trained medical personnel to operate them in many of the towns and cities. However, water was still scarce in most of the country. When the Turkmen broke from the Union in 1990, they found themselves with a medical situation in which 60 percent of the hospital maternity wards were without hot water, 40 percent without any running water, and two-thirds without adequate sewer facilities.

Religion. As with other once-nomadic people in the south of the former Soviet Union, the Turkmen are Muslims following their own plan within the Shi'ite sect of the faith.

Economy. Before World War I, Turkmen were dependent on their animals for food, clothing, transportion, and shelter. This lifestyle was discouraged after the war, as the Soviets turned their attention to the nearly one-third of the land that could be made arable by developing irrigation systems. Between 1915 and 1945 the Soviet Union doubled the land dedicated to growing cotton in the Turkmen Soviet Socialist Republic. The number of cattle, goats, sheep, and horses kept by Turkmen fell to one-fourth the pre-World War I numbers as the people turned to raising cotton, grains, grapes, and vegetables.

In addition, the Soviet Union encouraged the development of the mineral resources of the country. Many of the Turkmen found themselves living in towns and villages established for workers in the oil industry and in processing other minerals. By 1990, these workers were producing nearly 6,000,000 tons of oil yearly along with more than 200,000 tons of mineral fertilizers, and 5,500,000 tons of sulphur. Electrical generating facilities had been built to provide energy for these new industries. However, the percentage of Turkmen working in these industries is not comparable to the percentage of Turkmenistan Russians working in them, since many Turkmen prefer to raise crops and tend their smaller herds of animals.

For More Information

Gregory, James S. *Russian Land, Soviet People.* New York: Pegasus Press, 1968.

The Europa World Yearbook, 1991. London: Europa Publications Ltd., 1991.

Stewart, John Massey. *Across the Russias.* Chicago: Rand McNally and Company, 1969.

UKRAINIANS
(you kray' nee uns)

Slavic and Mongol people who first settled under a Viking prince
of Kiev in present-day Ukraine.

Population: 36,488,950 (in Ukraine, 1989 census).
Location: Ukraine in Eastern Europe, bordered by Byelarus, Russia,
Romania, Poland, and Czechoslovakia.
Language: Ukrainian.

Geographical Setting

Ukraine's varied terrain includes the Carpathian Mountains on the
southwest border, swampy western wetlands, and vast grassy plains
in the south and east. Through Kiev, the ancient capital, the historic
Dnieper River flows south to the Black Sea. The swampy Dnieper
lowland gives way in the east to the steppes, which extend deep into
Russia. As the river winds south, it cuts through the *chernozem*, or
black earth, of the southern steppe. This band of rich, fertile land
also stretches east into Russia proper. Though much Ukrainian land
is suitable for farming, it is for the wheat grown in the chernozem
that the country was called the breadbasket of the Soviet Union.

Ukraine's climate, moderated by its coastal setting, is more temperate than many other parts of the former Soviet Union. Rainfall,
also linked to the large bodies of water bordering the land, is similarly
greater than elsewhere. The Black Sea coast attracted Soviet vacationers; the Crimean peninsula held the dachas, or vacation homes,
of the Soviet political leaders.

This is the home of the Ukrainians. However, the need for agricultural expertise in other parts of the Soviet Union resulted in the
migration of thousands of Ukrainians to other parts of the near East,

Ukrainians

Ukrainians were sent to establish farms in many parts of the former Soviet Union (for example, thousands were sent to Uzbekistan). Still, more than 50,000,000 live in or near Ukraine.

while the need for industrial workers in Ukraine has resulted in the relocation of more than ten million Russians to Ukraine.

Historical Background

Origin. The Ukrainians and Russians of today can both trace their origins to a group known as Rus that formed a political organization in what is now the Ukraine in the eighth century A.D. Governmental headquarters were centered in Kiev. The Rus were a division of the Slavic people who began moving into southern Russia from the northern Carpathian Mountains as early as the 400s. By the 800s, they had established a network of trading communities, taking advantage of a vast river system through which traders ranged from the Baltic to the Black seas. In one of these communities, the people appealed to nearby Vikings for leadership and protection from hostile nomads. The Viking prince Rurik founded the first Russian ruling house at Novgorod. After his death in 879, his successor, Oleg, moved south, capturing the prosperous Slavic city of Kiev and making it his capital. Kiev led the group of cities which the Vikings gave the name "Rus." Traders of Kievan Rus transported furs, honey, and slaves along the Dnieper River to the Black Sea and from there to the Greek city of Constantinople, or Byzantium, where these goods were traded for gold, silk, wine, and spices.

Orthodox Christianity. More than the greatest trading hub of its day, Byzantium was also the seat of the Byzantine Empire, and the center of Orthodox Christianity. Its ancient culture attracted early Rus leaders, and in 988, Prince Vladimir married the emperor's sister, Anna, and converted to Greek, or Orthodox, Christianity. Vladimir destroyed the old pagan idols of the Rus—hurling them into the Dnieper River according to one story—and forced his subjects to embrace the new religion. From then on, Christianity would be a central feature of Ukrainian and Russian life.

Flowering of Kiev. Byzantine cultural influence also shaped Kievan civilization. For the first time, the Rus had an alphabet, modified from Greek by two Byzantine monks, Cyril and Methodius. With small changes, this "Cyrillic" alphabet is still used today. Kiev soon boasted churches to match the most beautiful in Constantinople; the distinctive "onion" domes of Russian Orthodox Churches reflect Rus adaptation of Byzantine architecture. Under Vladimir (died 1015) and his son Yaroslav, Kiev became a part of Christian Europe, a wealthy state with marriage links to France, Norway, England, and Hungary, as well as to the Byzantine royal house.

Tatar invasion. In the 1100s the Kievan state began to break up under a series of invasions by nomadic tribes. The people split into three branches. Older cities in the north asserted their independence and refugees from the invasions founded new cities in the forests of the northeast. In the 1200s, Asiatic horsemen, Tatars (a Mongol group) invaded the land of the Rus. Led by Genghis Khan and his successors, the vast Tatar armies advanced as far as Vienna in Austria. Eventually the Tatars established an empire on the steppes (grasslands) south and east of Ukraine. Kiev, in the Ukraine, already declining, was overrun in 1240. Much of the land of southern Rus was emptied of people, particularly the steppes in eastern Ukraine. Those who remained would mix with newcomers of succeeding generations to become the Ukrainians.

Foreign rule. For most of the next seven and a half centuries, Ukrainian land was under the control of various neighboring powers. In the north, the Grand Duchy of Lithuania occupied present-day Lithuania and Byelarus in the 1300s to form a powerful state that absorbed much Ukrainian territory. Southwestern Ukraine fell under Polish political and cultural domination. The Poles expanded their rule under a system of lords who chose the ruler of Poland from among themselves, allowing them to otherwise rule their serfdoms independently. When the lords became oppressive, some of the peasants moved farther southeast. The result was a Ukrainian people who influenced and were greatly influenced by both their Russian and Polish neighbors.

Cossacks. As Poland and Lithuania grew together in the 1400s and eventually united (1569), increasing numbers of serfs (peasants virtually owned by their landlords) rebelled against their Polish masters and fled east. There, in order to survive, they adopted the rough-and-ready life of the Tatar horsemen. By the 1500s, they had established a camp on the eastern bank of the southern Dnieper River. It was called the Zaporozhian Sech, or "clearing on the rapids." Later, other similar groups arose in southern Russia. Called Cossacks, they became an important element of Ukrainian and Russian history (see COSSACKS). The independent, almost militaristic, society of the Zaporozhian Cossacks is often considered the first Ukrainian state.

Russian empire. In the mid-1600s, the Ukrainians fought against Poland, which, along with Tatars from the east, had long threatened the area. However, to protect themselves from these two threats, the Ukrainians entered into union with the increasingly powerful Russian state (1654). Three years later, the Russians began an attempt to eliminate Ukrainian nationalism. Under this pressure, the Ukraine was divided in 1667 between Poland and Russia. Some Polish Ukrainians became known as Ruthenians. From the time of the final demise of the Zaporozhian Cossacks in 1775, and aside from a brief period (1917–1920) following the Russian Revolution and the German occupation (1941–1944) during World War II, Ukraine remained part of the Union of Soviet Socialist Republics, governed from Moscow, until 1991. As the Ukrainian Soviet Socialist Republic, it was ruled from Moscow. Throughout, however, Ukrainians resisted the Russians, even as the two societies became closely entwined.

Resistance was both cultural, in the maintenance of traditional ways, and political, in the struggle for independence.

Call for independence. During the nineteenth century, there was an outpouring of literature in the Ukrainian language. Ukrainian poets and writers of the era were preoccupied with problems of social justice and national freedom. Their leading spokesperson was the poet Taras Shevchenko (1814–1861), whose verses called on fellow Ukrainians to rise against the oppression of Russian tsars. Folk songs of protest were created during this time, and by the beginning of the twentieth century, the Ukraine had produced prominent artists in drama, painting, music, and writing. Partly inspired by such nationalist literature, a movement for independence from tsarist Russia grew in the Ukraine and was active at the time of the Russian Revolution in 1917.

Civil war and Bolshevik rule. Shortly after the revolution, civil war broke out among three factions of Ukrainians. The nationalist faction favored independence and separation from Soviet rule. Others supported the Bolsheviks in Russia, and a third group called for alliances with both Germany and Poland. The Bolsheviks succeeded in establishing their regime in the area by 1919 and on December 30, 1922, the Ukrainian Soviet Socialist Republic became a member of the USSR.

The first half of the twentieth century was a time of great suffering throughout the lands under Russian control. War and hunger claimed millions of lives, as did the dictatorship of Soviet leader Joseph Stalin. Stalin has been blamed for the famine which killed at least 5,000,000 Ukrainians in 1932 and 1933. The dictator sold Ukrainian wheat abroad, starving those who had grown it. As elsewhere in the Soviet Union, intellectuals and political and religious leaders also suffered in huge numbers, being either shot or sent to Siberian prison camps. At least 5,000,000 more died in World War I, after Germany invaded Russia through the Ukraine and Byelarus. Cities and towns were devastated in the fighting and under the German occupation. A slow but steady recovery followed the war years. By the 1970s, Ukrainians produced about 25 percent of the Soviet Union's economic output, with newer industries rivaling the productivity in agriculture.

Soviet disunion. In 1991, following reforms by Soviet leader Mikhail Gorbachev, the Soviet Union entered a period of political instability.

Ukraine and the other former Soviet republics declared their independence. In October 1991, Gorbachev proposed an economic treaty among the now independent states that would establish a common currency and a single banking system. Ukraine, after Russia the most populous and wealthy of the former Soviet republics, initially rejected this proposal, fearing domination by the much larger Russia. However, recognizing the difficult adjustments to a market economy ahead, Ukrainian leaders reversed their position in November and joined other states in signing this first step toward a reorganization of the Soviet Union into a Commonwealth of Independent States.

Culture Today

Sub-societies. With a population second only to that of the Russian Soviet Republic, the Ukrainians were the largest and most influential non-Russian nationality in the former Union of Soviet Socialist Republics. The large Ukrainian society is a mixed one made up of such distinct groups as the Lemky in western Ukraine, the Boiky in the east, the Volhynians in the north, and the Hutsuls in the southwest. These groups have different roles in the economic life of the region. For example, the Boiky are practiced cattle breeders, while the Hutsuls raise livestock but are also employed as craftsmen and builders. All the groups speak and write Ukrainian, a language that is a dialect of Russian but contains many words derived from the Poles.

It was in the 1500s that the term "Ukraine" came into use. Originally a Slavic word for "borderland" or "frontier," it referred at first to the land. Soon the people used it to refer to themselves, just as the more numerous Slavic groups in the northeast had taken over the earlier term "Rus." However, the glories of Kiev remain a proud memory for the Ukrainians—and a point of contention with the Russians, who also want to claim the old civilization. Beginning in the 1800s, nationalism has been strong among Ukrainians.

Economy. Approximately 36 percent of the Ukrainian people are employed in heavy industry. The Ukraine produced 40 percent of the Soviet Union's steel, and much of its manganese and titanium ores. Ukrainian workers manufacture automobiles, tractors, and industrial equipment. The republic is the largest coal-producing area among the former Soviet republics and is a base for other energy sources, one of which is nuclear power harnessed at plants designed and encouraged by the Soviet Union.

Chernobyl. North of Kiev is the Chernobyl nuclear power plant, where there was major leakage of radiation on April 26, 1986. A reactor exploded, sending a radioactive plume three miles into the air. Within ten days, radioactive particles had been deposited over western Europe, from Scandinavia to Greece. Workers struggled to extinguish the reactor fire and care for those stricken with radiation poisoning. In all, 31 lost their lives, mostly local firemen who were exposed to extreme danger in order to prevent flames spreading to a second reactor. Eventually, over 100,000 Ukrainians and Byela-russians were evacuated from within a 30-mile radius of the plant. Unable to ever return to their homes, they were resettled by the Soviet government. The health of the people is currently being monitored to assess the effects of this leakage.

Farming. Approximately 32 percent of the Ukrainian people are ag-ricultural workers. Called the "Big Breadbasket" of the USSR, their republic produced 25 percent of the Soviet Union's grain and 60 percent of its sugar. As part of the Soviet Union the family-owned small farms were collectivized and the agricultural worker became part of a large-scale production unit that filled quotas assigned by the Communist party. Surpluses were distributed by the workers among themselves.

Food and clothing. Crops produced on collective farms include sugar beets, flax fiber, sunflower seed, potatoes, and grapes. Small private plots of land alongside their traditionally neat and well-kept home-steads supplement the people's income. Ukrainians raise cattle, pigs, sheep, goats, and poultry for meat, milk, eggs, and use wool for cloth-ing. Traditional costumes are colorful and diverse. Women wear scarves with ribbons or flowers, blouses with full sleeves, and skirts fastened with a woven belt. All these garments featured rich em-broidery in bold colors. Today, these are most often worn on special occasions. Daily attire for women consists of a simple dress or skirt and blouse, still worn with a scarf or kerchief. The clothing is mass-produced, though women still often enliven it with embroidery. Men wear mostly simple outfits: inexpensive suits in the city, patched and sturdy work clothes in the country. As elsewhere in the Soviet Union, young people in the 1970s and 1980s have taken to Western fashion, favoring jeans, casual shirts, and sneakers or, more recently, Western-style running shoes.

Temporary housing for a war-displaced Jewish farm family in the Kherson region of Ukraine. *Courtesy of the Judah L. Magnes Museum, Berkeley, California.*

Long since disappeared are the simple mud huts that once distinguished the Ukrainian peasant. Today, workers on the many Ukrainian *kolkhosy* (collective farms) live in comfortable wooden cottages or modest apartments. Reacting to the large-scale migration to the cities, authorities have offered attractive housing and better pay to agricultural workers.

Family life. Although their land has been collectivized, the Ukrainians tend to live on scattered farms rather than in villages. The family itself is a small unit compared to that of other former Soviet peoples, usually only including the husband, wife, and children. Still, the extended family gathers on special occasions such as weddings. At such times the men drink vodka, the women visit and joke, and they all sing and dance. The family is the link to tradition. Ukrainians love music: each holiday or special occasion has its own songs. The songs are accompanied by folk instruments: the *bandura*, a stringed instrument that is plucked; the *tsymbali*, also stringed, but played with a light wooden hammer; and the *sopiika*, or flute. The wife has traditionally been a participant in the decision-making process of the family, acting more as an equal to the husband than in mainstream Russian families. There has also been a greater emphasis on the individuality of family members.

Religion. Until 1946, the Ukrainians practiced two forms of Christianity. One centered around the Russian Orthodox Church while the other was a church of the Uniate faith—Orthodox but using some ceremonies of the Roman Catholic religion. However, close ties of this church with the base in Rome has long been debated by Ukrain-

Shoppers visit a fruit and vegetable stand at the Krasky Partisan collective farm in Moldova. *From the Library of Congress.*

ian authors. Uniate bishops and clergy of the Ukraine were arrested after World War II and the religion was denounced in favor of Russian Orthodoxy. Today the church of the Ukraine is controlled by the leadership in Moscow. Under communism, religion was not encouraged. As a result it is most often the elderly who attend the few churches remaining. Kiev, for example, with more than 2,000,000 inhabitants has only 22 houses of worship.

Patterns of religious affiliation reveal cultural differences among Ukrainians. Lviv is the major city in western Ukraine. In the past it has been part of Poland, which is traditionally Roman Catholic. There were large numbers of Lviv residents who claimed membership in the Ukrainian Catholic Church which, founded in 1596, combines Catholic beliefs with Orthodox rituals. Stalin abolished this church in 1939 in spite of its 4,000,000 adherents. Some people now attend Roman Catholic services in Polish. In 1989, mass demonstrations in Lviv demanded the restoration of the Ukrainian Catholic Church.

Literature. For several centuries before becoming part of the Soviet Union, Ukrainian artists, poets, and authors wrote about their own independent society. At first, most writing was inspired by Ukrainian affiliation with the eastern Orthodox religion. The first printed works appeared in the sixteenth century. One of these, *The Lament of the One Holy Apostolic Church of the East* (Meletyi Smotrytskyi, 1578–1633), was a commentary on the Ukrainian struggles with Poland and with the Roman Catholic Church.

The first Ukrainian grammar texts appeared in the seventeenth century amid the beginnings of stories based on folklore. During this period many songs and ballads were written about the Cossacks. Still, the Ukrainian written language was not uniform until Ivan P. Kotliarevskyi (1769–1838) established a literary language with his plays, poems, and operas featuring Ukrainian settings and characters.

Ukrainian literature was largely based on folklore. Folk stories were collected and published in such works as *The Rusalka of the Dniester*, an almanac. In the modern age, the greatest writer in Ukrainian was the poet Taras Shevchenko, who lived from 1814 to 1861, and drew on folklore to write about the landscape and the Ukrainians' dramatic history. An ardent nationalist, Shevchenko often returned to themes of popular revolts and the Cossack wars against the Poles. As the Ukraine grew in population and industrialization in the early 1900s, writers such as I. S. Nechui Levitskyi and Ivan Franko began to write about the working class. Social themes

Women rest and gossip on a Ukrainian farm. *Courtesy of the National Anthropological Archive of the Smithsonian Institution.*

were a strong impetus for Ukrainian writers until the Ukraine fell under Soviet domination. Then, as in other parts of the Soviet Union, writing was restricted by the government to themes of "social realism" that were acceptable to the ruling party and the strong individuality of Ukrainian writers faded. More recently, Ukrainian writers have used their work to protest against Communist Party repression. In the 1960s and 1970s, many were arrested and sent to Siberian prison camps because of their views.

The arts. Ukrainian folk art varies by region, but most areas feature the traditional expertise in embroidery. Aside from decorative clothing, the people have created beautiful tapestries (wall-hangings). Other handicrafts include weaving, wood carving, brasswork, and pottery. Most famous, however, is the Ukrainian art of Easter egg painting. Although Moscow was the center for much of the musical creation and production in the Soviet Union, organizations like the Veryovka Ukrainian Folk Choir help to preserve old songs and dances. Founded in 1943, the choir tours throughout the world.

For More Information

Armstrong, John A. *Ukrainian Nationalism*, 3rd edition. Englewood, Colorado: Ukrainian Academic Press, 1990.

Edwards, Mike. "Ukraine." *National Geographic*, May 1987, pp. 595–611.

Edwards, Mike. "Chernobyl—One Year After." *National Geographic*, May 1987, pp. 632–653.

Manning, Clarence A. *The Story of the Ukraine.* New York: Philosophical Library, 1947.

UZBEKS

(ooz' becks)

Ancestors of Arabs, Turks, and Mongols who, at different periods of history, ruled the steppe land around the Syr Darya.

Population: 13,000,000 (1988 estimate).
Location: Uzbekistan (formerly Uzbek Soviet Socialist Republic); also Afghanistan and China.
Language: Uzbek, a Turkic language.

Geographical Setting

Encompassing Uzbekistan, one of the southernmost of the former Soviet Socialist Republics and extending into neighboring countries, the land of the Uzbeks is dominated in the east by an extension of the Tien Shan Mountains of China, out of which flows the Syr Darya, a river that crosses a broad steppe to the Aral Sea. The northeastern river basin forms the fertile Fergana Valley. The river then flows east around the edge of a desert, the Kyzyl Kum, before heading toward the Aral Sea. For the most part, the land is dry and subject to extremes of temperature. However, extensive irrigation projects of ancient and recent creation have converted much of the steppe into agricultural land upon which cotton and fruits are raised, and sheep grazed for meat and wool.

Historical Background

Origin. After the Russians and the Ukrainians, the Uzbek people are the third-largest national group in the old Russian-dominated region. These Turkic people appeared in the area they now inhabit very early in history. Samarkand, now a city of 200,000 people, was a capital

Uzbeks

The Uzbeks once lived throughout the old empire of Turkestan.

of the ancient Uzbek region that was captured by Alexander the Great in the fourth century. The city was taken in the eighth century by Arabs, who were followed by Seljuk Turks and the Mongol hordes of Genghis Khan. Under Arab influences, the city and region adopted the Muslim religion and Samarkand became the burial place of the cousin of Muhammad. Farther east and north, the city of Tashkent fell under Arab influence in the twelfth century. Later, Timur Leng, a Mongol descendant of Genghis Khan, ruled his dynasty from Samarkand.

The Mongols. Led by Genghis Khan, the Golden Horde from Mongolia invaded and then dominated Russia and eastern Siberia from the thirteenth to the fifteenth century. The khan, or leader, of the Golden Horde from 1313 to 1340 was called Uzbek, and the people were most probably named after this ruler. When the horde fell apart in the fifteenth century, the Uzbek, who were nomads, migrated south. They established themselves as rulers in the area and settled into an agricultural existence while also becoming skilled in com-

This exquisite mosque of past years, its minarets crumbled, stands in Uzbekistan. *From the Library of Congress.*

merce and crafts. In the seventeenth and eighteenth centuries, the Uzbeks developed three separate khanates (kingdoms): Kokand, Bukhara, and Khiva. Other groups such as the Tungus fell under their control and the khanates grew and flourished. Bukhara and Khiva became centers of culture and agriculture.

Russians. By the eleventh century, European Russians had become aware of this large group in the southeast. However, it was not until the nineteenth century that Europeans began encroaching on territory in central Asia, and most of the Uzbeks were incorporated into the Russian empire. Over 50,000 Uzbeks fled to Afghanistan during the Russian Revolution and the subsequent civil war against the Communist regime. Those who remained were defeated by the Soviets.

Soviet rule. The Uzbek Soviet Socialist Republic was officially formed on October 27, 1924. In the great purge conducted by Joseph Stalin from 1937 to 1938 leading Uzbeks, including Prime Minister Fayzullah Khodzhayev, were accused of conspiring against the Communist regime and were executed. The prime minister's name was officially cleared after his death. Completely absorbed into the Soviet system, Uzbekistan became a center of industry, leading in silk production, and producing cotton, copper, and heavy agricultural equip-

An ancient tower stands as a symbol of past grandure in Uzbekistan. *From the Library of Congress.*

ment. Reflecting these economic ties, Uzbekistan was an early member of the new Commonwealth of Independent States.

Culture Today

Education. Education—greatly advanced in the early days of the Uzbeks, but in decline under the various rules—has been one of the most substantial benefits of Soviet domination. The literacy rate of Uzbeks in the USSR today is 99.7 percent. More than 250,000 students attend Uzbek colleges, universities, and technical institutes. Ten million copies of 140 magazines are read each year by Uzbeks, and there are 260 newspapers in the country.

Economy. The capital city, Tashkent, has become a leading educational and economic center for peoples of central Asia. Much of the heavy industry of the republic—coal, petroleum, natural gas, crude steel, woven fabric, agricultural machinery—is centered there. Most of the industry is centered in the Fergana Basin, a valley through which the Syr Darya, a river flows between high mountains. North of this basin, the river flows through a land that was once desolate desert. Now irrigation projects have opened millions of acres for great agricultural enterprises. Almost two-thirds of the Uzbek people live in rural or small-town settings, mainly on collectivized farms. Work teams on an Uzbek farm are often all-male or all-female and specialize in raising a limited number of items, such as rice and cotton. Almost 70 percent of the cotton produced by the Soviet Union in recent years was grown in the Uzbek SSR. The Uzbek Republic also contributed one-half of the output of silk cocoons in the former Soviet Union and one-third of its lamb skins. Other agricultural products are wheat, maize, potatoes, and fruits such as grapes and dried apricots. The Uzbeks of Uzbekistan raise cattle, pigs, sheep, and goats while the Uzbeks of Afghanistan also raise camels. Most of Uzbekistan's agriculture is dependent upon irrigation. The Fergana Valley is an indication of the success of Uzbek agricultural industriousness. More than 270 miles long, much of the valley is irrigated by water from a giant canal that was built in just 45 days in 1939.

Food, clothing, and shelter. The national dish in Uzbekistan is *pilau*, or boiled rice. The dish may be cooked in more than 40 different ways with meat, vegetables, salads, raisins, carrots and various condiments. Pasta dishes, too, are particularly popular with Afghan Uzbeks and include *ash* (noodles and vegetable soup), *ashak* (ravioli with meat, cheese, or leeks), and *manty* (steamed-meat dumplings). Green tea (*kokchai*) is a common beverage. Uzbek farms and gardens provide apples, pears, muskmelons, pomegranates, and watermelons. Few meals are complete without kokchai.

Foods may be purchased at shops or bazaars, where bargaining for goods is a common practice. Silversmiths and goldsmiths, leatherworkers, woodcarvers, and rugmakers also sell their wares at these bazaars. It is claimed that the artisan always leaves one flaw in his

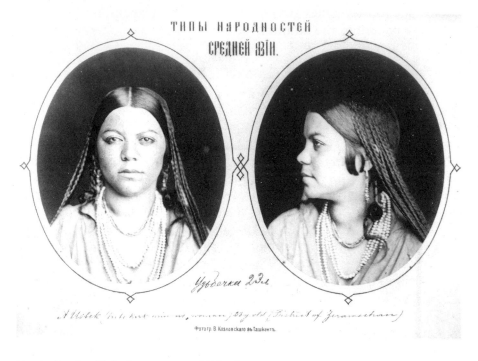

ТИПЫ НАРОДНОСТЕЙ
СРЕДНЕЙ АЗІИ.

Узбечка 23л.

A Uzbek (Sarte kirghis, woman) 23 y. old (District of Zeranschan)

Фотогр. В. Козловскаго въ Ташкентѣ.

Portrait of a Uzbek woman of 23. *Courtesy of the National Anthropological Archive of the Smithsonian Institution.*

or her work to acknowledge that only Allah (the deity of Muslims) can produce the perfect item.

Clothing may also be purchased at bazaars. Soviet Uzbeks mostly wear European-style garments. Traditional dress for men includes the *duppi*, a black skullcap with white embroidery, or a turban. The traditional outer garment is a long robe open in the front and tied together with a knotted scarf. An embroidered vest is worn underneath and the men are shod in high boots cut above the knees or low, boat-shaped, open-style shoes. The old-style dress for women includes colorfully embroidered head scarfs and short-sleeved knee-length dresses. Tie-dyed silk, Russian chintz, and striped patterns are popular among Uzbek women.

The three-generation household is typical in Uzbek families. It includes parents, unwed children, and married sons and their wives and children. Girls marry at young ages, but under Soviet law had to wait until the end of their schooling at age 17. Families normally raised four to ten children. Modern housing, however, has become less spacious, discouraging the existence of such large families.

The traditional house is a square, rectangular or domed structure made of mud bricks. The entire structure is fronted by a two-part wooden door and situated inside a walled compound. When they migrate to their summer quarters, most Uzbek seminomads live in *yurts*, or felt-covered tents with designs that face the inside. Some live in the *chapari*, which is a smaller tent built with only poles and matting. As Uzbekistan has become industrialized, many Uzbeks have moved to the cities in search of work. Here, prosperous workers build individual houses, while those less wealthy live in flats in the concrete-block housing developments erected by the government.

Religion. Most Uzbeks are Muslims. At one time the Uzbek city of Bukhara was the central Asian center of Islam. Surrounded by a wall of baked mud bricks with 11 gates, the city was enhanced by 360 mosques and many Muslim theological colleges. The city of Samarkand was also strongly Muslim and contained many blue-domed mosques and minarets.

Initially the Soviet government declared Muslim laws invalid, closed the mosques or religious centers of the Uzbek, and persecuted the clergy. In the last years of the Soviet Union, the Uzbeks were allowed to reopen their mosques and build new ones that reflected the religious independence the Uzbeks had always demanded. Along with their Islamic beliefs, the Uzbek retain previous beliefs in nature-spirits and shamans, religious leaders who converse with spirits to bring about good or evil. Curses are laid on people by sticking objects into dolls.

Recreation. Wrestling and horsemanship are popular sports among both nomadic and settled Uzbek. *Buzkashi* is a particularly popular game played between teams of whip-wielding horseback riders who aim to be first at lifting an animal carcass from a starting circle and carrying it to a goal. Other forms of recreation for the Afghan Uzbeks are launching falcons after game birds and hunting with hounds for gazelle, rabbits, and other desert animals.

The arts. The Uzbeks enjoy music—especially opera—and dance. The city of Taskhent is the center for the Alisher Navoi Bolshoi Theater of Opera and Ballet, the Khanza Uzbek Drama Theater, and the Operetta Theater.

Samarkand, the capital of the empire controlled by Timur (Tamerlane), is an old city with beautiful ancient structures. In other cities too, such as the capital, Tashkent, ancient mosques and public buildings are signs of the great architecture of the past. These old buildings are carefully preserved in Uzbekistan. Most of its active cities, however, are new. Tashkent has grown rapidly and has new wide avenues with modern buildings shadowing the old structures.

In crafts, Uzbek artisans create ceramic pieces, jewelry, gold embroideries, and carpets that are prized throughout the world.

Science. Once Samarkand, the ancient capital, was a center for the study of mathematics and astronomy. As early as the fourteenth century a great astronomical academy had been established there. The 12-yard-high sextant of the old observatory built in the time of Timur's son Ulugbek still stands as a monument to this early work. After a long dormancy, science is again a major subject of study in Uzbekistan today. The Uzbek Academy of Sciences has more than 30 active research institutes.

Government. Competition is present in both the politics and sports of the people. In Afghanistan, Uzbeks were engaged in combat against the Soviets, who invaded the country in 1979. Uzbeks also aided in preventing the Soviets from gaining any measure of control in the Afghan countryside. In the Soviet Union, they were represented by the Uzbek Communist Party. There is a continuing attitude of resentment toward the Soviet regime, but appreciation for the higher standard of living that resulted from its policies. Its economy closely tied to that of Russia, Uzbekistan in 1991 became a member of the Commonwealth of Independent States.

For More Information

Gregory, James S. *Russian Land, Soviet People.* New York: Pegasus Press, 1968.

Shalinsky, Audrey. *Central Asia Émigrés to Afghanistan.* New York: Afghanistan Council Asia Society, 1979.

Stewart, John Massey. *Across the Russias.* Chicago: Rand McNally and Company, 1969.

YUGOSLAVS
(yoo goh slahvs')

Citizens of the former nation of Yugoslavia.

Population: 24,000,000 (1990 estimate).
Location: Western Balkan peninsula and Adriatic coast.
Languages: Serbo-Croatian, Slovenian, Macedonian.

Geographical Setting

Yugoslavs

The Yugoslav entry tells of the several different peoples who came together under Tito to form the nation of Yugoslavia.

A little larger than Wyoming, Yugoslavia lies at the historic meeting place of five cultures: Germanic, Latin, Slavic, Greek and Islamic. Each culture has made its mark on the mostly Slavic people, where a turbulent past has left them with complex territorial problems. Politically, Yugoslavia since World War II has been divided into six republics. From northwest to southeast they were Slovenia, bordering Austria and Italy; Croatia, arching from the Adriatic coast deep inland; Bosnia-Herzegovina and Serbia, both landlocked in the interior; Montenegro, on the southern coast; and Macedonia, bordering Greece and Albania in the southern interior.

Geographically, Yugoslavia falls into three regions. The thin coastal strip runs along the Adriatic Sea. Rocky and mountainous, the coast has many bays and islands. The limestone rock, called *karst*, dissolves rather than erodes in water, creating spectacular caves and long underground rivers. The interior highlands comprise the Julian Alps in the northwest, the Dinaric Alps, which run parallel to the coast and inland from it, and the inland mountains of Bosnia-Herzegovina and southern Serbia. Finally, the Pannonian Plains spread from eastern Slovenia through northern Croatia and Serbia. The vast and fertile plains carry the country's two main rivers, the Sava and the Drava, which join the mighty Danube at or near Belgrade, the national capital.

Generally, climatic differences reflect these geographical divisions. The coast enjoys a Mediterranean climate, with hot, dry summers and temperate winters. In the mountains, winter snow and cold increase with altitude, while summers can be short and cool. The plains share the continental climate of central Europe, with severely cold, windy winters and hot summers.

Note: This entry focuses on Yugoslavs in general, emphasizing the relations between the country's widely differing cultural groups. For supplemental information on some of these groups, see the separate entries, **Serbs, Croats, Slovenes** and **Montenegrins**. This entry gives more background on the twentieth century, when the separate peoples first united in a Yugoslav (or "south Slav") state.

Historical Background

Two empires. Slavic tribes first arrived in present-day Yugoslavia around 600 B.C., absorbing most of the Romanized peoples who occupied the area in ancient times. The region had for centuries been part of the Roman Empire, but as the Slavs arrived the Christian Empire was breaking into two parts. In Western Europe, Roman Catholicism came to predominate, while the eastern Mediterranean was ruled by the Greek city of Byzantium. There the Greek Orthodox form of Christianity helped shape a culture very different from the West. The Slavs who arrived found themselves on the border between these uneasy neighbors. Each side wanted to win the Slavs over to its own form of Christianity. By about A.D 800, the Roman Catholic Franks had converted the Serbs. These religious differences and the resulting cultural tensions are still in effect today.

. . . replaced by two empires. By about the 1300s, these old powers had given way to new ones. In the north, the growing Austrian state, like the old Frankish one, was Roman Catholic. In the south, however, the Orthodox Byzantine Empire gradually succumbed to the Ottoman Turks, who conquered the territory once under Byzantine influence and created a mighty empire in the name of Islam, but were unable to press farther into Catholic lands. Austria held them off for the most part. Again, the frontier between two hostile cultures divided the Slavs in the same region as before. The Croats lived under Hungarian rule in the eleventh century, and later (1526) they and the Slovenes lived under Germanic Austro-Hungarian rulers (the Habsburgs). Serbs and the Macedonians lived under the Ottoman Turks.

An ancient, but still used church, in Yugoslavia. *Courtesy of Aleksandar Albijanic.*

For centuries, the border area between the Ottomans and those under Austro-Hungarian rule was often a wasteland or a transit area for refugees, as the two empires varied their boundaries on future Yugoslav soil.

Struggle for independence. The idea of a union of southern Slavs had originated in the eleventh century and continued to be championed through the centuries. Through much of the nineteenth century, the Serbs in the region led an almost continuous rebellion against Ottoman rule. In 1804, Serbia gained a measure of independence and began to build a powerful Serbian state. An intellectual reformation revived Serbian language and literature in the early 1800s. Then in 1842 Karadjordjević (Alexander) became Prince of Serbia. Although he was later deposed, accused of conspiracy, and imprisoned, Alexander did much to unite the Serbian people. By 1867, all Ottoman troops had been withdrawn from the region that would be known as Yugoslavia, until 1992.

Yugoslav kingdom. By the late 1800s, Austria's influence had grown and Turkey's declined. The assassination of the Austrian Archduke Franz Ferdinand in 1914 by a Serb triggered an Austrian invasion of Serbia—which eventually led to World War I. After the defeat of Austria and Turkey in 1918, the Serbian king Alexander proclaimed the Kingdom of Serbs, Croats, and Slovenes, with himself as monarch.

Friction developed in the kingdom's early years, mainly between Croats and Serbs. The Westernized, more prosperous Croats resented Serbian dominance of the government and military. The Serbs, for their part, felt that they had done the most to win the Slavs' independence and had the right to the largest role in governing. Leaders of the two groups could not agree, and in 1929 King Alexander assumed personal dictatorship and renamed the country Kingdom of Yugoslavia. He was assassinated in 1934, and the government fell to his brother, Prince Paul, since the heir to the throne, King Peter II, was underage. Paul aligned himself with the growing power of Germany, but in 1941 was deposed by the military, which, with Peter II as the titular head of government, realigned Yugoslavia with the Allies.

Occupation. The Axis powers (Germany and Italy) attacked Yugoslavia on April 6, 1941, and the Yugoslav army surrendered 11 days later. The entire country was occupied by the Germans and Italians, except for Croatia, where a fascist puppet regime (the *Ustachi*) took power. The Ustachi quickly initiated a policy to control the 1,000,000 Serbs under its rule—killing many of them, expelling others, or forcing Serbs to convert to Roman Catholicism. The Ustachi also persecuted Croatian Democrats and Jews.

Resistance. Though the army command had surrendered, the Yugoslavs had not finished fighting against the occupation. Two resistance groups arose, the Četniks and the Partisans. The Četniks, led by the Yugoslav army Colonel Draža Mihailović, were mostly Serbs who supported the monarchy and were the official army of the government in exile. The Partisans were organized by the Communist party of Yugoslavia (outlawed since 1921), under Josip Broz (Tito). Tito and Mihailović distrusted each other. Mihailović believed in delaying until his forces were strong enough to have a good chance of success, and he was a fervent anti-Communist. Tito urged all-out war to begin immediately. The two groups ended by fighting each other as well as the Germans. Tito's Communists ultimately prevailed. By 1945, they had driven the Germans and Italians from Yugoslavia and had executed thousands of Četniks and Croatian fascists. Having suppressed opposition, they were overwhelmingly voted into power.

Tito's decades. At first, Tito modeled the Federal People's Republic of Yugoslavia on Stalin's Soviet Union. Each of the old regions would become its own republic: Serbia, Croatia, Slovenia, Bosnia-Herzegovina, Montenegro and Macedonia. To limit Serbia's influence, her borders would contain two "autonomous provinces": Kosovo and Vojvodina. Though the six new republics theoretically retained some powers, authority was actually held by Tito and his cabinet.

In 1948, soon after World War II, relations broke down between Yugoslavia and the Soviet Union. A number of reasons contributed to the rift, most stemming from Tito's refusal to conform to Stalin's wishes in his foreign policy. Still in need of help rebuilding a country devastated by war, Tito did not hesitate to turn to the West. Yet he refused to compromise his own political philosophy. During the 1950s and 1960s, Tito formulated a policy of "nonalignment," in which nations such as India and Egypt followed his lead in avoiding becoming allied to either superpowers: Soviet Union and the United States.

Tito oversaw several new constitutions for Yugoslavia. Over the years, the republics and provinces gained more control over local government. He also assigned more power to workers in managing businesses and industries, and sometimes allowed public disagreement with his policies. Yet his government, like other Communist regimes, found it necessary to outlaw all organized opposition and to often repress dissent. While the strength of his leadership brought progress and relative prosperity, it also kept hidden the old tensions that continued to divide the people. Tito held Yugoslavians together until his death in 1980, but by 1991 differences between the Croats and Serbs had erupted into civil war, and by early 1992, under a United Nations peace-keeping body, the Croats and Serbs had agreed to disband the unity of Yugoslavia.

Culture Today

Nationalism and democracy. Although Tito's regime was more liberal than those in other Eastern European countries, Yugoslavia has been among the last to embrace democratic change. Part of this slowness comes from Yugoslavia's very independence from Soviet influence, and the resulting distance from the reforms that started under the Soviet leader Mikhail Gorbachev. More important, perhaps, is the fact that change itself has become an issue in disputes over na-

In some places, Yugoslav farmers lack machinery and still use animal-drawn wagons. *Courtesy of Aleksandar Albijanic.*

tional rights. Serbs—at 10,000,000 the largest national group—traditionally dominated the government and the army. Belgrade, the Serbian capital, is also Yugoslavia's federal capital, and Serbs see this as symbolic of their leadership. Thus, strong central authority means continuation of Serbian dominance. For reform-minded Croats and Slovenes, nationalism has been tied instead to democracy, which offers a chance for greater national expression.

Territory and rights. The question of national rights is also deeply connected with that of territory—which in turn arises from Yugoslavia's complex and turbulent past. The federal borders do not exactly match the ethnic ones. Thus, while most of the roughly 5,000,000 Croats live in Croatia, not all do. About 1,000,000 live in Bosnia-Herzegovina, a region made up of mixed Serbs and Croats, many of whom converted to Islam under Turkish rule. Another 100,000 live in Vojvodina, a province of Serbia. Similarly, about 600,000 Serbs live in Croatia, where their ancestors were settled by the Habsburgs as a barrier against Turkish raids (see SERBS, CROATS). Memory of the persecution of World War II has been described as an important reason for Serbia's attacking Croatia in 1991.

Kosovo. Also potentially explosive, however, is the situation in the Serbian province of Kosovo. Though Kosovo was the heart of medieval Serbia, today Serbs have mostly left the province. Those that remain are now outnumbered by ethnic Albanians, who demand self-rule. The Serbian leader Slobodan Milošević has denied their demands and in 1990 used army and police forces to control them. Kosovo was quiet during the civil war of 1991, but promises to be a continuing problem.

Vojvodina. The Vojvodina province of Serbia is another region with difficult issues to resolve. Here a strong Hungarian minority seeks to preserve its own language and customs, and would probably favor alliance with Hungary.

Religion. Religious and cultural identity have long been closely intertwined for the Yugoslavs. Their Roman Catholicism helps lend the Slovenes and Croats their Western European outlook; Orthodox Christianity brought the Serbs into the orbit of the Greek East. Likewise, the adoption of Islam by Serbs and Croats in Bosnia-Herzegovina meant that Turkish culture took hold there in a way that it did not in Croatia and Serbia. Having been granted autonomy by the Ottoman Empire from the 1700s on, religion and religious leaders played important parts in Croatian and Serbian nationalism. This tendency continues today. Finally, the family has always been central to religious life for the Yugoslavs, and became especially so during Turkish occupation, when many churches were closed.

Family life. The basic social unit was traditionally the *zadruga* or extended family group. This large cooperative household, which was the base of village organization, shared work and property, with leadership most often falling to the oldest male (whose powers were limited). In most of rural Yugoslavia, the zadruga lasted into the early twentieth century. During centuries of foreign rule, the zadruga allowed the Slavs to preserve their cultural and religious traditions by offering strength through cooperation. Today, the same spirit survives. In the 1960s and 1970s, when Yugoslavs moved to cities in large numbers, many stayed with relatives until finding housing, which was scarce. Those who moved to cities in turn helped the ones who stayed in the country, either by sending money or by returning to work on the family farm during free-time.

Nets are more effective than hooks when lake fishing in Montenegro. *From the Library of Congress.*

Food, clothing, and shelter. Diet varies by region (see individual entries). As might be expected, the cultural melting-pot makes for lively cuisine. Turkish influence is strong in Bosnia-Herzegovina, Austrian in Slovenia, and Greek in Macedonia. Grilled meats and plum brandy (the national drink, called *šljvovica*) are common everywhere. In Serbia, the meat will be served with a salad of tomatoes, onions, peppers and parsley; along the coast, thin-sliced ham called *Dalmatinski pršut,* or Dalmatian prosciutto, precedes the meal. Other Italian-style dishes are found along the coast, as well as excellent seafood.

A peasant farmer in Yugoslavia poses in front of his house in his everyday dress. *From the Library of Congress.*

Traditional costumes (see individual entries) appear at the many summer folk festivals and on special occasions. The colorful costumes incorporate details specific to certain regions, so that a knowledgeable observer can identify the wearer's religious and cultural background and place of origin.

Housing has been scarce, especially in the cities, owing to recent migration from rural areas. A phenomenon still seen throughout the country is *divlja gradnja* ("wild building"). Built without official (and expensive) permits, these often large homes may be unfinished for years, with the family occupying only a section.

Literature and the arts. Until the country was united, Yugoslavian literature was divided among the various societies there. The great poet Ivan Gundulić (1589–1638) represented the Italian-influenced area around the city of Dubrovnik in his drama *Dubravka*, and in *Tears of the Prodigal Son*, Jovan Rajić (1726–1801) represented the influence of the Russian Orthodox Church. The Serbs influenced by Hungary were represented by Dositej Obradović (1742–1811), who is recognized as the father of modern Serbian literature. Croatian literary talent reached its peak with Count Ivo Vojnović (1857–1929), another resident of Dubrovnik, whose most famous work was *A Trilogy of Dubrovnik*.

Under Tito, writers and artists expressed themselves more freely than in most other Communist countries. In literature, some of the most important novels after World War II examined the war and its destructive effects. Two examples are *Far Away Is the Sun*, by Dobrica Ćosić, and *The Poem*, by Oskar Davičo. Opera, drama and classical music are very popular, as are exhibitions of painting and sculpture. There is a thriving film industry, centered in Zagreb, the capital of Croatia; also Zagreb is the home of an annual film festival of international reputation. Folk arts are important, and Yugoslavs boasts a wealth of beautifully designed and decorated churches. These ancient religious centers attract many tourists.

Language. For the historical development of Serbo-Croatian, the shared language for which Serbs and Croats use different alphabets, see the separate entries on Serbs and Croats. Other languages are Slovenian and Macedonian, Slavic languages closely related to Serbo-Croatian. Like religion, language has been associated historically with nationalist movements.

Economic trouble. A significant part of the current unrest stems from economic inequality between the wealthier, more advanced north (Slovenia, Croatia) and the less developed and often downright poor south (Serbia, Bosnia-Herzegovina, Montenegro, and Macedonia). As tensions increased in the late 1980s, Serbia and Slovenia, for example, boycotted each other's goods. By the end of 1989, Yugoslavia's inflation rate had reached 1,500 percent and its standard of living had gone back to levels of the 1960s.

Civil war. In June 1991, Slovenia and Croatia declared independence from the Yugoslav federal system. The federal army, controlled by and mostly composed of Serbs, invaded Croatia soon after. Many Croatian towns were destroyed or damaged by shelling and bombing, and some street-fighting continued despite a cease-fire. Yet while the soldiers and militias (unofficial armies) were fighting, the Serbs and Croats who shared the villages often helped each other through a difficult time.

Note: As this book goes to press, Slovenia has been recognized as a separate nation, as has Croatia after a bloody war and a United Na-

Yugoslav dress is widely varied, from the older dress of this elderly man to the Western costume of his walking partners. *Courtesy of Aleksandar Albijanic.*

tions-guided cease-fire. Macedonia has declared for independence and has been recognized by other nations except for Greece, where the name Macedonia is claimed to be a Greek heritage. Bosnia-Herzegovina has also declared for independence and is in bitter war with the Slavic "national" army.

For More Information

Andrejevich, Milan. "Kosovo: A Precarious Balance between Stability and Civil War." *Report on Eastern Europe*, October 18, 1991.

Danforth, Kenneth C. "Yugoslavia: A House Much Divided." *National Geographic*, August 1990.

Doder, Dusko. *The Yugoslavs*. New York: Random House, 1978.

Jordan, Robert Paul. "Yugoslavia: Six Republics in One." *National Geographic*, May 1970.

Nyrop, Richard F., editor. *Yugoslavia: A Country Study*. Washington DC: Department of the Army, 1982.

Singleton, Fred. *A Short History of the Yugoslav Peoples*. Cambridge, England: Cambridge University Press, 1985.

Viorst, Milton. "A Reporter at Large: The Yugoslav Idea." *New Yorker*, March 18, 1991.

COUNTRY BRIEFS

ALBANIA
(al bay' nee uh)

Population: 3,500,000 (1988 estimate).
Location: The Balkan Peninsula, bordered by Greece, Yugoslavia, and the Adriatic Sea.
Language: Albanian.
Principal cities: Tirana (capital), 220,000; Durres, 80,000; Scutari, 80,000; Elbasam, 75,000.

The smallest of the Balkan countries, Albania has been independent for only short periods in its long history. Settled by people from Greece before 600 B.C., captured by the Romans in 167 B.C., then dominated by the Turks, the country won a short independence of 17 years under George Castriota (Skanderbeg) in the 1400s before falling again to Turkish rule. Then in 1912, Albanians were able to

declare their independence, and to proclaim a republic in 1925. In 1928, president Ahmed Bey Zogu named himself king of an Albanian monarchy and took the name King Zog. This kingdom was to be overrun by Germany and Italy in World War II. Resistance to the Axis takeover was led by Albanian Communists, and in 1944 the Communist leader, Enver Hoxha took command of the government. An agreement to unify with Yugoslavia was developed in the next two years, but was never implemented because Joseph Stalin of the Soviet Union opposed it.

The independent spirit that has kept alive the Albanian language and customs through the centuries has been evident under communism. At first recognized officially by many world powers under the condition that free elections be held, Albanians kept Enver Hoxha in power without true elections. This action lost support of the United States and placed Albania squarely under the influence of the Soviet Union. However, Albanians were determined to succeed under a Stalinist form of communism, and when the Soviet Union relaxed its adherence to the old doctrine in 1961, Albania was denounced by

Albanians and Greeks make up most of the population of Albania.

the Soviet Union. The following year, Albania broke relations with the Soviets. China replaced the Soviet Union in trade and guidance, but Albania broke that relationship in 1976 and began to turn to the West for support and trade relations.

Today, the rugged mountain-filled country is totally nationalized. Albanians mostly subsist by farming and sheep-herding in a land that is two-thirds mountains with many short rivers that rush out of the mountains toward the Adriatic Sea, sometimes flooding large areas of the farmland and pastureland. The rocky coast has few ports and is often covered with swampland, further isolating this small country.

In the 1980s and 1990s, the Albanian government has been trying to establish some trade relations with Western countries. However, few people from foreign countries are permitted to visit the country, and those who are allowed to visit travel mostly only on very closely guided tours. These tours do not include people from the United States, a country still considered to be an obstacle to Albanian independence. In the late 1980s and early 1990s Albania has been subject to internal revolts over economic and religious matters.

ARMENIA
(ar men' ee uh)

Population: 3,045,000 (1987 estimate).
Location: The land bridge west of the Caspian Sea, bounded by Georgia, Azerbaijan, Iran, and Turkey.
Languages: Armenian, Russian.
Principal cities: Yerevan (capital), 1,400,000; Leninakan, 225,000; Kirovakan, 180,000.

Ancient Armenia, as it was known in biblical times, was a large area in present-day Turkey, Iran, and the Soviet Union. After the rule of the region by Alexander the Great, it became part of Persia. By 190 B.C. it was partitioned by its own princes into two kingdoms. Reunited, it became the first country in this area to officially embrace Christianity (A.D. 286). Later, this region became part of the lands

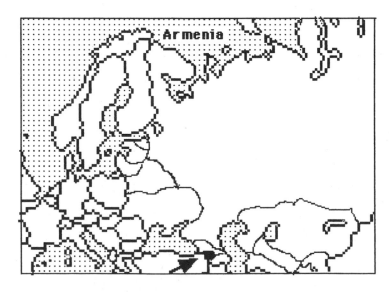

governed by Genghis Khan, Tamerlane, and finally by the Ottoman Empire. During the Russo-Turkish War of 1877–1878, Armenia became the subject of debate and was eventually divided among Turkey, Iran (Persia), and Russia. The Armenians in Turkey were subject to pogroms for their extermination or complete subjugation. Many were killed and others fled to the Russian and Iranian areas of the country. In 1922 Russia's section came into the Soviet Union as part of the Transcaucasus Republic. In 1936 this region was divided and Albania became the smallest Union Republic in the Soviet Union, with only 11,506 square miles of land—slightly larger than the state of Maryland.

Armenia is a land of many high mountain peaks and a mountain lake, Lake Sevan, that empties into both the Razdan River and the Araks River, which separates the Armenian republic from Turkey.

Since 1922, the Armenian Republic has been dependent as a republic on other republics in the Union for financing its development and for trade. It has been bound to Azerbaijan by joint use of mountain pastures along their border for sheep-grazing.

Ninety percent of the people of Armenia are Armenian. More than 5 percent are Azeri and 2 percent are Russian.

When Armenians held their first multiparty election after the final breakdown of the Communist economy in 1991, they elected a moderate leader, Levon Tér Petrosyan, to be their president. Petrosyan promised to cooperate with other republics to build a new Soviet economy. Armenia became one of the first to sign a joint economic pact with seven other Soviet republics, even though it is separated from the other signing republics by Azerbaijan and Georgia, both of which did not elect to join the economic alliance.

A major problem for Armenians, and one which they hope to submit to the United Nations for resolution, involves the former Autonomous Soviet territory of Nagorno-Karabakh. This state lies within Azerbaijan but has long been inhabited by Armenians. In 1991, the dispute over this bit of land erupted into war, and since Nagorno-Karabakh is near the Azerbaijan border with Georgia, the struggle threatens that state also.

AZERBAIJAN
(az er bai' jan)

Population: 8,000,000 (1988 estimate).
Location: On the land bridge between the Black Sea and the Caspian Sea at the Soviet-Iran border.
Languages: Azerbaijani, Russian.
Principal city: Baku (capital) 2,000,000.

Azerbaijan lies in a lowland south of the Carpathian Mountains bordered by the Caspian Sea and Iran. It once included the old Russian territories of Baku and Elizavetpol along with Dagestan in present-day Georgia and the northwest portion of Iran. In April 1920 the Russian land inhabited by the Azeris was unified, and in 1922 it was admitted to the Soviet Union as part of the Transcaucasus Soviet

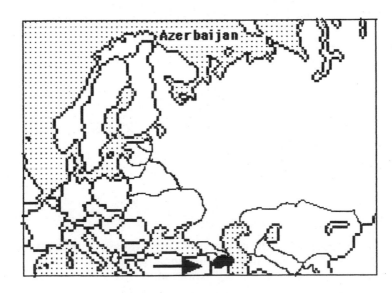

Republic. In 1936, this area was further divided into three Soviet Union republics and Azerbaijan regained its identity.

The Soviet Azerbaijian Republic was once largely dependent on the agricultural potential of its lowland area. But under Soviet rule, the small region became industrialized and its mineral resources developed. Today, a large pipeline carries petroleum pumped from regions near the capital city of Baku to the port city of Batumi in the Republic of Georgia. The mountain areas also yield iron, bauxite, and copper.

Under the Soviet system, these resources were held and their uses controlled by the government in Moscow. With the realignment of the Soviet Union in 1991, Azerbaijan has been hesitant to form new alliances that would endanger the rights of the republic to develop its own economy.

A small section near the Armenian border lies in Azerbaijan but is inhabited by Armenians. This area is a semi-self-governing area labeled under the Communist system an Autonomous Oblast. Lying

Azerbaijan's seaports attract workers from Russia and other nearby countries. The people of this country include 78 percent Azeri, 8 percent Russians, and 8 percent Armenians.

near the border with Georgia, this area has been the subject of dispute with Armenia for many years. With the abandonment of communism by the government in Moscow, and the independence of the republics, the conflict over this region, Nagorno-Karabakh, has erupted into war between the two republics. This war has also threatened to disrupt affairs in Georgia.

BULGARIA
(bul gar′ ee uh)

Population: 10,000,000 (1988 estimate).
Location: Southeastern Europe bounded by Yugoslavia, Greece, Turkey, the Black Sea, and Romania.
Language: Bulgarian.
Principal cities: Sofia (capital), 1,200,000; Plovdiv, 380,000; Varna, 300,000; Burgas, 200,000; Ruse, 190,000; Stara Zagora, 160,000.

In the fourth century A.D., Tatar settlers founded a nation on the Volga River with a capital near present-day Kazan. Later these people

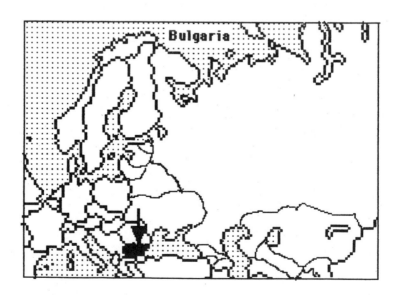

moved to the land between the Bog and Danube rivers. Here they founded a second Bulgaria by the seventh century. By the ninth century the small group had adopted Christianity and merged with the greater Slavic population. When this region was overrun by Russians, the Bulgarians established a third kingdom between the Balkan Mountains and the Danube River. For nearly 500 years, from 1390, Bulgaria was ruled by the Turks. Made an independent country, but still tributary to Turkey in 1878, Bulgaria began self-rule under Alexander, a German prince. In 1875, territorial difficulties with Russia led to defeat and Alexander's alliance with Russia led to rebuilding of the kingdom under Prince Ferdinand. Ferdinand successfully opposed Russian influence.

Long under Turkish influence, Bulgaria became an independent nation through the Treaty of San Stefano in 1878, but its boundaries were not settled because Turkey and Russia quarreled over the territory. In the early 1900s the country was a monarchy. However, alliance with the Germans in World War I resulted in the loss of some Bulgarian land. A settlement with Russia (which had declared

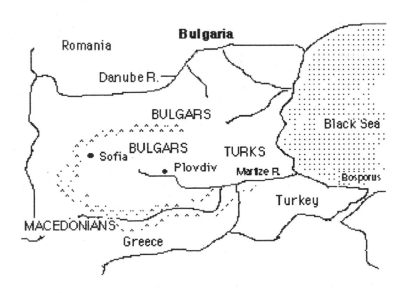

Most of the people of Bulgaria are Bulgars. However, there is a 10 percent Turkish minority and there are some Macedonians.

war with Bulgaria during World War II) fixed Bulgarian boundaries and positioned Bulgaria solidly with the Communist countries. By 1946 the country had become a people's republic along the lines of the Soviet Union. Since Bulgaria had a long-standing bond with Russia because of its earlier aid in freeing Bulgaria from the Turks, the country soon severed its relations with Western countries. It was not until 1959 that Bulgaria began to establish a diplomatic relationship with the United States.

In the 1980s and 1990s Bulgaria has struggled with internal disputes over ethnic and religious issues. The Bulgarian government attempted to deny Jews freedom of religion and then quarreled with the large Turkish-Muslim minority in the country.

Bulgaria is a land of rugged mountains and fertile river valleys. The Danube River flows along its northern border, separating Bulgaria and Romania. The Balkan Mountains rise in the center of the country and cross east to west. The more rugged Rhodope Mountains separate Bulgaria and Greece in the south. Between the two mountain ranges, the Martisa River cuts a broad, fertile valley on its course from the Balkan Mountains through Turkey. In this valley, Bulgarians raised wheat, corn, rye, tobacco, vegetables, oats, and cotton along with hogs. Sheepherders graze their flocks in the foothills of the mountains.

Under Soviet guidance, Bulgaria began to industrialize its economy. The mountains provided coal, copper, lead, zinc, iron, manganese, and lead, and these fueled manufacturing of metal products, chemicals, and machinery. As a result, city populations swelled, housing became limited, and pollution grew to be a serious problem for the country.

BYELARUS
(byel a rus')

Population: 10,100,000 (1987 estimate).
Location: Eastern Europe bounded by Lithuania, Latvia, Russia, and Ukraine.
Languages: Byelarussian, Russian.
Principal cities: Minsk (capital), 1,525,000; Gomel, 465,000; Mogilev, 345,000; Vitebsk, 335,000.

Located in flat land through which the armies of Europe and Asia have frequently marched, the country of Byelarus has been part of several major European powers. In the 1400s this land was part of a much larger-than-today Lithuania, and later, as the Grand Duchy of Lithuania faded, the region was incorporated into Poland. It was taken to be part of Russia in 1793. By the 1800s, however, the people

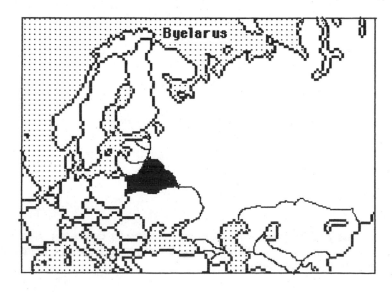

of "White Russia" had begun to develop a sense of national identity. Before 1917 this area formed several different provinces of Russia. The Soviet Union merged the provinces of Minsk, Vitebsk, and Mogilev, and added parts of Grodno and Gomel to form the Byelorussian Soviet Socialist Republic. The old provinces had grown up around cities and towns that still have these names.

Earlier, Mongols had crossed the land, but like most of its invaders, used Byelarus as a battleground and passageway to more attractive areas. Because of the land's frequent use in battles, many of the older cities and towns grew up around strong forts. The remnants of these structures mark Byelarus today. Even churches came to be fortified against the frequent incursions of foreigners.

As part of the Soviet Union, Byelorussia was encouraged to industrialize. Minsk became an important railway stop between Warsaw and Moscow. Lumber mills, paper mills, and iron, machine, and textile factories were built to supply the people of the Soviet Union with necessary supplies. These industries tied Byelorussia firmly to

Byelarus

Byelarussians are 79 percent of the population in Byelarus. Scattered throughout the country are Russians (12 percent), Poles (4 percent), and Ukrainians (2.5 percent).

the government of Moscow. However, as communism in the Soviet Union faded and the central government weakened, the leaders of Byelorussia joined the other republics in declaring their independence. The country was renamed Byelarus.

However, the interdependency on trade with other republics was a strong force, and Byelarus joined Armenia, Tajikistan, Turkmenistan, Kyrgyzstan, Uzbekistan, Kazakhstan, and Russia in an economic treaty of October 1991. This was a possible first step toward rebuilding a Soviet Union along free-market principles. In a second step toward economic reconstruction, the president of Byelarus joined the presidents of Ukraine and Russia and other former Soviet republics in signing an agreement to form a Commonwealth of Independent States.

CZECHOSLOVAKIA

(chek o slo vak′ ee uh)

Population: 16,500,000 (1988 estimate).
Location: Central Europe, bounded by Germany, Poland, Ukraine, Hungary, Austria.
Languages: Czech, Slovak.
Principal cities: Prague (capital), 1,270,000; Bratislava, 420,000; Brno, 400,000; Ostrava, 340,000; Kosice, 225,000.

The region that is now the home of Czechs and Slovaks was long divided into a number of principalities. These were first united by the leader Samo in A.D. 627. Until 1230 the nation of Bohemia was ruled by an elected king; the kingship then became hereditary. Ruling under the direction of the German emperor, Bohemia still maintained its separation from that state. Until 1620 Bohemia was a troubled

kingdom, fighting frequently with Poland and attempting to remain apart from the German Empire. In 1620 it became part of the Austrian Empire and remained Austrian until the Austro-Hungarian Empire was dismantled after World War I. In 1919 the Czechoslovakian border was expanded to include Sudetenland, an area populated mostly by Germans. This was an opening for Adolf Hitler, who in 1938 claimed the area for Germany after secret pacts with Britain, France, and Italy. Later Hitler invaded the country on the pretense that Czechoslovakia was home to German people. Their country restored after World War II, the Czechs and Slovaks found that a part of their old land had been given to the Soviet Union. By 1946, Czechoslovakia had been deeply influenced by the Soviets and the election that year installed the Communist party as the governing body, with party chairman Edvard Beneš as president. He was replaced by Klement Gottwald, who became prime minister of the Communist state and who was replaced in 1953 by Alexander Dubček, followed in 1968 by Dr. Gustav Husák, who ruled until 1988.

Czechoslovakia

Czechoslovakia is divided among Czechs and Slavs, but includes a few Germans and Hungarians. Nearly two-thirds of the people are Czechs, and one-third Slovaks.

In 1989, a coalition of Czechs and Slovaks staged what has been called the "velvet revolution," in which the Communists were dislodged from government. Two distinct peoples, Czechs and Slovaks, chose to cooperate in forming a new government even though their cultures showed many differences.

The land of Czechs and Slovaks is a land of mountain ranges, none reaching altitudes greater than 8,711 feet. Mountains ring the northwestern section, break the center of the country with rows of mountain ranges, and separate the eastern section from Poland. Czechs live in the west within the socialist republics of Bohemia and Moravia. Slovaks live in the less-populated eastern section of the country.

The Slovaks have long resented their more affluent countrymen, who outnumber them two to one and therefore controlled the government. From 1939 to 1944 they formed an independent Slovak fascist state.

ESTONIA

(es to′ nee a)

Population: 3,800,000 (1988 estimate).
Location: The Baltic Sea coast bounded by Latvia and Russia and across the Gulf of Finland.
Languages: Estonian, Russian.
Principal cities: Tallinn (capital), 500,000; Kurgan-Tyube, 60,000.

Except for a short period of its long history, Estonia has been ruled by other peoples. It was divided between the Danes and Germans in the thirteenth century. The land fell completely to the Germans through its purchase by the Teutonic knights in 1346. In 1561 it fell to the Swedes, and was formally ceded by Sweden to Russia in 1721. It became a union republic in the Soviet Union in 1940. Through all

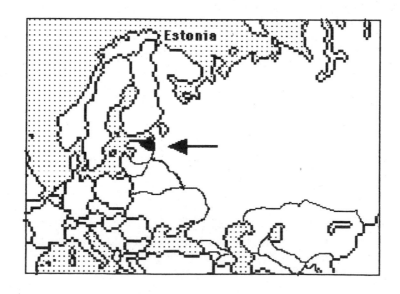

these governments, the Estonians have managed to preserve their culture, language, and feelings of national identity.

The nature of the land makes this unity even more impressive. The land is mostly meadows and heaths broken by forests, making traverse difficult. In addition, there are 1,520 islands in the country, which tends to isolate small groups of people.

In the late 1980s, Estonia joined the other Baltic States in their expressions of interest in self-government. In 1990, this expression grew to declarations of independence by Estonia, Latvia, and Lithuania. As Lithuania pressed this demand, the Soviet Union resisted. Russian troops in all the countries were bolstered, ports were blockaded, and public demonstrations were suppressed. But the Soviet policy of *perestroika* stimulated the revolutions. When Communist hardliners seeking to replace the Moscow government attempted a coup on August 19, 1991, the result was a Soviet military takeover in parts of Estonia, Latvia and Lithuania. Estonia responded with a new declaration.

Russians have joined Estonian workers in Estonia. The people of that country are 65 percent Estonians and 28 percent Russians, with a few Ukrainians and Finns.

On August 20, 1991, Estonia's parliament declared independence despite the Soviet military presence. On August 21, the Soviet troops withdrew their forces and the Estonian people took to the streets in celebration. Finally, on September 6, 1991, the independence of the three states was officially recognized by the Soviets. The Baltic countries also refused to recognize or sign the Union Treaty, which was to define the relationships of the republics to the central government.

Estonia's head of state (Arnold Ruutel), the parliament, and the people began the difficult task of rebuilding a country that had become almost totally dependent on the Soviet Union for energy, management, and supplies. Some immediate concerns of the country are problems such as defining Estonian citizenship, training personnel for many of the jobs held by Russian officials, establishing an Estonian currency, and setting up diplomatic relationships and embassies with the nations of the world. Thirty-five percent of the people of Estonia are immigrants from other parts of the former Soviet Union—30 percent from Russia. Defining the citizenship status of these people has become a primary concern for Estonian leaders.

GEORGIA
(jorg' uh)

Population: 4,200,000 (1988 estimate).
Location: Between the Black Sea and the Caspian Sea south of the Caucasus Mountains.
Languages: Georgian, Russian.
Principal cities: Tbilisi (capital) 1,200,000; Kutaisi (225,000); Batumi (150,000).

The area that is now the Republic of Georgia has a long history of submission to other people. Their early ancestors paid homage to Alexander the Great. They were united for more than a century under King Pharnabazus and his successors, but then were invaded by the Roman warriors Pompey and Trajan. Subsequently, Georgia was a Sassanide dynasty for 300 years before the land was overrun by Arabs

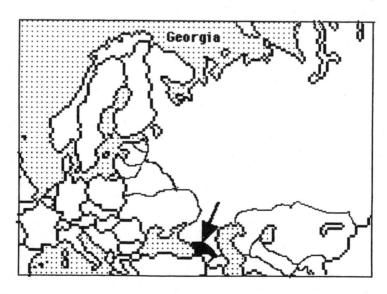

in 787. Again in the eleventh century, the country was invaded, this time by the Turks, soon to be displaced by the Mongols. Independent Georgia reached its height in the twelfth century when Queen Tamara won Russian support by marrying a Russian prince. Alexander II replaced George VII, who had driven Timur Leng (Tamerlane) from the country. Alexander II divided the country into two parts under his two sons. This began a division that brought the country 26 princely realms. The division weakened the country so that some princes swore allegiance to Russia for protection. In 1799 the king of Georgia resigned in favor of the emperor of Russia, and in 1802 it was proclaimed a Russian territory.

Georgia is a small country of 29,000 square miles, but is rich in mineral resources and in agriculture. The country rises to the Caucasus Mountains in the north, but is mostly a fertile plain reaching from the Baltic Sea to the Caspian Sea. Once the region was most famous for its warm mineral springs and fine beaches along the Caspian Sea. Many people from the Soviet Union came to this area to

Georgians (69 percent of the population), Armenians (9 percent), and Russians (7.5 percent) make up the people of Georgia. Five percent of the people are Azeri.

vacation. However, during its participation in the Soviet Union, Georgia developed strong industries and began to ship petroleum—pumped in Azerbaijan—from its port at Batumi. Georgia has its own energy source in rich coal mines. Iron and manganese are mined in the mountains, and these metals are used to manufacture automobiles. The nearly Mediterranean climate allows Georgians to grow citrus crops, as well as bamboo, tobacco, and grapes.

Seeking to gain a measure of self-government, Georgia declared its independence from the Soviet Union and established free elections. In May 1991, Zviad Gamsakhurdia was chosen president. He immediately started actions to make Georgians economically self-sufficient. As with other economies emerging from the former Soviet Union, Georgia's economy was bound to the rest of the Soviet republics and the Soviet ruble was the country's money standard. Changing the economy that had developed for 70 years under Communism proved to be difficult for all the republics. President Gamsakhurdia's plan called for austerity in Georgia until adjustments could be made. However, some people were unhappy with the change, and others, its pace. One unit of the national guard rebelled and demanded the president's resignation. This has resulted in a great deal of turmoil in the country, with President Gamsakhurdia accusing Communist hardliners of stirring up unrest.

HUNGARY
(hun′ ga ree)

Population: 11,200,000 (1988 estimate).
Location: Central Europe, bounded by Czechoslovakia, Ukraine, Romania, Yugoslavia, and Austria.
Language: Hungarian.
Principal cities: Budapest (capital), 2,540,000; Debrecen, 222,000; Miskolc, 220,000; Szeged, 200,000.

Between A.D.893 and 901, bands of Magyars from the east invaded the land that is now Hungary and drove out the Slavs who were already established there along the Danube River. Prevented from sweeping farther west by King Otto of the Germans, the Magyars settled on a wide plain crossed by the Danube and Tisza rivers and surrounded by low mountains of the Carpathian and Alp systems.

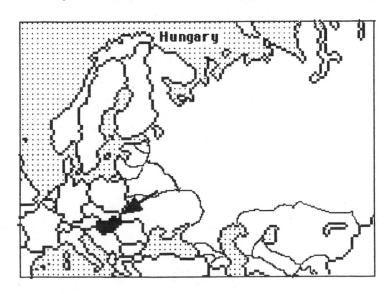

Led by Arpád, the Magyars formed loose bands along the rivers and across the plain, where they were joined by other peoples who migrated into the plains. From about 900 and continuing for the next century, Hungary was governed by nobles who ruled their serfdoms independently. In the year 1000 Stephen (now St. Stephen) was named king and succeeded in uniting the nation. With little interruption, there followed a series of powerful kings who expanded Hungarian territory and advanced its people. The Golden Bull (1222), a charter of human rights, was granted to the noblemen by King Andrew II three years before a similar charter, the Magna Carta, was signed by the king in England. Then in 1301 the line of rulers from the Arpád family was broken and the king became an elected officer chosen by the nobles.

By 1500 the power of the Hungarian kings had decayed and Hungarian land was divided between the Ottoman Empire and the Austrian Habsburgs. Nearly 400 years later, Hungary was joined to Austria under a dual monarchy (1867) in which the Emperor of Austria was also the King of Hungary.

Hungary

Most of the people of Hungary are Magyars.

In the twentieth century, Hungary first made an alliance with the Germans in both world wars. After the first war, a 1920 settlement in the Treaty of Versailles restored the country, but with only one-third of its former land. In 1944, the Hungarian government broke an alliance and was invaded by Germany. Following the war, Hungarians established a republic in which the Communist party won the elections. This party ruled under the counsel and direction of Soviet leader Joseph Stalin. When he died, Imre Nagy attempted to lead the country toward a more open society. Because Russian troops had occupied the land since 1947, Nagy was rebuffed but later reinstated. In 1956, the Soviet troops intervened in an attempt to quell the liberalization movement. Rebellions continued, as seen in 1986 when more than 100 people staged a protest against industrialization requiring a new dam on the Danube River.

Once a land nearly totally devoted to raising wheat and other farm products, and to grazing livestock, Hungary under Russian influence was encouraged to develop its industrial potential. Particularly attractive to the Soviet Union was the abundant coal in the mountain areas. Mining of coal was expanded and the coal used to provide energy for textile and other manufacturing industries. However, technology provided by the Soviet Union was frequently of old designs and did little to preserve the environment. As a result, Hungary in the 1990s has many cities covered with soot and air pollution from ill-managed coal mines and poorly constructed industrial plants.

KAZAKHSTAN
(keh zak′ stan)

Population: 14,000,000 (1988 estimate).
Location: Southern region of the former Soviet Union, bordered by Kyrgyzstan, Uzbekistan, Turkmenistan, the Caspian Sea, and Russia.
Languages: Kazakh, Uzbek, Russian.
Principal cities: Alma-Ata (capital), 1,130,000; Karaganda, 650,000; Chimkent, 400,000.

One of the Muslim republics of the former Soviet Union, Kazakhstan includes a great central steppe and a southern desert set off in the southwest and southeast by mountains. It is a land crossed by the Syr Darya, the Ural, and Irtysh rivers and many tributaries. It is also a land of salt lakes, among them the Aral Sea and Lake Balkhash.

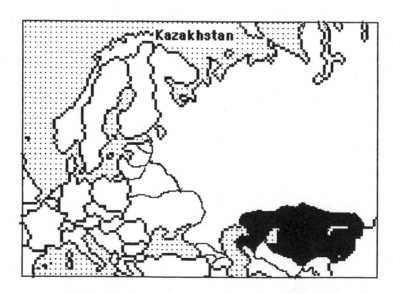

Kazakhstan

Farm workers imported from Ukraine and Russia outnumber the Kazakhs in their own land. Russians (41 percent), Kazakhs (36 percent), Ukrainians (6 percent), and Tatars (2 percent) make up most of Kazakhstan's population.

Two-thirds of the people of this region are Kazakhs. They were people of the Mongol hordes that swept across Asia and Europe in the thirteenth century. The region was part of the Ottoman Empire until the 1700s, but gradually, between 1730 and 1853, came under Russian rule. Then in the twentieth century, while part of a larger southern Russian Turkestan, the people began to move toward more independence. By 1920, the Kazakh-Kyrgyz in the area were prepared to build a self-governing republic, and in 1936 this republic was admitted to the Soviet Union.

In the 1970s and 1980s, the Soviet Union, seeking greater food productivity in the steppes, sent large numbers of Ukrainians and Russians into Kazakhstan to develop large irrigation systems. Wheat and fruits were the major products to be developed. Kazakhs also produce coal, tungsten, copper, zinc, and petroleum. But a major occupation remains herding and related industries, such as leather-working.

A major industry in central Kazakhstan, and one that poses difficult questions of ownership as the Soviet Union is divided, is the major space exploration station and launching center, Baikonur. This station, the large investment in agriculture, and the fact that Kazakhstan is the third-largest in area of the former Soviet Republics, make the country an important key in any attempts to reorganize a new union.

KYRGYZSTAN
(kir geez′ stan)

Population: 4,000,000 (1988 estimate).
Location: South of Russia, bounded by Kazakhstan, China, and Tajikistan.
Languages: Turkic, Russian.
Principal cities: Pishpek (Frunze), 640,000; Osh, 210,000; Dzhalal Abad, 80,000.

Inhabited as early as the thirteenth century by Mongols who adopted a Turkic language, the land of the Kyrgyz was annexed to Russia in 1864 as part of Russian Turkestan. By 1873, a Russian fort had been built and a town had begun to grow around it called Pishpek. In 1926, Kyrgyzstan was recognized by the Soviet Union as an autonomous

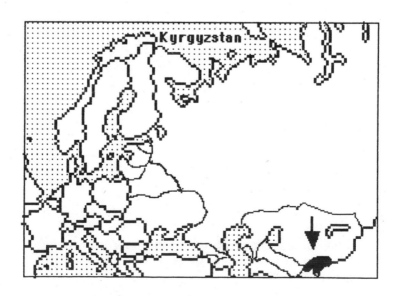

region, and by 1936 the area had been made a Union Republic of the Soviet Union. Pishpek, renamed Frunze became its capital.

The people of Kyrgyzstan are mostly Muslims, and like their neighboring Muslim states in the Soviet Union, were not easily persuaded to abandon their religion and receive orders from Moscow. In fact, Kyrgyzstan and other Muslim lands acquired by the Soviet Union remained governed by their own leadership derived from their tribal and nomadic past. They often did not even pay taxes to the Union.

Frunze is the governmental base for a land that is mostly mountainous. The Tien Shan Mountains extend into Kyrgyzstan from China and the Alai Mountains cross the southwest. The mountains of Kyrgyzstan have peaks ranging in altitude from 16,000 to more than 23,000 feet, many with glaciers standing permanently on their slopes. The Chu and Naryn rivers flow through deep valleys in the mountains and provide fertile soil for such crops as wheat, tobacco, and rice. But most of Kyrgyzstan land is productive for raising cattle,

Kyrgyzstan

Kyrgyz form the largest group of any of the peoples who live in Kyrgyzstan. Russians, Ukrainians, Uzbeks, and Tatars together nearly match the Kyrgyz population.

sheep, goats, yaks, and rugged, small horses. The mountains are rich in coal, mercury, and other minerals, as well as petroleum.

Once largely nomadic people famed for their black tents, today one-third of the people live in cities, with Pishpek the only large one.

The people of Kyrgyzstan, already more independent than some of the other former Soviet Union Republics, were prepared to break with the tough management of the Soviet Union and form an independent state. However, their government has joined with other former republics, including all of their Muslim neighboring states, in accepting economic ties, guided by a single bank and a single currency based on the Soviet ruble.

LATVIA
(lat' vee uh)

Population: 4,500,000 (1988 estimate).
Location: Baltic Sea coast, bounded by Estonia, Lithuania, and Bye-larus.
Languages: Latvian, Russian.
Principal cities: Riga (capital), 900,000; Jelgava, 80,000.

On August 19, 1991, a failed coup to overthrow the Soviet govern-ment leadership led to the weakening of the Communist central gov-ernment. The turmoil that followed resulted in the country of Latvia officially gaining independence from the Soviet Union on Friday, September 6. This historic day reflected years of struggle by the Baltic States to regain their independence since the Soviet occupation in 1940. It had been preceded by years of agitation for more freedom,

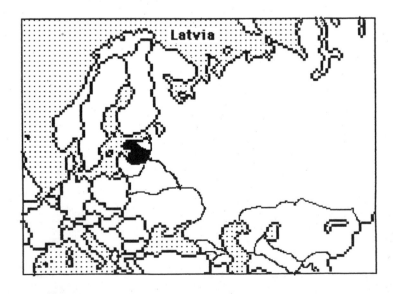

which gained momentum with the reforms initiated by Soviet president Mikhail Gorbachev's policy of *perestroika,* or "openness."

In 1990, all three of the Baltic States had declared a transitional independence. The Baltic countries also refused to recognize or sign the Union Treaty, which was to define the relationships of the republics to the central government. When a coup was attempted by Communist hardliners in Moscow on August 19, 1991, the Soviet military began to take over parts of Latvia, Estonia, and Lithuania with naval blockades and the seizure of communication centers. On August 20, 1991, Latvia's parliament declared independence, and clashes outside the parliament occurred in protest to the military presence. On August 21, the Soviet troops withdrew their forces as the Latvian parliament outlawed the Communist Party in their country. The Latvian people took to the streets in celebration of their independence while tearing down statues of Lenin and other remnants of the past Communist occupation of Latvia.

Latvia

Latvians make up 54 percent of the population of Latvia. A large percentage is Russian (33 percent). Most Russians live mostly near the seaports around Ruga. This area also attracts Byelarussians, Poles, and Ukrainians.

Latvia's prime minister (Anatolijs Gorbunovs), parliament, and the people face many challenges ahead to rebuild their country. Of all the Baltic countries, Latvia has the greatest proportion of ethnic Russians residing in the country, more than 33 percent of the population. Problems such as defining Latvian citizenship, training personnel for many of the jobs held by Russian officials, establishing a Latvian currency, and setting up diplomatic relationships and embassies with the nations of the world are some of the immediate concerns of the country. Latvians' strong national solidarity—formed through the centuries of foreign occupation—may be a great advantage in building an independent Latvia.

LITHUANIA

(lith′ oo a′ nee uh)

Population: 3,700,000 (1990 estimate).
Location: Baltic Sea coast bordered by Latvia, Byelarus, Poland, and Russia.
Language: Lithuanian.
Principal cities: Vilnius (capital), 550,000; Kaunas, 405,000.

Lithuanian tribesmen, who were early settlers on the land along the Baltic Sea between the Vistula and Salis rivers, spoke a language unlike that of their neighbors. Eventually they established their own kingdom between Slavs on one side and Germans on the other. In the thirteenth century, the Lithuanian king, Ringold, united the people and expanded Lithuanian influence through present-day Byelarus and Ukraine to the Black Sea. By the fourteenth and fifteenth cen-

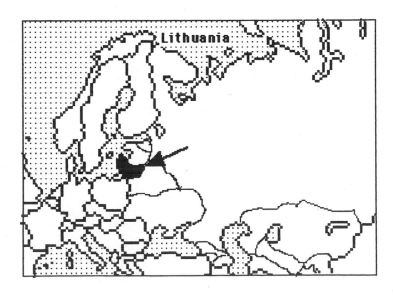

turies, Lithuania had united with Poland to become a superpower in Eastern Europe. A formal union between the two countries was formed in 1569, but this agreement increased Polish influence in Lithuania, and resulted in a decline of each power rather than a strengthening. In the 1770s, Poland-Lithuania was divided among their neighbors and Lithuania was itself divided between Prussia and Russia. Russia sought to eliminate the old society. The Russians abolished the word Lithuania in 1840, and prohibited the use of the Lithuanian language with its Latin alphabet. The part of Lithuania under Prussia retained its language until the region was taken over by the Germans under Otto von Bismarck. Still, Lithuanians held hopes for regaining their national identity. World War I offered the opportunity. Lithuanians established a government and demanded independence, which was granted by the Allied powers in 1922.

The Lithuanian problems were not over, however. In 1939, Russia demanded and received an agreement that it could use Lithuanian ports on the Baltic Sea. For a time, matters in Lithuania were further complicated by Poland's claim that the capital city, Vilnius, was Pol-

Lithuania

Eighty percent of the people of Lithuania are Lithuanians; 9 percent are Russians; and 7.5 percent are Poles.

ish territory. With that foothold, the Soviet Union took complete control of Lithuania and its neighbors, Latvia and Estonia, in 1940. For 50 years, Lithuanians sought independence while controlled forcibly by the Soviet military. Finally, with power in Moscow weakening and the Communist economy on the verge of collapse, the three small countries were able to declare their independence in 1990. That was the beginning of the reorganization of the Soviet Union, and despite the economic problems of the entire region, Lithuania has refused to join the former Soviet republics in an economic pact, preferring by 1991 to completely dissociate themselves from the former Soviet Union.

MOLDOVA
(mol da' va)

Population: 3,500,000 (1988 estimate).
Location: The western edge of the former Soviet Union bordered by Romania and the Ukraine.
Languages: Romanian, Russian.
Principal cities: Kishinev (Chisinau: capital), 680,000; Belgorod, 300,000.

In its history, Moldova has seldom been a self-governing nation nor have its boundaries been fixed. In the fourteenth century, Vlach and Hungarian peoples founded a nation there that was united under the guidance of Hungary and Poland. The land came under the control of the Turks in the sixteenth century and was united to neighboring Walachia by Michael the Bold to form Romania. For most of the

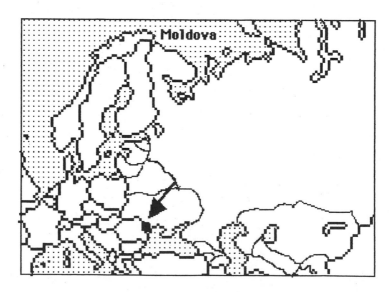

eighteenth century the region was governed by Greeks for the Ottoman Empire. Then in 1774 the land was divided. A region known as Bukovina fell to the Austrians while Bessarabia came under Russian domination. In 1861 Moldova and Walachia were united to form the country of Romania. Again in 1917, Bessarabia was taken by the Russians. In 1940, Romania ceded its claims to the small area that is now Moldova to the Soviet Union and in that year it became an Autonomous Republic within the USSR.

Moldova is a rich agricultural land, but is one of the most densely populated republics that made up the Soviet Union. In a plain between the Dniester River on the northeast and the Prut River in the southwest, Moldova is a land of sugar beets, sunflowers, vineyards, cotton, potatoes, and grains. The agriculture has provided a base for industries such as food-processing. For its industrial growth, Moldova is bound to the Ukraine by shared hydroelectric sources along the Dniester River.

Moldova

Besides Moldovans, who are 64 percent of the population, Ukrainians (14 percent) and Russians (13 percent) are the largest groups in Moldova. There are also Gagauzi, Jews, and Bulgarians living there.

The mixed heritages of Moldovans has resulted in confusion during the 1991 attempts to reorganize the Soviet Union. Moldova declared its independence (August 27), established its own rule, and refused to sign a cooperative economic pact with other Soviet Republics. However, the fate of this small state is undecided. With their country probably not large or wealthy enough to sustain itself, Moldovans are divided. The majority favor reuniting with Romania. However, the 700,000 Russians and Ukrainians who have settled in Moldova want it to remain a self-governing trans-Dniester republic, while cooperating with Ukraine.

POLAND
(po′ land)

Population: 39,500,000 (1988 estimate).
Location: Central Europe, bounded by the Baltic Sea, Russia, Ukraine, Czechoslovakia, and Germany.
Language: Polish.
Principal cities: Warsaw (capital), 2,175,000; Lodz, 1,050,000; Gdansk, 890,000; Kraków, 820,000; Poznań, 660,000; Wrocław, 650,000; Szczecin, 440,000.

Much of Poland is a flat, fertile land sloping gradually to the Baltic Sea. For centuries it has been almost completely devoted to farming and herding.

A land settled in the tenth century A.D. by Slavic people who withstood Mongol invasions and a series of weak kings dominated

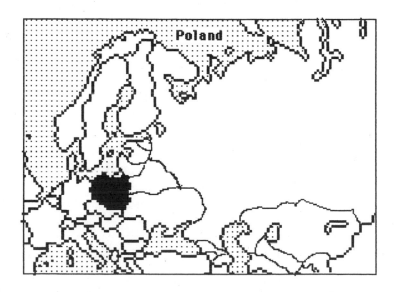

by the nobles in a collection of serfdoms, Poland grew into a great empire stretching from the Baltic to the Black seas. The peace-loving people of Poland have been torn, dominated, and exploited throughout history by Germans on the west and Russians on the east. For example, in the seventeenth century, after reaching its greatest influence through its merger with Lithuania, Poland fell and was divided three ways among Austria, Germany, and Russia. Then during World War I, western Poland was claimed by the Germans. At this time Poland included Silesia, Vilna, and some of the Ukraine and Byelorussia.

Modern Poland was established as a republic in 1918, but between 1926 and 1939 was ruled by a military government. In 1939, at the beginning of World War II, Germany claimed more Polish western land while Russia reclaimed the Ukraine and Byelorussia. From this close vantage point, Russia was influential in founding the Polish Committee of National Liberation in 1944. This committee was to guide Poland in the postwar years.

Poland

Most of the people of Poland are Poles. A few are Germans and Ukrainians.

Poland became a Communist state after World War II (1947), and joined the Warsaw Pact in 1955. It joined the Soviet Union in attacks on Czechoslovakia in 1968. However, the Polish workers were not satisfied with the economic results of a dictatorial communism. In the 1970s and 1980s, they showed their discontent with massive strikes. The Communist rulers retaliated with force and by outlawing labor unions. However, Polish workers united under a single labor union umbrella, Solidarity (1981), and continued to press the government for reforms. Finally, in the late 1980s, free elections were held in the country. Under a new government, Poland undertook massive economic reforms designed to feed the people while moving Poland toward participation in the world market. These reforms were too sudden and the results too slow to develop for many Poles, and the next election resulted in the leader of Solidarity, Lech Wałęsa, taking power in 1990. Still, Polish people were impatient for improvement. In 1991, the Polish people were again unhappy with their elected government.

ROMANIA
(roh main′ ee uh)

Population: 23,500,000 (1988 estimate).
Location: Southeast Europe bounded by Moldova, the Black Sea, Bulgaria, Yugoslavia, and Hungary.
Language: Romanian.
Principal cities: Bucharest (capital), 2,200,000; Brasov, 352,000; Timisoara, 324,000; Iasi, 315,000; Cluj-Napoca, 316,000; Constanta, 312,000; Galati, 305,000; Craiova, 297,000; Ploesti, 250,000.

Before 1881, Romania was part of the Ottoman Empire. It became an independent nation in that year, but its borders have changed frequently since that independence. After World War I, Romania nearly tripled in size because of annexations of neighboring lands. However, by 1940 the country had been forced to cede some of its

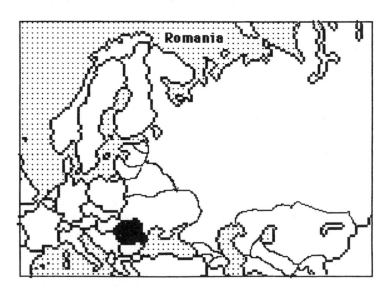

newly acquired land to the USSR. Bessarabia and northern Bukovina were made part of the Soviet Union, a portion of Transylvania fell to Hungary, and southern Dobruja was restored to Bulgaria. In that same year, a Nazi-style organization, the Iron Guard, began to be a strong influence in the country. The Iron Guard forced the abdication of the king and installation of a dictator, Ion Antonescu, under whose rule Romania sided with Germany in World War II. In 1944 the country found itself in the Russian sphere of influence, and King Michael of Romania was forced to accept a Communist government. The king abdicated his throne in 1947 and Romania became a people's republic. It allied itself firmly with the Soviet Union through the Warsaw Pact of 1955.

Under Soviet influence and controlled by Soviet troops, the country began to expand its economy from an agricultural base to an industrial one. Romanian industry mined bauxite, manganese, oil, and natural gas and manufactured textiles, chemicals, iron, steel, min-

Romania

Romania, until its domination by the Soviet Union, was an agricultural center of Europe. Soviet industrialization brought workers and managers from Russia, Ukraine, and Hungary to join Germans who were already powerful in the country.

ing equipment, and agricultural machinery for the Soviet Union. In the 1970s this movement for economic change was slowed by severe floods that crippled the country for several years. For many years, the country's development was controlled by the central government led by a dictator. Although a follower of the Marxist-Leninist doctrine, the dictator did not always agree with the Soviet Union in international policies. In December 1989 Romanians rebelled against their dictator, Nicholae Ceauşescu, and the government was overthrown to be replaced by a more liberal president. The old dictator was tried for crimes against the people and executed in 1989. The new president immediately undertook strong economic reforms to rebuild a country devastated by floods and government corruption. To aid in this rebuilding, he needed help from a government made up mostly of old Communist party leaders. Rebuilding included privatization of industry and land; in less than a year, farmland owned by peasant farmers more than doubled in acreage. The privatization of industry required much reorganization, and at first the productivity of this industry declined.

The people of Romania, however, were impatient for a more stable economic life. In 1991 Romanian coal miners, struck and marched on the capital. By October 1991, these workers had forced the prime minister of the country to resign in hopes that more conservative government officers would continue government support of the mining industry.

RUSSIA
(rush' uh)

Population: 170,000,000 (1988 estimate).
Location: Northeastern Europe and northern Asia.
Languages: Russian and more than 100 other dialects.
Principal cities: There are more than 40 cities with populations of more than 500,000 and 11 cities of more than 1,000,000 people—Moscow (capital), 12,650,000; St. Petersburg, 5,650,000; Novosibrisk, 1,545,000; Sverdlovsk, 1,540,000; Kuybyshev, 1,480,000; Volgograd, 1,305,000; Chelyabinsk, 1,275,000; Saratov, 1,145,000; Perm, 1,125,000; Rostov-na-Donu, 1,125,000; Ufa, 1,080,000.

Although encompassing four-fifths of the land of the former Soviet Union, and housing 60 percent of the Soviet people in an area that stretches 2,500 miles north to south and 7,000 miles east to west,

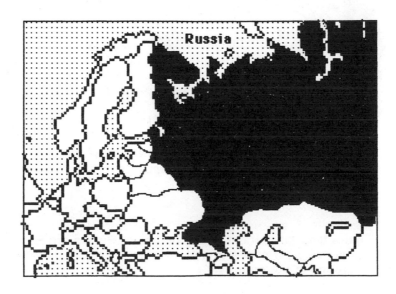

today's Russia is not as large in land mass as the Russia of the late 1800s.

Russian Slavs began to settle this area between the third and eighth centuries A.D. They were joined by Scandinavians who, in the ninth century, formed a kingdom based at Novgorod and, later, at Kiev (now in Ukraine). The early Russians established small independent groups under princes. These were easily overrun by Mongols beginning in 1237. However, by the fourteenth and fifteenth centuries, the princedoms around Moscow had become sufficiently strong to drive out the invaders, and by 1550 had been united into a single empire under Ivan IV. Still, it was not until the reign of Peter I (Peter the Great) that Russia began to acquire neighboring lands earnestly. Under the rule of Peter I, Russia moved to gain access to the Baltic Sea by acquiring Lithuania and the Ukraine, Estonia, and the region of present-day Petrograd from Sweden in 1721. Then at the end of the 1700s and the beginning of the 1800s, a series of military adventures incorporated many areas into the Russian Empire—two-thirds

Russia

Neighboring Countries

Former Soviet Republics

Although more than 80 percent of the people of Russia are Russians, most of whom live west of the Ural Mountains, there are more than 100 ethnic groups in the country.

of Poland in 1795, Finland (1809), Bessarabia (1812), Georgia and Dagestan (1813). Some of the Ottoman Empire was included in the 1860s and 1870s. Throughout this expansion, Russians were ruled by tsars, sometimes despotically, and the Russian people remained in poverty. In 1917, Communist leaders led a successful, if bloody, revolution. The brutality begun in that revolution continued through the rules of Lenin and Joseph Stalin. Under these Communist leaders the Union of Soviet Socialist Republics was established—with Russia by far the largest of the republics.

The land of Russia begins with two great plains in Europe that extend to the Ural Mountains and then through a great steppe eastward to the Pacific Ocean. The southern Asian borders are marked by mountain ranges. Its size and history have placed Russia in an awkward leadership position with the fall of communism in the 1990s. The Russians successfully thwarted a hardline Communist coup in 1991, but left a shattered Soviet Union. Fear of their large neighbor—based on Russia's expansionist history—has made it difficult for other former republics to follow Russian lead in reshaping the Soviet Union. Wealthy countries such as the Ukraine and Georgia are reluctant to strike agreements that suggest Russian domination again. At first, only the Muslim Soviet republics, which refused always to be dominated by Moscow, were willing to sign treaty agreements with Russia that would begin to reshape the union. Later in 1991, the other Slavic republics (Byelarus and Ukraine) followed Russian leadership in attempting to reform the former union into a Commonwealth of Independent States.

372

TAJIKISTAN
(ta jik′ i stan)

Population: 4,969,000 (1988 estimate).
Location: Asia, bounded by Uzbekistan, Kyrgyzstan, China, and Afghanistan.
Languages: Russian, Tajik.
Principal cities: Dushanbe (capital), 600,000; Leninabad, 175,000.

Throughout their early history, the Tajik people were nomadic herders, except for some who settled in agricultural pursuits in the river valleys. These tribes were overrun by Mongols and Turks and forced to move to the mountainous region of present-day Tajikistan. The region was part of the ancient state of Turkestan, a land of large trading centers as early as the fourth century. Mongols under Timur Leng (Tamerlane) ruled the region from the thirteenth century. When

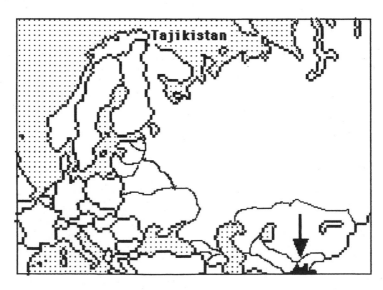

this empire declined, the people, left in poverty and loosely organized under tribal leadership, were assimilated into the Russian Empire between 1868 and 1895.

The Pamir Mountains and the Trans Alai Mountains pass through the region with peaks as high as 24,000 feet. The Amu Darya River lies on the border with Afghanistan and its tributaries have cut deep valleys in the mountains. These valleys are the homes of Tajik farmers who grow cotton, wheat, barley, and livestock. As in other parts of the Soviet Union, much attention was paid to industrialization in Tajikistan. Mining for lead and zinc became an important part of the economy.

Tajikistan is one of a group of southern republics of the former Soviet Union in which Islam is the dominant religion. The binding force of the doctrines of this religion are so strong that the Soviet Union never succeeded in replacing religion with loyalty to the central government—even though the land became part of Russia in 1895, was incorporated into the Russian Soviet Federated Socialist Re-

Tajikistan

More than half (59 percent) of the people of Tajikistan are Tajiks, but there are large minorities of Uzbeks (23 percent) and Russians (10 percent) spread throughout the country, along with some Tatars.

public in 1924, and became a separate Union Republic in 1929. In other aspects, however, Soviet socialism became a strong force in the region.

By 1991, when Soviet President Mikhail Gorbachev suspended activities of the Communist party in the Soviet Union, Tajikistan had already elected a president, Kudreddin Aslonov, who embarked on a pattern of political reforms. However, President Aslonov was joined in government by a parliament consisting mostly of Communist party members. In spite of Gorbachev's actions against the party after the attempted coup of August 1991 failed, the Tajik parliament refused to accept the Communist party suspension. President Aslonov was forced to resign and a new, more autocratic government was installed. The result has been turmoil in this Muslim state. The people have rebelled against the new government, seeing it as a return to the oppressive actions of the earlier Soviet Union.

TURKMENISTAN
(turk men' ih stan)

Population: 2,800,000 (1988 estimate).
Location: Southern edge of the former Soviet Union bordered by Kazakhstan, Uzbekistan, Afghanistan, and Iran.
Languages: Turkomen, Russian.
Principal cities: Ashkhabad (capital), 375,000; Mary (Merv), 90,000; Nebit-Dag 85,000; Krasnovodsk, 60,000.

Tribes of Turkish people inhabited this region by the fourth century A.D. and were part of the great empire of Timur Leng (Tamerlane) after the thirteenth century invasion by Mongols. By the eighteenth century, the empire had faded and southwardly moving Russia was able to take control of the land. This is an ancient land important in Hindu and Persian tradition. The city of Mary (Merv), situated

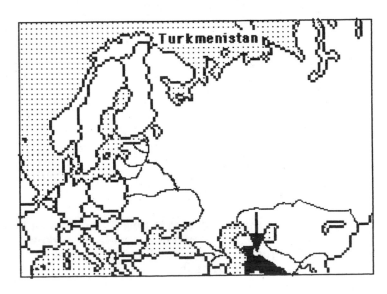

at an oasis, is considered in both Hindu and Persian folklore to be the beginning place of humans.

In 1881, Russians defeated Turkic tribes in the desert region south of Russia, organized the land under the Soviet Union in 1924, and formed the Turkmen Soviet Socialist Republic in 1925. Thus, this section of the Soviet Union has a century-long bond with the Russians.

Even though the country borders the Caspian Sea, a lack of water has kept this republic sparsely populated. Inland from and east of the Caspian Sea is one of the harshest deserts in the world, the Kara-Kum. Southward, mountains separate Turkmenistan from Iran and Afghanistan. On the east, a large river, the Amu Darya, separates Turkmenia and Uzbekistan, and is depended upon for much of the agriculture and industry in the country.

Under Soviet direction, a large canal was begun from the Amu Darya just north of Afghanistan to eventually reach across the Kara-

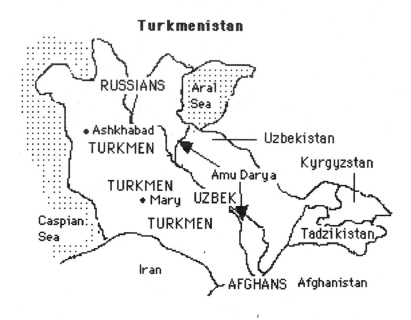

Turkmenistan

Since the tenth century, the region that is now Turkmenistan has been inhabited by Turkic tribes known collectively as Turkmen. These people make up 68 percent of the population; 13 percent are Russians and 8.5 percent are Uzbeks.

Kum toward the Caspian Sea. The Amu Darya valley, the canal, and, in the southeast, the Murgab River have been developed into large irrigation systems that support production of wheat, cotton, barley, fruits, and sheep. Along the Caspian Sea and inland into the desert, mineral resources are mined, and oil is produced near the city of Nebit-Dag.

Economic dependency on the Soviet Union—because of the Union's commitment to providing water sources—was strong. As a result, when communism collapsed and the Soviet Union fell into disarray in 1991, the newly independent republics signed an economic agreement as a first step toward reforming the union. Under this treaty, eight former Soviet republics will share a national bank and the basic unit of money, the ruble. By the end of 1991, Turkmenistan had joined other former republics in a Commonwealth of Independent States.

UKRAINE

(you crane′)

Population: 44,000,000 (1991 estimate).
Location: Eastern Europe, bounded by Byelarus, Russia, Romania, Czechoslovakia, Poland.
Languages: Ukrainian, Russian.
Principal Cities: Kiev (capital), 2,740,000; Donetsk, 2,185,000; Kharkov, 1,865,000; Dnepropetrovsk, 1,560,000; Odessa, 1,190,000; Zaporozhye, 855,000; Lvov, 745,000; Gorbovka, 710,000; Krivoy Rog, 685,000.

Except for brief periods of time, Ukraine land has always been ruled by others—in recent years by the Soviet Union and before that by Russia and Poland. An early kingdom established by the Swedes at Kiev grew to be an independent Slavic state that was absorbed by

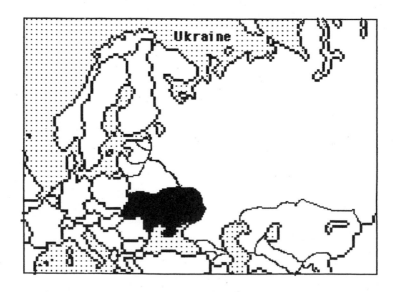

Russia in two stages—the region east of the Dnieper River in 1686 and that west of the river in 1703. Ukraine's borders have been changed often—western Ukraine fell to Poland in the Treaty of Riga (1921) to be regained by Russia in 1939; Bessarabia and Bukovina were added to it in 1940 and Moldavia was taken away. Rulers have attempted to eliminate the Ukrainian language and customs, but instead have furthered the sense of nationalism in the region. Ukrainian language has been maintained, and Ukrainian literature has grown.

Under the Soviet Union, Ukraine grew from its region of mostly fertile, rolling plains to include Ruthenia across the Carpathian Mountains and the Crimea, a peninsula in the Black Sea made famous by meetings between leaders of Allied powers after World War II at the city of Yalta. These additions made Ukraine second in size only to Russia among the republics of the Soviet Union united in 1922.

One-fifth of the people of Ukraine live in the very large principal cities, and many more live in cities of 250,000 to 500,000. Particularly in the Donets Coal Basin near the Black Sea, Ukraine was a major industrial supplier of the Soviet Union. Iron, chemicals, textiles, and

Ukraine

More than 10,000,000 Russians and nearly 500,000 Byelarussians share the land throughout Ukraine with the 36,000,000 Ukrainians.

all sorts of machinery are produced in Ukraine's factories. Once an agricultural land, now more people live in the cities and work in industry than those that live by agriculture.

With the abandonment of communism in the Soviet Union and the weakening of the central government, Ukrainian leaders chose to form an independent nation that could be a powerful industrial force in Europe. In October 1991, after most of the republics had declared their independence, eight of the republics signed an economic treaty. This treaty was to establish a common currency that would have value on the world market and to form a single central bank. Ukraine at first refused to join, fearing that the country would again be dominated by their much larger neighbor, Russia. However, trade in the Soviet Union had long been mostly between republics, and Ukraine was a major partner in the union. For example, Ukraine supplied the Soviet Union with 55 percent of its iron. These economic ties bound Ukraine with the other republics, so that in November 1991, after assuring themselves of fair treatment by internally troubled Russia, Ukraine joined the other republics that had signed the economic pact. This pact was a first step in reconstructing the union with a free-enterprise economy. Other steps, however, failed and in December 1991, Ukraine joined Byelarus and Russia to form a Commonwealth of Independent States.

UZBEKISTAN

(ooz bek ih stan')

Population: 13,000,000 (1988 estimate).
Location: South of Russia, bounded by Kazakhstan, Kyrgyzstan, Tajikistan, Afghanistan, and Turkmenistan.
Language: Uzbek, a Turkic language.
Principal cities: Tashkent (capital), 2,260,000; Samarkand, 380,000; Andizhan, 285,000; Namangan, 285,000; Kokand, 175,000.

Tashkent is an ancient city, built in the seventh century at an oasis that receives water from streams feeding the Amu Darya. Another ancient city, Samarkand, at an oasis fed by the Zervashan River, was once the center of a Muslim culture and the capital of the empire of the Mongol leader, Timur Leng. After the fall of this empire, these and other cities were the centers of emirates held by Turkish im-

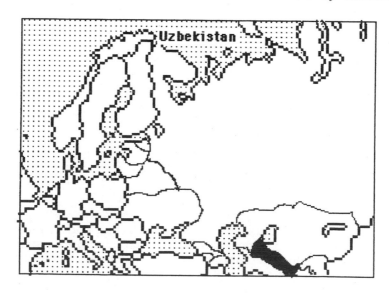

migrants to the land. In the 1800s Russians occupied first Tashkent, then the emirates at Samarkand, Bukhara, and Khiva. By 1873 the emirates were all paying tribute to the Russian rulers. In 1917 the Soviet Union set up conditions for Uzbekistan to become a republic within the union, and in 1924 the old emirates combined to form the Uzbek Soviet Socialist Republic.

Ties between the Uzbeks and the rest of the Soviet Union were strong. The Soviet structure aided in developing vast irrigation systems for the Uzbek farmers and herders. In return, Uzbekistan provided more than half the cotton used by the Soviet Union, about half the rice, and 60 percent of the union's medicinal herbs. The Soviet Institute for Scientific Research has developed plant strains that are more resistant to the very cold winters of Uzbekistan. Still, sheepherding is the major occupation in some areas. Karakul sheep, which produce Persian lamb fur, are raised in Uzbekistan. Much of Uzbekistan's industry is related to agriculture and the processing of

Uzbekistan

Of the people of Uzbekistan, 69 percent are Uzbek and 11 percent are Russian. Tatars, Kazakhs, and Tajiks each contribute 4 percent of the population, while 2 percent are Kara-Kalpaks who live in their own section in the north.

animal and plant products. Uzbekistan was also a provider of oil for the former Soviet Union.

Like its neighbors, the Muslim republic took the Communist control from Moscow lightly and always commanded a measure of independence. The leaders of independent Uzbekistan of 1991, did not share the fears of Russian domination expressed by Byelarus and Ukraine. Instead, Uzbekistan joined other Muslim states in signing an economic agreement to employ a single central bank and establish the ruble as an internationally exchangeable currency. Subsequent 1991 developments resulted in Uzbekistan joining other republics in the Commonwealth of Independent States.

YUGOSLAVIA

(you go slav′ ee uh)

Population: 24,000,000 (1988 estimate).
Location: Southeastern Europe, bounded by Austria, Hungary, Romania, Bulgaria, Greece, and Albania.
Languages: Serbian, Croatian, Slovenian.
Principal cities: Belgrade (capital), 1,400,000; Zagreb, 800,000; Sarajevo, 450,000; Skopje, 420,000; Ljubijana, 310,000; Novi Sad, 270,000.

In 1882 King Milan reinstated the kingdom of Serbia, which had been organized first in the thirteenth century under Urosh the Great, but had been under Turkish rule since 1459. This country achieved its greatest power in 1912 in an alliance with Bulgaria, Montenegro, and Greece to fight Turkey. This glory was short-lived, however. In

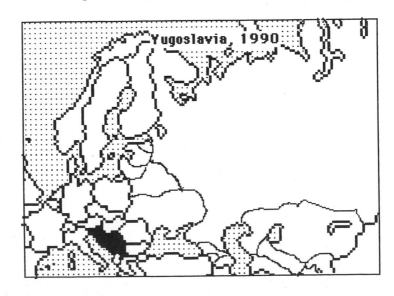

1914 the ruler of the Austro-Hungarian realm was assassinated and the blame was placed on two Serbs. Austro-Hungary declared war on Serbia, but hesitated when Russia came to that country's rescue. Germany seized the opportunity to declare war on Russia, and World War I began. Following the war, a new country, Yugoslavia (the name means "southern slavs") was organized but not formally recognized until boundaries with other countries were finally determined in 1929. In the 1930s, the predominantly Serbian government was tormented by Croat and Slovene demands for more autonomy. A new constitution was drawn in 1939 and the new alignment overthrew the government, which had allied itself with Germany and Italy. From 1941 through 1945, the Croats were virtually an independent nation. During this period there was a great deal of conflict between the minority Croats and Slovenes and the majority Serbs. In 1945 a Communist republic closely affiliated with the Soviet Union was formed under Marshal Tito (Josip Broz), who was able to control the quarreling

Croats and Serbs live in all regions of the old state of Yugoslavia. Bosnians and Herzegovinans, for example, only make up 44 percent of the population in the area of Bosnia-Herzegovina. Serbs and Croats are 56 percent of the population there.

factions. Shortly, however, Tito differed with Yugoslavia's Soviet partner and Yugoslavia was expelled (1948) from the Cominform, the umbrella structure for Communist governments associated with the Soviet Union. From that time until 1980 Yugoslavia was held tightly under the military dictatorship of Marshal Tito. Upon his death, the country again fell into disunity.

The Yugoslavia of Tito had a narrow coastal plain. It was separated from Italy by the Julian Alps in the north and from Albania by the North Albanian Alps in the south. The northern part of the country was inhabited mostly by Croats and Slovenes. Serbs and Montenegrins were predominant in the center of the country, and there was a strong Turkish and Muslim population in the south.

By 1990 the Croats were again demanding independence and the Serbian-controlled army began to press for their submission. Memories of their earlier conflicts, although more than 40 years past, have added to the fires of civil war. In spite of efforts by other European countries to arrange a peaceful settlement of the problem, and despite United Nations pleas for a cease-fire, the rebellion of the Croats and military suppression by the Serbs erupted frequently in 1991. By the first month of 1992, Serbs, Croats, and other groups in Yugoslavia had agreed to dissolve the nation.

Slovenia and Croatia have successfully pursued their struggle for independence. Both of these new small countries have been recognized by the United Nations, as has Bosnia-Herzegovina, although fighting between Bosnians and Serbs continues in that former Yugoslav state. Macedonia, the southernmost Yugoslav state, has also declared independence.

Glossary

Ashkenazim The group of Jews who trace their ancestry to Central and Eastern Europe.

Bohemia The mountain-encircled western part of Czechoslovakia that was once an independent nation.

Byzantine Empire An empire founded by Zeno (474–491) in competition with the Rome-based Roman Empire. Its capital was Byzantium and later Constantinople, the headquarters of the eastern Christian church.

Byzantium An ancient city of Turkey, which was the earliest site of the headquarters of the Eastern Roman Empire.

Dacia An ancient kingdom, roughly equivalent to modern-day Romania, that was made a province of the Roman Empire by Trajan in A.D. 107.

Dalmatia A section of the Adriatic coast in Yugoslavia.

glasnost A late Soviet Union policy of openness, particularly openness and honesty about the history of the Communist rule in the Soviet Union.

Golden Horde The armies of Genghis Khan that swept over eastern Europe and Asia in the thirteenth century.

hajj A pilgrimage to the holy city of Mecca required of all Muslims who are able to make the trip.

jihad A holy war—the commitment of Muslims to defend other Muslims in the event of attacks on them.

kolkhozy Collective farms under the Union of Soviet Socialist Republics, in theory owned and operated by the workers but actually directed by government edicts and quotas.

koran The holy book of the Muslims.

Moldavia (now Moldova) A section, now independent, on the border between Ukraine and Romania that once included Bessarabia and Bukovina, and once was a part of Romania.

Mongols Members of any of the nomadic tribes of Mongolia that came together under the great Khans to conquer much of Asia and Eastern and Central Europe.

Moravia A western section of Czechoslovakia that, with part of Silesia, formed the Sudetenland claimed by Germany early in World War II.

namay The commitment to daily devotions in Islam.

Ottoman Empire Established in the thirteenth century from a sultanate in Central Asia, the Empire included most of the territory of the Byzantine Empire by the sixteenth century.

patriarchal Pertaining to a social system in which descent and succession are traced through the male line.

peristroika A policy of change advocated by the Soviet leader Mikhail Gorbachev to relax central government control of industry and economics in the Soviet Union.

pesme One of the many Serbian folk songs.

pogrom An officially organized or tolerated attack by one people on another, such as the attacks on Jews in Poland and Germany in the years just before and during World War II.

Roman Empire An empire based in the ancient city of Rome, beginning in 27 B.C., that grew to have more than 40 provinces and to control most of the Mediterranean area. The Roman Empire controlled most of Europe south and west of the Danube River.

Romany The language spoken by the Gypsies.

saun The Islamic requirement for fasting during the month of Ramadan.

Sephardim The group of Jews of Spanish heritage.

shahada One of the basic tenets of Islam—the requirement for frequent recitations of faith.

shtetl A Jewish village in Central Europe in which all the villagers worked together cooperatively.

social realism A point of view of Soviet Communists that guided art, literature, music, and theater during the period of the Soviet Union. Social realism called for the arts to deal with "real" social issues to the glorification of workers and industrialization.

sovkhozy State-owned and -operated farms in the Soviet Union.

Sudetenland The Sudetic Mountains on the north borders of Bohemia and Silesia claimed by the Germans in 1938 and 1939.

Tatars Mongolian peoples who, under Genghis Khan overran Eastern Europe and Central and Western Asia in the thirteenth century; thus Mongols who joined Genghis Khan.

Torah The holy book of the Jews.

Transylvania A northwest and central plateau region of Romania bordered on three sides (north, east, and south) by the Carpathian Mountains and the Transylvanian Alps. Transylvania has long been contested for by Romania and Hungary, but is now part of Romania.

tsar (czar) A king or emperor. Most often associated with the leaders of Russia before the 1917 takeover by the Communists.

ustase A right-wing group of Croatians responsible for destroying thousands of Serbs in present-day Croatia during World War II. The name is drawn from the founder of the movement, Ustachi.

yurt The round tents that were the common abodes of nomadic herders in the Tien Shan mountains—Kyrgyz, Tajiks and others.

zadruga An extended family in Romania and Yugoslavia.

zakat In Islam the demand for the faithful to give alms.

Zionist A Jew who supported the idea of an independent state for the Jews in Palestine.

Bibliography

Armstrong, John A. *Ukrainian Nationalism*, 3rd edition. Englewood, Colorado: Ukrainian Academic Press, 1990.

Backman, Ronald D., editor. *Romania: A Country Study*. Washington, DC: American University Press, 1991.

Balassa, Iván and Gyula Ortutay (Maria Bales, Kenneth Bales, and Laszlo T. Andras, translators). *Hungarian Ethnography and Folklore*. Budapest: Corvina, 1984.

Berlin, Isaiah. *Russian Thinkers*. New York: Viking Press, 1978.

Blunden, Godfrey. *Eastern Europe: Czechoslovakia, Hungary, Poland*. New York: Time Inc., 1965.

Borody, Stephen. *Hungarians: A Divided Nation*. Yale Russian and East Europe Publication #7, 1988.

Borsody, Stephen, editor. *The Hungarians: A Divided Nation*. New Haven, Connecticut: Yale Center for International and Area Studies, 1988.

Burant, Stephen R., editor. *Hungary: A Country Study*. Washington, DC: American University Press, 1990.

Caldwell, Erskine, and Margaret Bourke-White. *North of the Danube*. New York: Viking Press, 1939.

Candea, Virgil. *An Outline of Romanian History*. Bucharest, Romania: Meridiane Publishing House, 1977.

Ceaușescu, Ilie. *War, Revolution, and Society in Romania: The Road to Independence*. New York: Columbia University Press, 1983.

Clébert, Jean-Paul. *The Gypsies*. Baltimore: Penguin Books, 1967.

Creton, Edward. *Russia*. London: Longmans, 1986.

Doder, Dusko. *The Yugoslavs.* New York: Random House, 1978.

Dömötör, Tekla, editor. *Hungarian Folk Customs.* London: Collets, 1988.

Fekete, Márton, editor. *Prominent Hungarians: Home and Abroad.* München: Aurora Editions, 1965.

Friend, Morton. *The Vanishing Tungus: The Story of a Remarkable Reindeer People.* New York: Dial Press, 1973.

Georgescu, Vlad, editor. *Romania: Forty Years, 1944–1984.* New York: Frederick A. Praeger, 1985.

Gerutis, Albertas, editor. *Lithuanians: Seven Hundred Years.* Annapolis, Maryland: University of Maryland Press, 1969.

Gillon, Adam and Ludwik Krzyzanowski, editors. *Introduction to Modern Polish Literature: An Anthology of Fiction and Poetry.* New York: Twayne Publishers, 1964.

Illés, Lajos, editor. *Nothing's Lost: Twenty-five Hungarian Short Stories.* Budapest, Hungary: Corvina Kiadó, 1988.

Illyés, Elemér. *National Minorities in Romania: Change in Transylvania.* New York: Columbia University Press, 1981.

Jackson, John H. *Estonia.* Denver, Colorado: Greenwood, 1979.

Jordan, Robert Paul. "Yugoslavia: Six Republics in One." *National Geographic,* May 1970.

Kecskemeti, Paul. *The Unexpected Revolution.* Stanford, California: Stanford University Press, 1961.

Kerner, Robert J., editor. *Yugoslavia.* Berkeley, California: University of California Press, 1949.

Kostelski, Z. *The Yugoslavs.* New York: Philosophical Library, 1952.

Lampe, John R. *Bulgarian Economy in the Twentieth Century.* New York: St. Martin's Press, 1986.

Lubachko, Ivan S. *Belorussia Under Soviet Rule 1917–1957.* Lexington: University Press of Kentucky, 1972.

Macartney, C. A. *Hungary: A Short History.* New York: Frederick A. Praeger, 1956.

Maclean, Fitzroy. *Holy Russia.* New York: Atheneum, 1979.

Manning, Clarence A. *The Story of the Ukraine.* New York: Philosophical Library, 1947.

McClellan, Woodford, editor. *Russia,* 2nd edition. New York: Prentice-Hall, 1989.

Mikasinovich, Branko, Dragan Milivojevic, and Vasa D. Mihailovich, editors. *Introduction to Yugoslav Literature.* New York: Twayne Publishers, 1973.

Nemcová, Jeanne W., editor and translator. *Czech and Slovak Short Stories.* London: Oxford University Press, 1967.

Owen, Gale R. *Rites and Religions of the Anglo-Saxons.* Totowa, New Jersey: Barnes and Noble, 1981.

Popescu, Julian. *Romania.* New York: Chelsea House, 1988.

Potapov, I. P., and M. G. Levin, editors. *The Peoples of Siberia.* Chicago: University of Chicago Press, 1964.

Recheigl, Miloslav, Jr., editor. *Czechoslovakia Past and Present,* Volumes 1 and 2. The Hague, Netherlands: Mouton and Co., 1968.

Reményi, Joseph. *Hungarian Writers and Literature.* New Brunswick, New Jersey: Rutgers University Press, 1964.

Shipler, David. K. *Russia: Broken Idols, Solemn Dreams.* Harmondsworth, England: Penguin Books, 1989.

Sinor, Denis. *History of Hungary*. New York: Frederick A. Praeger, 1959.

Tong, Diane. *Gypsy Folktales*. New York, Harcourt Brace Jovanovich, 1989.

Vakar, Nicholas P. *Belorussia: The Making of a Nation*. Cambridge: Harvard University Press, 1956.

Vowles, Hugh P. *Ukraine and Its People*. London: W. and R. Chambers, 1939.

Wood, Alan and R. A. French, editors. *The Development of Siberia: People and Resources*. London: The Macmillan Press, 1989.

Woods, J. Douglas and David A. E. Pelteret, editors. *The Anglo-Saxons: Synthesis and Achievement*. Waterloo, Ontario, Canada: Wilfrid Laurier University Press, 1985.

Yarmolinsky, Avrahm, editor. *Two Centuries of Russian Verse: An Anthology from Lomonosov to Voznesensky*. New York: Random House, 1966.

Index